A Textbook of Event Management

A Textbook of Event Management

Logan Gaspar

RANDOM

RANDOM PUBLICATIONS

NEW DELHI (INDIA)

A Textbook of Event Management

ISBN 978-93-5111-440-6

Published in 2014 in India by
RANDOM PUBLICATIONS
4376-A/4B, Gali Murari Lal, Ansari Road
New Delhi-110 002
Phone : +91-11-43580356, +91-11-23289044
e-mail: randomexports@gmail.com, sales@randompublications.com, info@randompublications.com

Type Setting by: Friends Media, Delhi-110089
Digitally Printed at: Replika Press Pvt. Ltd.

Preface

Events and occasions are an integral part of human life. We simply cannot bypass them as they touch almost all aspects of our social existence. Birthday celebrations, social gatherings, engagements and weddings are events we celebrate at the personal level. During academic years there are school events such as annual day functions, inter and intra school contests, sports day celebrations, followed by college and university level festivals. In the sphere of work, there are annual general meetings, exhibitions, marketing campaigns, conferences, product launches and brand development activities. Other events such as fashion shows, cultural programs, talent hunt shows, promotional campaigns, religious gatherings and so on also play an important role in our life. And what's more, all of us have been a part of these events from time to time. We either organise these events or take part in the show. Either ways we want these occasions to go on as per our expectations and in doing so we often seek professional help. However, we do not pay much heed to the people who assiduously put in their effort and creative talent to make these events memorable and successful. They are the event managers. Event management is a multifaceted activity. Major constituents of this profile include creativity, meticulous planning, relationship management, advertising and marketing and much more, all rolled into one seamlessly choreographed process.

The recent growth of festivals and events as an industry around the world means that the management can no longer be *ad hoc*. Events and festivals, such as the Asian Games, have a large impact on their communities and, in some cases, the whole country. The industry now includes events of all sizes from the Olympics down to a breakfast meeting for ten business people. Many industries, charitable organizations, and interest groups will hold events of some size in order to market themselves, build business relationships, raise money or celebrate. Event management is considered one of the strategic marketing and communication tools by companies of all sizes. From product launches to press conferences, companies create promotional events to help them communicate with clients and potential clients. They might target their audience by using the news media, hoping to generate media coverage which will reach thousands or millions of people. They can also invite their audience to their events and reach them at the actual event. Event managers can supervise diverse corporate events, such as product launches, press conferences, corporate anniversary parties, meetings, conferences, and marketing programs such as road shows and grand opening events. In addition, they can coordinate special corporate hospitality events such as concerts, award ceremonies, film premieres, parties to launch new products or services, fashion shows, commercial events, and even private (personal) events such as weddings and religious services. Event management firms can handle a variety of specific event-related services, which can range from a few select services for clients with limited budgets, to handling all creative, technical and logistical aspects of an event. The event manager is the person who plans and executes the event. Event managers and their teams are often behind-the-scenes running the event. Event managers may also be involved in more than just the planning and execution of the event, but also brand building, marketing and communication strategy. The event manager is an expert at the creative, technical and logistical elements that help an event succeed. This includes event design, audio-visual production, scriptwriting, logistics, budgeting, negotiation and, of course, client service. It is a multi-dimensional profession. An event architect is an event manager that becomes involved at the early initiation stages of the event. Specially for larger public events, at the initiation stage, the event architect needs to make crucial choices and decisions related to the creative concept and design of the event. In depth technical design knowledge and full understanding of how to communicate a company´s message across a public are needed in order to make the event effective.

The book is intended to assist students and teachers who are interested in this subject.

I would like to thank my team for standing beside me throughout my career and writing this book. My special thanks go to "Random Publications" who have published the book.

—Logan Gaspar

Contents

1. Introduction to Event Management 1

- Marketing Tool 1
- Event Planning 4
- Event Scheduling 6
- Sustainable Event Management 6
- Environmental Impacts and Legacy 7
- Perfect Venue: The Key to a Successful Event 8
- Corporate Events-A Company's Selling Campaign 10
- How to Plan a Corporate Event on Maui 11
- Planning an Event the Professional Way 12
- How to Grow Event Attendance 13
- How to Plan a Charity Walk or Run 14
- The Planning Phase 14
- Resources and Staff 15
- Finding Participants 16
- Online Fundraising Tips for Events 18
- Event Management Systems Help Administrative and Event Planning Professionals 20
- What to Give as a Gift to the Professional Speakers at Your Event 21
- Steps for Planning a Seminar and Training Event 22
- Capture a Big Crowd With Your Captivating Business Event 24
- Selecting Conference Venues Wisely 28
- The 1 Thing You must do if you Attend Events 30
- 3 Secrets on Getting the Most Out of Attending Events 31
- Why You Must Attend Events to Grow Your Biz 33

- Event Hire Companies-Adding Life, Colour and Zest to Your Parties 34
- Best Event Planning Tips 37

2. Planning and Policies **41**

- Mexican Priorities: Gaming, Tourism and Energy 41
- Tourism Development Priorities in North East England 43
- Northumberland Tourism 43
- Tourism Tyne & Wear 44
- Tourism and the Imperatives of Sustainable Development 46
- Mekong Tourism Office Defines Priorities 48
- Tourism Planning 50
- Abu Dhabi Races Ahead with Tourism Plans 63
- Kerala Tourism plans 'Onam Road Show' 65
- South African Tourism Plans to hold in-country Road Show in India in August 2009 66
- CR-T1021: Tourism Plans and Investment Designs in Wild Protected Areas 67
- Tourism Plans Road Show in Middle East 67
- Tourism Plans for Andamans go on, Tsunami Notwithstanding 68
- Madhya Pradesh Lines up Big Tourism Plans 70
- Puerto Rico Tourism Plans Major European Expansion 72
- Dubai World scraps most of its Rwanda Tourism Plans 73
- Banahaw Ecotourism Plans Studied 73
- India: Sikkim to Expand Tourism Plans 74
- L.A. Port has Big Tourism Plans for Waterfront 75
- Tourism as a Development Strategy 76
- Tourism Strategy Objectives 77
- Tourism Development Strategy: 2001-2010 80
- East London Tourism Development Strategy and Action Plan 2004-2006 81
- Dcms Sustainable Development Strategy: Sectors Tourism 81
- Tourism's Potential as a Sustainable Development Strategy 82
- Tourism Development Strategies 84

- Development Strategy to the Challenge of a "Plan de Excelencia" 88
- National Sustainable Development Strategies 93
- United Nations Department of Economic and Social Affairs Division for Sustainable Development 95
- Tourism Development Strategy (2006 – 2010) 95
- Target Market 96
- Tourist attractions (events + nature) 96
- Tourism Development Strategy 100
- 2008 Economic Development Strategies-Agritourism Industry 104
- The Ministry of Tourism 106
- Mot and other Ministries' Training Needs 107
- Ministry of Tourism 108
- Training Needs for MOT and Other It event Ministries 109
- Recommendations for Travelling and Education For the Private Sector 111
- Survey of Training Needs In 'the Cambodian Travel and Tourism Sector 112

3. Market Plan of Travel Business 115

- Two Sides of Tourism Planning 115
- Steps in the Planning Process 116
- Tourism Management Organizations and Services 119
- Concluding Remarks 127
- Strategic Framework for Tourism 128
- Vision and Objectives 128
- Overall Guiding Principles for the Tourism Plan 128
- Strategic Directions – Tourism Positioning 129
- Rationalize and Modernize Juneau's Approach to Tourism 130
- Current Management Approach 130
- Alternative Models for Tourism Management 131
- Update the Comprehensive Plan 131
- Motivation of Nature Tourism 132
- Tourism Marketing 139
- What is Marketing 139

- Recreation and Tourism Marketing 140
- The Marketing Plan 141
- Overall Business Objectives 141
- Market Environment Analysis 142
- Economic Conditions 143
- Laws and Government Actions 143
- Technology 143
- Competition 143
- Business and Community Profiles 144
- Market Segmentation (Identification) 144
- Marketing Objectives for each Segment 145
- Marketing Strategy (Mix) 146
- Promotion 148
- Marketing Budget 150
- Implementation 150
- Conclusion 151
- Information Supply in Tourism Management 152
- The Transmission of Market Research Data in the Internet 155

4. Event Marketing Strategies: Public Relations 157

- Media Coaching Can Help 157
- Project Managing for a Special Event 160
- Event Promotion Tip: Using the Seminar to Sell Your Consulting Services 161
- Marketing Workshops Success: The Mental Side of the Product Sales Game 162
- Seminar Marketing Advantage: Know What You MUST Know about the Competition! 163
- Event Promotion Tip: 5 Things You MUST do to get people to Come to your Next Event 165
- Project Management Using Event Chain Methodology 167
- Event Management-Corporate and Personal Events 171
- Event Management of Conferences 172

5. Event Organization 173

- Organization of Events 173
- Event Marketing in the Internet 214
- Event Marketing for Private Events 214

- Event Management Software 215
- Event Planning Software 215
- Air Show 216
- Exhibition 219
- Art Exhibition 220

6. Event Marketing **226**

- Announcing Events 227
- Plan for the Event or Flounder 228
- Super Lead Generation Event 228
- Trade Show Success 231
- The Ins and Outs of Trade Show Exhibits 232
- Engagement Marketing 233
- Relationship Marketing 237
- Approaches 240
- Personalized Marketing 245
- Evangelism Marketing 247
- Types of Events 249
- Bidding for Events 250
- Preparing the Event Proposal 251
- The Event Director 254
- Financing the Event 255

7. Event Management of Corporate Events **257**

- Event Manager for Corporate Events 257
- Event Management of Trade Shows 260
- Event Management of Seminars 261
- Planning of Meetings 263
- Event Management of Team Building Events 264
- Event Management of Press Conferences 267
- Event Management of Networking Events 268
- Event Management of Product Launches 272
- Event Management of VIP Events 274
- Topics of Theme Parties 276
- Annual Shareholders Meetings 278
- Event Management of Award Ceremonies 280
- Event Management of Incentive Events 282
- Event Management of Private Events 286

- Event Management of Weddings 287
- Event Management of Birthday Parties 288
- Event Management of Wedding Anniversaries 289
- Event Management for Family Events 290
- Event Management of Personal Events 290

8. Online Event Marketing Strategies 292

- Exhibit Marketing Mistakes: Ten Tips on How to Avoid Them! 293
- Reduce Event Management Cost with Online Registration Software 299
- Reduced Over-Purchase of Merchandise and Food 300
- Marketing Optics can Cloak Reality 301
- Planning Your Fundraising Campaign-How Nonprofits Raise More Funds Online in a Global Recession 302
- 10 Reasons Meetings and Events are Important in Tough Times 304
- Short Changing Your Trade Show ROI by NOT Planning 309

9. The Event Budget 311

- Typical Event Expenditure 312
- Selling the Event 313
- Managing Event Staff 315
- Event Safety 318
- Promote Events Through Social Media – Part One 320
- Event Chain Methodology 323
- Event Chain Methodology Principles 323

Bibliography 325

Index 327

1

Introduction to Event Management

Event management is the application of project management to the creation and development of festivals, events and conferences. Event management involves studying the intricacies of the brand, identifying the target audience, devising the event concept, planning the logistics and coordinating the technical aspects before actually executing the modalities of the proposed event. Post-event analysis and ensuring a return on investment have become significant drivers for the event industry.

The recent growth of festivals and events as an industry around the world means that the management can no longer be *ad hoc*. Events and festivals, such as the Asian Games, have a large impact on their communities and, in some cases, the whole country. The industry now includes events of all sizes from the Olympics down to a breakfast meeting for ten business people. Many industries, charitable organizations, and interest groups will hold events of some size in order to market themselves, build business relationships, raise money or celebrate.

Marketing Tool

Event management is considered one of the strategic marketing and communication tools by companies of all sizes. From product launches to press conferences, companies create promotional events to help them communicate with clients and potential clients. They might target their audience by using the news media, hoping to generate media coverage which will reach thousands or millions of people. They can also invite their audience to their events and reach them at the actual event.

Services

Event management companies and organizations service a variety of areas including corporate events (product launches, press conferences, corporate meetings and conferences), marketing programs (road shows, grand opening events), and special corporate hospitality events like concerts, award ceremonies, film premieres, launch/release parties, fashion shows, commercial events, private (personal) events such as weddings and bar mitzvahs. Clients hire event management companies to handle a specific scope of services for the given event, which at its maximum may include all creative, technical and logistical elements of the event. (Or just a subset of these, depending on the client's needs, expertise and budget).

Event Manager

The event manager is the person who plans and executes the event. Event managers and their teams are often behind-the-scenes running the event. Event managers may also be involved in more than just the planning and execution of the event, but also brand building, marketing and communication strategy. The event manager is an expert at the creative, technical and logistical elements that help an event succeed. This includes event design, audio-visual production, scriptwriting, logistics, budgeting, negotiation and, of course, client service. It is a multi-dimensional profession.

The event manager may become involved at the early initiation stages of the event. If the event manager has budget responsibilities at this early stage they may be termed an event or production executive. The early stages include:

- Site surveying
- Client Service
- Brief clarification
- Budget drafting
- Cash flow management
- Supply chain identification
- Procurement
- Scheduling
- Site design
- Technical design
- Health & Safety.

An event manager who becomes involved closer to the event will often have a more limited brief. The key disciplines closer to the event are:

- Health & Safety including crowd management,
- Logistics
- Rigging
- Sound
- Light
- Video
- Detailed scheduling
- Security.

As an Industry

Event Management is a multi-million dollar industry, growing rapidly, with mega shows and events hosted regularly. Surprisingly, there is no formalized research conducted to assess the growth of this industry. The industry includes fields such as the MICE (Meetings, Incentives, Conventions and Exhibitions), conferences and seminars as well as live music and sporting events. The logistics side of the industry is paid less than the sales/sponsorship side, though some may say that these are two different industries.

Technology

Event management software companies provide event planners with software tools to handle many common activities such as delegate registration, hotel booking, travel booking or allocation of exhibition floorspace.

Education

There are an increasing number of universities which offer courses in event management, including diplomas and graduate degrees. In addition to these academic courses, there are many associations and societies that provide courses on the various aspects of the industry. Study includes organizational skills, technical knowledge, P.R., marketing, advertising, catering, logistics, decor, glamor identity, human relations, study of law and licenses, risk management, budgeting, study of allied industries like television, other media and several other areas. Certification can be acquired from various sources to obtain designations such as Certified Trade Show Marketer (CTSM), Certified Manager of Exhibits (CME), Certified in Exhibition

Management (CEM), Global Certification in Meeting Management (CMM), Certified Meeting Professional (CMP) and the Certified Special Event Professional (CSEP).

Career opportunities are in the following Industries :

1. Event Management
2. Event Management Consultancy
3. Hotel, travel and hospitality Industries
4. Advertising Agencies
5. Public Relations Firms
6. Corporations
7. News Media
8. Non-profit organization
9. Integrated Marketing & Communications
10. Event Budgeting and Accounting.

Categories of Events

Events can be classified into four broad categories based on their purpose and objective:

1. Leisure events e.g. leisure sport, music, recreation.
2. Cultural events e.g. ceremonial, religious, art, heritage, and folklore.
3. Personal events e.g. weddings, birthdays, anniversaries.
4. Organizational events e.g. commercial, political, charitable, sales, product launch, expo.

Event Planning

Event planning is the process of planning a festival, ceremony, competition, party, or convention. Event planning includes budgeting, establishing dates and alternate dates, selecting and reserving the event site, acquiring permits, and coordinating transportation and parking. Event planning also includes some or all of the following, depending on the event: developing a theme or motif for the event, arranging for speakers and alternate speakers, coordinating location support (such as electricity and other utilities), arranging decor, tables, chairs, tents, event support and security, catering, police, fire, portable toilets, parking, signage, emergency plans, health care professionals, and cleanup.

Steps to Planning an Event

The first step to planning an event is determining its purpose, whether it is for a wedding, company, birthday, festival, graduation or any other event requiring extensive planning. From this the event planner needs to choose entertainment, location, guest list, speakers, and content. The location for events is endless, but with event planning they would likely be held at hotels, convention centers, reception halls, or outdoors depending on the event. Once the location is set the coordinator/planner needs to prepare the event with staff, set up the entertainment, and keep contact with the client. After all this is set the event planner has all the smaller details to address like set up of the event such as food, drinks, music, guest list, budget, advertising and marketing, decorations, all this preparation is what is needed for an event to run smoothly. An event planner needs to be able to manage their time wisely for the event, and the length of preparation needed for each event so it is a success.

Event Planning as a Career

Event planning is a relatively new career field. There is now training that helps one trying to break into the career field. There must be training for an event planner to handle all the pressure and work efficiently. This career deals with a lot of communication and organization aspects. There are many different names for an event planner such as a conference coordinator, a convention planner, a special event coordinator, and a meeting manager. To read more about people involved in event planning and production. Event planners' work is considered either stressful or energizing. This line of work is also considered fast paced and demanding. Planners face deadlines and communicating with multiple people at one time. Planners spend most of their time in offices, but when meeting with clients the work is usually on-site at the location where the event is taking place. Some physical activity is required such as carrying boxes of materials and decorations or supplies needed for the event. Also, long working hours can be a part of the job. The day the event is taking place could start as early as 5:00 a.m. and then work until midnight. Working on weekends is sometimes required, which is when many events take place.

Publications and Resources

Many business-to-business trade publications exist to help event planning and production professionals become educated about the issues and trends in their industry. Many are controlled circulation publications available at no cost to qualified event professionals. Qualification is based on multiple variables like job title, company type, industry segment or geographic region, and is at the publisher's discretion.

Event Scheduling

Event scheduling is the activity of finding a suitable time for an event such as meeting, conference, trip, etc. It is an important part of event planning that is usually carried out at its beginning stage.

In general, event scheduling must take into account what impact particular dates of the event could have on the success of the event. When organizing a scientific conference, for example, organizers might take into account the knowledge in which periods classes are held at universities, since it is expected that many potential participants are university professors. They should also try to check that no other similar conferences are held at the same time, because overlapping would make a problem for those participants who are interesting in attending all conferences.

When it is well known who is expected to attend the event (e.g. in the case of a project meeting), organizers usually try to synchronize the time of the event with planned schedules of all participants. This is a difficult task when there are many participants or when the participants are located at distant places. In such cases, the organizers should first define a set of suggested dates and address a query about suitable dates to potential participants. After response is obtained from all participants, the event time suitable for most of participants is selected. This procedure can be alleviated by internet tools.

Sustainable Event Management

Sustainable Event Management is the process used to produce an event with concern for environmental, economic and social issues. An event is a mass gathering of people for a purpose.

Sustainability in event management commonly addresses environmental impacts of the production, the impacts of events on community, and its economic legacy.

The concept of sustainable development is relevant to the production of events. A common interpretation of sustainability in event management can be seen in through concern for environmental impacts.

Environmental Impacts and Legacy

Purchasing

Procurement, Sourcing, Supply Chain, Materials Use.

The materials, supplies and products used to produce an event all have the potential for negative environmental impacts. Through environmentally preferably purchasing reductions in these impacts can be achieved back up the supply chain. Options to reduce environmental impacts of purchasing can be achieved through such things as; using products which have an eco-label, including organic, fairtrade, FSC or other sustainable forestry products, VOC free, chemical free cleaning products, PVC free, eco-paints, sustainably produced meat/chicken/pork/seafood, products made from sustainable and recyclable materials, etc.

Energy

The energy used to produce an event can be provided directly through the mains/grid power or through mobile or portable power generators. Reducing the environmental impacts of event production can be achieved through reducing the amount of energy needed or to provide energy through renewable or zero emissions sources.

Waste

Reducing the total amount of waste going to landfill or incineration is the aim. This can be done through preventing waste from being created in the first place, or through diverting waste from landfill/ incineration through recycling, composting biodegradable waste (or sending to biogas facilities) and through salvage and re-purposing.

Water & Sanitation

The amount of water used at an event and focusing on its reduction is the key to sustainability in event management in this topic. Reducing the amount of sewage and grey water produced is also an aim.

Transport

The impact of the audience's travel to an event is often seen as one of the largest environmental impact. CO2 emissions as a direct result of transport is the measure used to gauge this. To reduce the impact of audience transport to and from an event, public transport use, filling up all the seats in the car, and coming on foot or by bicycle where appropriate, can be encouraged.

Biodiversity

Protecting the natural environment, both flora and fauna and the ecosystems in which they live is an important aspect to the environmental management of event production.

Venue, Accommodation and Destination

Ensuring that the choice of destination, accommodation and venue is suitable for the requirements of the event and the attendee demographic can be key in reducing unnecessary travel and boosting local economy. By sourcing local suppliers, the carbon footprint of the event will be reduced dramatically as suppliers will need to transport themselves, products or services to the event

Perfect Venue: The Key to a Successful Event

Familiarity can breed boredom. Fortunately with thousands of venues across the country there settle for the mediocre. With a little forethought and the help of this article you will be able to host a truly memorable event.

Plan Ahead

The first step is to plan well in advance of your event. The best venues can be very busy at peak times of the year so for peace of mind you need to book early. However if you have left it late do not despair. It is more important to know exactly what you are looking for because this will help you narrow the choices and find the perfect venue. With such an enormous variety of venues in the country-perfect is out there.

What kind of Event are you Hosting?

The type of event you are hosting will completely affect your choice of venue. It goes without saying that full scale awards ceremonies require a different venue to intimate business meetings. Know what the event is and what you hope to achieve from it. Dinner Dances, AGM's, Product Launches, Company Fun Days, Large Exhibitions, Small Exhibitions and Christmas Parties all need to be treated differently. Don't take your staff to the same place each time!

What do you Want to Achieve from Your Event?

Be honest with yourself about your aims for the event. If you want a basic functional venue that will simply suit your needs then opt for that. If however you want to wow your delegates with an ostentatious display of wealth then it is important you pick your venue accordingly.

Know the Size of your Gathering

The number of people you expect to attend is very important. You will not want to book out the main hall at the London Aquarium if you are only expecting a few.

Conversely you do not want to pick a venue that is too small for your delegation. Many venues have flexible capacities so if you expect your numbers to fluctuate then explain this to the venue managers. Some venues even have moveable walls to accommodate the right numbers of people.

Location-Parking and Accessibility

Access to your venue is crucial. Is it easy to find, or well sign-posted? Is there a railway station nearby? Are there sufficient car parking arrangements? Are you near the Airport? Know your delegates because it is no good having a beautiful country venue if none of your delegates drive and the nearest railway station is miles away.

Budget

Does the meeting venue fit your budget? As with everything your choice will ultimately boil down to cost. Be aware of any extras that need to be considered e.g. data projectors, AV equipment and lighting and find out when payment will be required.

Ask about the rates on offer. Many venues offer 24 hour rates, Dinner, Bed & Breakfast rates and Day Delegate rates. This could considerably reduce your bill. It is also important to find out about the venue cancellation policy in advance just in case you are forced to withdraw.

Personality of Venue

The personality of your venue is difficult to quantify nevertheless it is important. Try asking the following questions: Does the venue have air conditioning? Is there natural daylight in the venue? Is the restaurant/bar what you're after? Are refreshments provided? Remember it's important that you choose what's right for your delegation.

Check for Yourself

If you can; visit the venue in advance. Speak to the staff, check out bar prices and get a feel for the place. Do not despair if you do not have the time or inclination to do this yourself there are many companies that specialise in finding the perfect venue for you.

Corporate Events-A Company's Selling Campaign

Events and different affairs are integral parts of a growing business organization. Success and failure of the events can produce positive or negative effects on the industry position of a firm. Knowing how to prepare one social gathering is very vital; whatever type it is-massive, fancy or simple events must be prepared to please the guests.

The guests in a company affair can differ in size and in the types of attendees. It can have thousands of guests or just a handful of important dignitaries. The guests could be people of the high echelon of the business firm such as board of directors and investors or they can just be simply the workers, customers and suppliers. The aura could be lavish or just intimate. But the variety does not extend to the result. There should be just one outcome-a successful gathering. This will largely depend on the planners. There are companies that assign their employees to do the planning, with occasional consultation with the boss. But this could be a risky approach. Even if the employees are good and talented, the approach of an expert is very much different and more reliable. It is then advisable that every company should consult a company event planner. Experience and talent of these professionals are always a guarantee for a successful social undertaking.

Celebration of any company affair entails a number of things-the theme, the purpose and the general objective of the event. The expert planner will be able to devise the strategy to make the event conform to the said theme and objective. They suggest the venue options, the food and the activities. The food usually is one important aspect of any party's success. The event planner will meticulously attend to all the details of the catering. This does not only involve the food, but the crew as well. Past experiences disclose that failure of social events happen because catering fell short of the expectation. In any party, small or big number, there must always be enough or even more than enough food for all the guests. The timing of serving the food is also crucial. The venue should also be just right for the number of people-not too big to disperse the guests. It should be noted that there should be enough room for them to circulate and socialize. The decorations also create an impression. Therefore, these should conform to the chosen event theme. As a party coordinator has expertise, she can synchronize the decorations, the theme and the program of activities. Event designing has much to consider and only an expert in the field can do the job perfectly and flawlessly. If the company consistently hold social functions, it is best to have a regular events planner. This way, the company is sure to render variations in style which will make their parties enigmatic. Thus invited guests would come to savor another experience extraordinaire...

How to Plan a Corporate Event on Maui

Are you planning to have the annual business or corporate event on the island of Maui, Hawaii? If so, you are in for a treat, as the island is ripe with unique entertainment for Maui corporate events. From the relaxing to the entertaining and celebratory, Maui offers memorable diversions for everyone!

In fact, Maui has been awarded the most family friendly and single friendly vacation spot on Earth, many times over! Maui offers five star accommodations, affordable accommodations, world renowned beaches, destination worthy spa services, a multitude of golf courses, reef snorkeling, whale boat tours, and of course, the world famous Pan-Pacific cuisine.

Maui also hosts many Hawaii and Maui inspired art galleries for the islands most established artists. There are local agricultural tours, for the environmentally inspired team. And there is also a variety of evening entertainments for the whole family, from famous local music entertainers, to Circ De Soleil produced theater.

There are many coordinating services on Maui that specialize in creating celebratory events, visitor entertainment, and Maui corporate parties.

Maui corporate events generally take place in a resort hall, in a private beach tent, or on an estate location. Many popular Maui corporate event entertainments include, hula dancing, fire spinning, tropical bar services and henna temporary tattoos using your corporate logo design.

It is important to find qualified event specialists when planning your Maui celebration, as there many mishaps to planning events and activities site unseen. For instance, many locations can claim that they have the capacity and set up that you require for your party, but in reality, a lot can be lost in translation.

Having an on-site coordinator that you can trust, allows you to sit back while someone else investigates and translates your companies needs. Luckily Maui has many reputable event coordinators that will work with you to create an amazing vacation event for your most valued employees...

Planning an Event the Professional Way

Everybody has his or her own talent. You, too, have your exceptional forte but do you have the capability to organize an event for your office and company? If not, then it is better to resort to an expert in this undertaking-hiring a professional event and conference organizer. Coordinating for a social gathering is a complex task, the planning and preparations may require time and effort. And if you are not adept to the task, your party might end up as a fiasco. And if your gathering is a marketing tool, you might end up losing instead of gaining clients. So do not risk the chance-better to hire a professional events planner rather than do it yourself.

The skilled party coordinator is adequately equipped with the proper personal knowledge and experience to do the planning and eventually execute every detail of the plan for a successful event. Therefore, the expertise of this coordinator will enable your organization or company to achieve the optimal result. Aside from a guaranteed success of your event, you will enjoy the benefits of being stress-free and you can even save money.

You know that you can be relieved of the stress because everything about the event will be undertaken by the planner. He or she will take charge of arranging for the venue, the food and the program of activities. This planner will also handle the invitations for the guests, as well as the sitting arrangement of the visitors. And if the affair would require more time such as a week-end or overnight, your coordinator can also take care of the lodging and travel arrangements of the guests. They can tackle all these jobs with ease and facility. If you are not going to hire the expert, can you do the complexities of the planning and execution of the plans?

You are not to hire any planner that you meet. Be sure that in choosing your special coordinator, he or she must possess the important characteristics such as effective communication skill, capability to tackle problems and details, industry in the fulfilment of the task and patience. When you choose your professional planner, be sure to get some feedbacks first. And if many endorse the services of one particular coordinator, then this may be the right expert for your parties. Once you have found your coordinator, she or he can be your party specialist in all your events. Parties are not the only forte of these arrangers. They can also be behind any conference or meetings-be it a big or small crowd. Whatever the size and venue of the party, your planner can always design specific plans customized for your need...

How to Grow Event Attendance

Build Your Email List-Your number 1 marketing priority should be maintaining and growing your email contact list. Email marketing is a highly effective and low-cost way of getting the word out about your event. Make it easy for visitors to your website to subscribe to your email newsletter. On event day, make sure you provide a paper newsletter subscribe list when you are checking everyone in. Make sure when you design your email newsletters that you include a very clear call-to-action for the recipient to "Share this Email with a Friend".

Social Media-Build a Facebook page for your event and include references to it on your website and all marketing materials. Offer incentives for those who become a fan of your Facebook page. For example, offer a deal where those who are on your list of Facebook fans will receive a special commemorative t-shirt when they check in on event day. Your Facebook fans have their own circle of online friends who will notice their association with your event and naturally want to learn more.

Recruitment Incentives-Offer registrants a gift if they can convince their friends to participate. Group discounts are also a great way to recruit people who may be on the fence about attending. A common group discount would be a family deal where 4 people can attend for the price of 3.

Discount Coupons-With a down economy, if your potential attendees are on a tight budget, they may be thinking about waiting until next year to attend. Help them out and offer promotional coupons for a registration discount.

Early-bird registration fee-Offer discounts for those who register early. Collecting more attendee data early in the registration process will also help reduce the amount of work for your staff in the last days prior to the event.

Offer Online Registration-Registering for your event online can be as easy as just a few clicks saving your attendees a stamp or trip in the car down to the event office to submit their paper entry. With online event registration, participant data and payment are collected instantly and a confirmation email is automatically sent out saving your staff time and resources.

Send one last email prior to the close of online registration-Make sure to identify those email list subscribers that have not yet registered and send them one last reminder about 1 week prior to the event.

Partnerships with other event organisers and clubs-Seek out other organisations that cater to the same types of people that would be interested in your event. If you're planning a cycling event, do some research online to find all of the cycling clubs in the area. You may be able to work out an arrangement where the club manager will promote your event to his members if you in turn promote his club to your event participants.

Post-Event Festival-Considering how competitive the events industry has become, event organisers are doing everything they can to make their event stand out above the rest. One way of doing this is to host a party or festival after your event and offer additional activities beyond the main event. Activities could include a concert, prize draw, games for kids, booth space for your sponsors to hand out free samples or food tasting from local restaurants. Allowing your attendees to bring friends and family to the party is a great way to recruit new participants for the following year's event.

Make it a fundraising event-Your event is sure to provide your attendees with an unforgettable experience but why not also send them home with a feeling that that have done something for the greater good? Choose a local charity and donate a portion of event proceeds to the cause. If you want participants to be more hands-on, organise a fundraising competition and ask that they solicit their friends and family for donations. Those who are asked to make a contribution may also decide that they want to participate in the event...

How to Plan a Charity Walk or Run

Charity events in any form are always popular, but increasingly, many organisations are choosing to recruit their fundraisers through more interactive events such as walks and runs. A charity walk or run is not only a healthy way for your participants to raise money for a good cause, but also a very visible way of publicizing your charitable cause to the community. If a charity run or walk seems like a good fit for your organisation, here is an overview of some things you may want to keep in mind when planning the event.

The Planning Phase

Choosing a Route

When planning a mass participation event such as a walk or run it is important that you first take some time to carefully consider the route your participants will be following. Your choice of route will play a central roll in other decisions you make concerning resources, staff size, security, transportation, volunteers, signage, and ultimately the satisfaction of your participants.

When mapping out the course, first determine the type of event you would like to hold. Most fundraising events try to be as inclusive as possible because, simply put, more fundraisers translates into more donations for your cause!

If your goal is to be as inclusive as possible that means you want people of all ages and physical abilities to be able to participate in your event. That said, when choosing your route it is a good idea to not only look at a map but get out there and actually walk the course yourself. When surveying the road, pay attention to elevation gain, traffic, road conditions, and any other factors that could potentially make participating in your event strenuous for the less physically able. You may also benefit from contacting a local running or walking club for suggestions of routes that may fit your participant's ability levels. Some common route distances for charity events are 5k, 10k, Half Marathon and Marathon.

Resources and Staff

The number of participants and spectators you expect on event day as well as length of course are the two main factors that will determine the size of your volunteer staff and resources needed. Here is a list of items commonly used by event walking and running events:

- Two way radios
- Rope, tape and cones for course marking
- Signage for start and finish areas
- Signage for services and support areas
- Portable toilets
- Trash cans
- Food
- Water
- Tents
- Tables
- Stage for awards ceremony
- PA system
- Generator.

Looking at your course map, you will be able to strategically position your water stops, trash cans, portable toilets, concessions stands and so on. When placing these resources, keep in mind that many people will want to gather around in the finish/celebration area after the event so you may need additional resources in that area. When planning for food and water for your participants, you may want to ask a local market to sponsor the event in the way of donated oranges, bananas and water that you can position along the course.

For your spectator concession stands, you will need to determine what types of food you will sell and if you will need to prepare or cook food on site. There are many companies that you can hire to staff and prepare food at your concession stands or you could use your volunteers.

Legalities of a Charity Walk or Run

Speaking of special permits, there are several legalities to consider when planning a charity walk or run. Now that you have chosen your route, have you looked to see if you need permission to use this planned route? You may need to speak with the local council or the person who owns the land. Have you checked to make sure there are no other events planned on your route come event day? Have you obtained liability insurance for your event? Ideally, your insurance should cover any medical problems that occur during the event as well as damage to the land and surrounding property. With the size of event you are expecting, are you required to schedule police presence or request road closures? Do you have permission from the organisation you are raising money for to use their logo and name?

Considering every city, town, or district have their own set of regulations, how you address them will depend on local law and requirements. What we highlighted above are only some of the larger items you should investigate. We would suggest contacting your local council for more information.

Finding Participants

Marketing

Now that you picked an event location and have all of the necessary approvals and permits, its time to start spreading the word! Traditional event marketing consists of mail, tv, radio, newspaper advertisements and signs posted up about town. These methods can be effective, reach large audiences, and should be looked into but they can come at a high cost. Don't let that get you down though-the internet has spawned many highly targeted, low-cost, and sometimes free marketing channels that are ideal for creating a buzz about your charity event. Here is a list of some web marketing options that you may want to consider:

Build a website-This is a must. Nowadays, any successful event has an official website where they can direct the public, media and interested sponsors for more information.

Facebook, Twitter, Social Media-There are countless online communities and fan pages out there that are filled with people passionate about the same cause you are raising money for. Get involved with these people and immerse yourself in the online conversation. Build a Facebook Fan Page or Twitter page for your event, invite your new online friends and encourage them to recruit their friends to get involved for the cause.

Submit Your Event to an Online Events Calendar-There are many websites that will give you a free event listing on their online calendar. Submit your event profile to as many of these as possible and make sure to include a link back to your website in the description.

Email Advertising-Does your organisation already have a list of members who subscribe to your monthly newsletter or email announcements? Send your contact list an attractive HTML email with information about your event and a link to your. Make sure to include "share" buttons in your emails to make it easy for the recipient to pass it on to a friend. Also, on your website, Facebook page and Twitter page, include a feature where the visitor can join your mailing list.

Participant Registration

Something important to consider from the start of the planning phase is how you will collect contact information, entry fees, and fundraising commitments from people who want to participate. Until recently, most events collected participant data and entry fees in person in the event office with a paper registration form. To streamline the staff workload that comes along with paper-based registration, you may want to find a technology provider that specialises in event management software and online event registration.

An integrated online event management system will allow you to build a custom online registration form, link to that form from your website, and collect your participant contact data online. We would suggest that the technology you choose include a merchant gateway integrated with the registration form so that you can seamlessly and securely collect payment online during the registration process.

Depending on your technology provider, the data collected on an online registration form should be captured and stored in a database that you can log into, manage the data, run reports, email participants and process cancellation refunds if needed.

If you hope to grow the size of your email database, it is very important that you make the Email question compulsory so that every online registration has an email address associated with it in your database. You will be able to use this email to send out reminder emails about changes to the event schedule or important notices about fundraising. Any fully integrated online event management system will also need the email address to send out an automatic confirmation email letting the registrant know that their payment has been accepted and spot saved for event admission.

Fundraising Tools

Some more advanced event management systems include an online fundraising platform that you can integrate with your online registration form. What's great about this is that every person who registers online will automatically have an online fundraising website created for them. The fundraiser can customise their website, ad images, set a fundraising goal, blog about their progress and training for the event, and communicate with their donors. The donor can visit the fundraising site and make an online donation with their credit card at which point the donation amount is added to the fundraisers goal total and money is sent to the charitable organisation. Many organisations are moving their fundraising efforts completely online because the general consensus is that people are likely to donate more if they are able to do it online from the comfort of their own home...

Online Fundraising Tips for Events

Online fundraising is quickly overtaking direct mail as the preferred method of collecting donations for charity events and non-profit organisations. As the younger "wired" generation grows up, we can safely assume that they will prefer to donate online almost exclusively. Are you doing enough to offer your donors and fundraisers the latest in online giving tools?

Here are some of the benefits to online fundraising:

- Immediacy-The donor can learn about the cause and is enabled to make a contribution immediately while the thought is fresh in their mind.

- Administrative Efficiency-The non-profit organization receives the funds immediately along with donor contact information.
- Instant Gratification for the Donor-An acknowledgement is instantly sent to the donor by way of automatic confirmation email.
- Analytics-The key to successful fundraising is knowing who your donors are and what interests them. Collecting donations online allow you to observe their behaviour in navigation of your website, track what they are reading prior to making the donation and what type of call-to-action resonates the most with them. Using this information to parse your contact lists will enable you to optimise your fundraising campaign by tailoring your message and call-to-action to different types of donors.

Here are some tips if you are just getting started with an online fundraising campaign:

- Consider All Marketing Channels-Reference your online giving option in newsletters, brochures, your website, signage and radio/TV advertisements.
- Leverage Social Media-Sites like Facebook are cheap and effective ways to cultivate a word-of-mouth marketing campaign and grow your fan base.
- Your Website-Include your mission statement, goals, objectives and what work your organisation has accomplished to further your cause. Explain how you will use the funds you raise and include photos and testimonials from your fundraisers, donors and beneficiaries.
- Provide lots of ways to Donate...but focus on pushing the online channel. Collecting as many donations online as possible will automate your workload and minimise volunteer staff time and resources needed. Make your 'Donate Online' button large and above the fold (top half of the page). You have the attention of your audience and they are looking for a way to contribute as quickly as possible-don't make them hunt for a way to give.
- Reward Your Donors-Offer a gift or incentive in return for a donation. Consider something as simple as a subscription to your organisation's monthly newsletter or an invitation to a gala dinner for those who donate over a certain amount.

- Find a Robust Online Giving Platform-Choose an online donation service that allows your fundraisers to build a personalised fundraising web page. Enabling your fundraisers to build a personalised space online where they can add photos, their own personal story and blog about their experiences raising money for the cause will really get them excited to share with all their friends and family.
- Encourage Your Fundraisers-Offer prizes to fundraisers who collect the most donations. Many online donation services offer a way to track the total amount each fundraiser has gathered on their personal page from friends and family.

Make it fun and get creative! With all of the relatively cheap (many times, free) online tools and marketing opportunities available nowadays, any organization can optimize their fundraising campaign...

Event Management Systems Help Administrative and Event Planning Professionals

For anyone who has had to deal with the hassles of registration and scheduling for a variety of events, an investment in event management systems can easily streamline this process.

There are many aspects to planning an event and making sure it goes smoothly. Whether you are planning a conference, competition, trade show, seminar or any other event, there are certain aspects that are common to their management and maintenance. These include not only scheduling of the location, guest registration, and working with a budget, but dealing with changes in location, cancelations, and updates. Event management systems make this whole process easier. Many of them provide a way to integrate your own best practices as far as registration and scheduling. They also provide content management systems that you can use to add your own content.

Many of the processes involved in event management are automated by these systems, including scheduling at a glance, change notifications, and payment systems. Users can use this software for space planning for these events as well, and the reservation of the resources needed for each event. They can use the event management software to arrange for services for the event as well, such as catering. This software frequently includes web calendars that can be published for ease of scheduling. Event management software can also print online tickets for attendees. All of these benefits offered by this software can reduce the headaches involved in keeping track of these important details. Anyone who is responsible for event scheduling will appreciate the way this software helps them prevent double booking any facility and all of the time and inconvenience that such a situation can cause. Whenever an event is held, most event planning and administrative professionals know that reporting needs to be done on the event. Event management systems provide a way to provide reports in a variety of standard formats, including HTML, MS Excel, and CSV. They also provide for the approval of funds for these events. This software is also coded to provide tools for auditing to ensure compliance with established processes. If you are in the event planning business or you perform event planning as part of your job duties, event management systems can reduce the time and resources required to manage and plan your important events. The ease with which you will be able to manage your events with event management systems makes them a worthy investment...

What to Give as a Gift to the Professional Speakers at Your Event

As a professional speaker, over the years, I have been given many different kinds of gifts after my seminar from the meeting planner. Some of these gifts are useful and some I have no idea what I will do with.

After a seminar or motivational speech, many meeting planners present you with a mug, water bottle or a T shirt with the company or association logo on it. It is a nice token of appreciation however most people have little use for it. I must have 20 logo mugs in my cupboard, and those are just from recent years.

I remember one year I was the motivational keynote speaker a conference in Newfoundland and the meeting planner gave me a coffee table book. Too big to fit in my carry-on, I left it in my hotel room. A week later, the hotel sent it back to me in the mail.

These gifts are expensive, they require a lot of work to put them together and who knows where they will end up. Before going to the trouble to give any gift, ask yourself why you are giving it. Because you will feel bad if you don't?

Is it because you have to present them with something at the end(the check would be fine)? As far as I know most motivational speakers don't feel entitled to a gift anyways. Here are some of the best gifts for a professional speaker I have received:

* Recently I got a solar charger (very cool!) with the association logo on it. When on the road, you can charge you cell phone, IPod, computer, etc
* A simple thank you card signed by the entire conference planning committee
* A miniature wooden lectern
* Original art from local artists
* A contribution made in my name to a worthy cause
* Photos taken of the event in a little book
* A star bucks coffee card-A favourite gift, everybody likes coffee
* A bottle of wine from the region. Was great, except that I couldn't take it in my carry on
* Many conference speakers speak to raise their profile in the industry, so articles featuring them, or articles summarizing their message are a real memento.
* One conference did a humorous caricature of me, holding the company logo. I still have it, ten years later.
* Gifts like fruit in the hotel room before you arrive are great especially if a speaker arrives late and all food places are closed
* The best gift by far is A follow up thank you letter and a referral to another speaking engagement or event.

A professional speaker doesn't give motivational speeches for the presents anyways. The real gift is being there and contributing to the event...

Steps for Planning a Seminar and Training Event

As we head into 2011, most organizations prepare to plan their goals. Included in this is continuing professional development. Corporate meeting planners are busy this time of year planning seminar, convention or training event (s). Here is a really simple list to Consider in building effective continuing professional development events:

1) Decide on your Goal. Will the event be for skill building like leadership, inspiration, or training like new advances in technology, compliance training, etc? Brainstorm first and plan each of your seminar, training or conventions into specific available dates in your calendar. Create a focus and theme for each meeting or convention.

2) Organize the key players. For each meeting or event, decide who needs to be a part of the seminar. If you are looking for specific skill training, consider what experts need to speak. If you are looking to build rapport and create motivation, than hire a motivational speaker. If you need after dinner entertainment, hire after dinner humorous keynote speakers. From here you create the agenda.
3) Decide on meeting space. For a smaller event, a boardroom may be sufficient. Larger convention space is available through hotels which also provide lodging accommodations for out of town delegates. You may need to create a request for proposal for different potential venues to get the best rates and service for your meeting.
4) Create a list of potential participants. Who needs to be at each seminar, meeting or event? Is it leadership? middle management? technical support? front line professionals?
5) Determine logistics. Some professional, guest or seminar speaker require PowerPoint, and others don't. It is best to equip each room just in case. Standard set up are microphones (lapel, handheld and/or podium), power point projector, computer, screen. Will you have internet access for presentations? You may need to hire an AV technician Company

Remember food and beverage and room set up.

Convention Industry Council has established a series of tools that should be viewed as an excellent source of best practices

Create your promotion strategy: How will you let people know about the event? Consider the audience. Some ideas:

A company or association newsletter, email promotion blast, social media, mass media, company website.

Create your specific promotions: Once you have decided on and coordinated the key players, leadership expert, keynote motivational speaker, seminar speakers, etc. It is time to get the word out about your event. Promote the keynote and seminar speaker, continuing professional development goals, and your theme

Set up a registration list: How will you handle payment? in advance or at the door, online? Coordinate and streamline the registration efforts.

Prepare signage: For specific rooms. Meet many times with the hotel or special event manager to organize and coordinate the fine details. Be clear on who does what. You many need to reduce or increase food and beverage, chairs, tables, number of rooms etc based on registration numbers.

Prepare name badges, the convention meeting agenda, keynote and seminar speaker bios and handouts.

Get all PowerPoint presentations and set up all last minute logistics. Be prepared that speakers may change their slides, last registrations may be high, you may have last minute room changes, AV challenges. If you go through this list and are prepared your Continuing Professional Development event, speaker, and agenda will be an inspiration and success...

Capture a Big Crowd With Your Captivating Business Event

Businesses to capture a big number of customers sponsor business events. The objective is to attract the attention of many clients-existing and prospective. The type of events is usually promotional. So if this is the purpose of your company, you need to take care of several things to ensure its success and of course, the primary purpose of attracting the biggest crowd possible.

The business event can either be indoor or outdoor. For both occasion, there is a need for exhibition set-up. In some occasions, there is a need for putting up booths. Whatever is established, you have only one ultimate purpose-get the patronage of clients.

The event should have an appealing theme. And in many cases of business events, the attending guests expect a lot-food, freebies and promotional items. But you cannot go all the way in your give-aways because there is a specified budget for the purpose. You will have a hard time doing this. You can crack your head planning for the success of the event. To this, there is one solution-a viable one that will attract the clients and satisfy all attendees. Aren't these two the main purpose of the event?

An experienced events planner can make your event the center of attraction. It will not only magnetize the crowd, it will even charm them to have loyalty and patronage for the product your company is promoting. The events planner is an experienced professional who knows how to fascinate guests. This is their expertise.

The events coordinator knows what types of crowd to target. Would it be the masses or the people of the high echelon in the society? Or is this party for the middle class? The theme can be based on the customers. Banners and streamers are among the things to be set-up. Your coordinator will know how to give to the venue an aesthetic appeal.

The prime purpose is to gather as much guests as possible. The planner will take charge of the advertisements; she makes sure that people will know about the event. She will ascertain that a big number of guests will flock to the business promotional event. Every guest is a prospective consumer of the product being promoted. And with many consumers, there will be more sales and eventually more income for the firm.

A secondary purpose is to satisfy the guests. The contentment of the guests will lead to sales. The planner knows this and she will endeavor to meet the expectations of the attending customers. And most of all she will attain the goal on the specified company budget...

The Right Place to Exhibit-A Strategic Approach

Business Week Magazine reported that "a trial and error approach to selecting a place to exhibit results in an average of 2.5 exhibit participations before you choose the right event." When you multiply that by the thousands of dollars and incredible amount of human resources to participate in a show, the cost of choosing the wrong place to exhibit is massive.

Here is a two step approach to choosing the best places for you to exhibit.

Step 1-Understand Your Objectives

Everything starts with your objectives. Understanding your objectives will influence all your choices.

Step 2-Define Your Audience

Who do you want to attract to your exhibit? If your answer is "Anyone with a pulse and a wallet," your response may be misleading you. Rarely will one product or service be appropriate for everyone. Follow this plan to ensure you select the right events the first time.

Establish a Customer Profile

The best place to start is to clarify who your real customer is. Understanding your existing customers and how they perceive the features and benefits of what you have to offer is the place to begin. This involves an in depth demographic and psychographic analysis of the person who is most likely to help you achieve your objectives.

Demographics answer the question, "Who is my customer?" It is an analysis of all the pertinent data that defines the characteristics of your customer. For a business-to-business transaction, the qualifiers may include: size of company, type of products sold, revenue, budget, number of employees, number of branches, ownership, industry sector, and so on.

Psychographics answer the question, "What do they do?" This is a chance to examine your target audience's attitudes, beliefs, and emotions. In the business-to-business marketplace, psychographic elements include: social responsibility, environmental conscience, business style, position within an industry, innovations, affiliations, employee relations, workforce type, management style, employee remuneration, shareholder relations, and so on.

Rank Your Customer Profiles in Order of Priority

The next step is to determine which targeted group will deliver the greatest return on your investment. Let's say you have identified three distinct users of your product or service. Ask which will give you the biggest bang for your buck. Now, when faced with various potential show selections, you can simply examine the audience quality, see where it fits in your priority, and decide.

Let's assume the following:

- Customer profile 1 is your "A" priority.
- Customer profile 2 is your "B" priority.
- Customer profile 3 is your "C" priority.

Choose the Right type of Event

Choosing the right event is a matter of style, taste, logistics, budget, ability, and geography. Geography is an important factor since it refers to your marketing reach and begs the question "Where is the best place to reach my targeted customer?" Think of your geographic reach as three tiers: regional, national, and international.

Tier 1: Regional Events

If you select a regional show, you might be able to influence visitors from as far away as 200 miles from the site.

Tier 2: National Events

National events attract an audience from across the country. They are usually wider in scope and focus.

Tier 3: International Events

In the international arena there are fewer events, but they are designed to attract visitors from a wider geographic area. These events are usually well established and well known in the industry, and because they are often timed according to business cycles, they become a must-see event for attendees and attract all levels of decision-makers.

When you choose your event you may also want to include such factors such as market priority, competitor profile, ability to generate leads or take orders, media opportunities, networking, access to an exhibitor's list, reputation of the show, show organizer's promotion strategy, sponsorships layout, and timing. Your list of factors should include the things that best meet your criteria for success.

Establishing a Selection Criteria

Your criterion generally falls into two broad categories: Strategic and tactical. Strategic considerations are where you should place your emphasis. Audience profile and geography are, for most exhibitors' crucial strategic elements.

The tactical elements revolve around logistical elements that can often be overcome. Show layout, move-in and move out considerations fall under this category.

Take each of your strategic and tactical elements and rate each on a continuum of 1-10, with one being a "nice to" but not critical to your success to ten being a "must have" element that is critical to your success.

The following provides an example of how your ranking might look:

Strategic Considerations

High Ranking Elements (weighting of X3) would be considered as the "must-have" elements that drive a company's decision to participate in a particular show. If the show is missing any of these elements, the odds are that it is not worth participating in.

Examples of "High Ranking" Elements:

- Market Priority
- Audience Fit
- Exclusivity of Opportunity.

Important Ranking Elements (weighting of X2) include those elements that significantly extend the reach and impact of your exhibit program, and contribute to the overall strength and viability of show selection.

Examples of "Important Ranking" Elements:

- Ability to contribute to lead generation
- Opportunity to impact audience
- Reputation of Show/Credibility of Show Organizer.

Tactical Considerations

Other Ranking Elements (Weighting X1) are usually attributed to specific activities and are considered less important on their own, but support the overall objectives of the exhibit program.

Examples of "Other Ranking" Elements:

- Show Organizer Promotion Strategy
- Competitor Presence
- Exhibitor Profile Opportunities
- Media Opportunities
- Networking opportunities with targeted decision-makers
- Access to Attendee Lists.

Use the Ranking Criteria and Evaluation Grid

To obtain a copy of the Evaluation Grid please contact the author at barry@siskindtraining.com

Finding the right show is difficult. Don't jump at the first opportunity that knocks on your door. You have lots of choices. Take your time and do your homework. The right show is a blend of audience, cost and logistics. Good event selection is a solid base upon which the rest of your exhibit program is built...

Selecting Conference Venues Wisely

There is an ever growing choice when looking for conference venues in the UK at present. Every possible type of venue now suggests that it is capable of being a conference venue, ranging from farms to 5 star hotels, from rugby grounds to racecourses. The problem a conference organiser faces is how to narrow down this choice. The first thing to bear in mind it the suitability of conference venues to your requirements. While a fancy 5 star hotel may sound very appealing, you have to be confident that the layout can work for your event. For example, some conference venues are unable to supply break out rooms close to the main area, causing logistical issues for the organiser. It is important to ensure you check the internal layout of conference venues and not just the beautiful brochure pictures taken from the outside. It is also important to look into the IT capabilities of conference venues. Many of the newer properties that offers the facility for conferences are not fully equipped with an in-house IT and audio-visual team. Unless you are prepared to bring this team in yourself, ensure you have a venue that is experienced in this area.

There is no easier way to ruin a conference than to have constantly failing Audio Visual through the key-note speeches. A good conference venue finding agency should always be able to suggest independent technical teams, but its far easier if conference venues can provide this service themselves. The overnight delegate needs are also a key factor when choosing conference venues. There is little point impressing your guests with a 15th century coach house for the main event, only to then have to bus them 30 miles to the nearest accommodation for the evening. This is where the more traditional conference venues come to the fore. As with many industries where new players have tried to break into an established market, there are very few that succeed. By far the most successful and well organised conference venues are the large hotel chains and bespoke city centre venues.

While the information that agencies and conference venues can provide by email, over the phone or by post, there is no substitute for visiting the conference venues before you decide. What many people do not realise is that you can view several venues for free without any obligation to decide there and then. A common preconception is that the venue will be over zealous in their efforts to convince you to sign the deal immediately. At reputable conference venues this practice is now extinct. With all of the above in mind, and with many more factors to be taken into account, it can seem a daunting task trying to find the right conference venues for your events. While there can be advantages to completing this whole process yourself, most people nowadays use a conference venue finding agency.

These agencies can range from system based call centres, to small knowledgeable regionally focussed agencies. These agencies can arrange several viewings in one day based on your requirements. Their key advantage is often their geographical knowledge, they can match your requirements to a range of conference venues in a specific geographic area (usually the key consideration when organising a conference, and a decision that is unlikely to be changed once made). To get a guide on the quality of these agencies, it's a good idea to ensure you have all of your key requirements listed, plus a few nice to have extras, when you first contact them.

A good agency should get back to you within a day with a range of venues that fit your needs. If they haven't taken the time to know your requirements, and have come back with totally unsuitable conference venues then try a different agency immediately, it wont take long to find an agency who you can confidently use over and over again, saving you many hours of fruitless searches and sales pitches, and leaving you to get on with organising the conference itself...

The 1 Thing You must do if you Attend Events

If you're going to spend the money to go to events, this is the Number One thing you MUST do or you're just throwing money out the window. Actually it's three things. Ready? Look, if you're one of these people who go to events, gets a stack of business cards, comes home and piles it on your desk with all the other business cards you've accumulated over the years, you are leaving a TON of money on the table. (Or in this case, on your desk.)

I can't tell you how many clients I've gotten from events who told me the biggest reason they hired me over some other copywriter or marketing strategist was simply because I followed up with them. And some other copywriter or marketing strategist they had met at an event and had a good connection with, never got considered because they didn't follow up.

So with that said, let me share my system for follow up after events.

1. I take all of the business cards out of my purse.
2. I call one of my team members, who comes over to my house and picks up the cards. (Note — if your team members don't live near you, you can also stick the cards in the mail.)
3. She inputs the cards into my database.
4. I don't add emails to my list unless I've made it very clear that's what I'm going to do (for instance, I'm speaking or I have a booth with a fish bowl for cards). But what I DO do is...
5. Mail them a Newsletter Postcard each month.

Some of you might be getting my Newsletter Postcard. It's an oversize postcard that has an article, a little note from Nick the border collie, and a testimonial. It's a template so it doesn't take long to put together each month. The nice part of direct mail is the connection. Many people who get my postcard take it with them to read. (How often does that happen with email newsletters?) And I can put people on my direct mail list who would never stay on my email list. \

Now, if adding direct mail feels too big or complicated to you right now, let me give you some alternatives.

1. Reach out personally to everyone on your list through an email or a mailed card (like through Send Out Cards). You can have your assistant help you with this or systemize it so you add a little personal note but the rest of it is the same.
2. After you've reached out, ask them if it's okay to be added to your ezine list. I'm really not of the mindset that you should add people to your email list unless you've made it clear that's what you're going to do. But that's me, I know some of my colleagues disagree with me. I would rather have people add themselves or tell me they want to be added.

If they don't respond or don't want to be added to your e-zine list, I would look for them on social networking sites (Facebook, Linked In, Twitter) and connect with them there.

And if you have someone who told you they're interested in hiring you, most definitely contact them. In fact, you should probably plan to contact them at least 7 times (if not more). No, you don't have to pick up the phone — dropping an email or adding them to your mailing list is also fine (although I would reach personally at least a couple of times with email or by phone).

I can guarantee if you make a point of following up with people you meet at events, you will see a much bigger payoff than if you don't.

3 Secrets on Getting the Most Out of Attending Events

You've got your suitcases packed, your airline booked and you're on your way to a live event.

But you're a little nervous: You've already spent a bunch of money, you're about to spend a bunch more on hotels and food, not to mention the time away from your business and life. Will this turn into a good investment (i.e. help your business grow) or will it end up being just a waste of time and money?

That's an excellent question and as someone who has attending more than her share of events with fabulous (and not-so-fabulous) results, let me share my 3 secrets to getting the most out of your attending events. Set your intentions on what you want to get out of the event. Are you looking for joint venture partners? New clients? New ideas or information you can implement in your business? Is there someone you really want to meet in person? All of the above? Something else entirely?

It doesn't matter how you define a successful event, what's important is that you actually spell out what you want to have happen and make it as clear as possible. If you're not clear on what you want, then your results could end up being equally murky. You want to visualize exactly what would have to happen for this to be a successful event for you. Let me take a moment and share a quick story about this. At an event I recently attended, I was walking through the dining room at dinnertime and I saw a woman sitting by herself. I went up to her and asked if she wanted some company, which she did. It turned out she had set the intention for meeting ME at this event and we've ended up doing a couple of joint ventures together. Isn't it amazing once you set the intention how the Universe actually delivers it?

Don't just hang around your "crowd": There's no question that one of the reasons why I love going to events is I can reconnect with all my old friends and colleagues. However, as much as I treasure the face-to-face bonding, I also want to meet new friends and colleagues too. Make a point of having either lunch, dinner, drinks, etc. with a new group each day. That gives you the opportunity to meet new people without going too far out of your comfort zone. (Now, if the thought of that is making you break out into a cold sweat, take a deep breath. Bring a friend with you, just don't only talk to your friend. Or only do this once or twice in the few days you're there and slowly work your way up. You'll probably discover the vast majority of the people at these events are just as eager and just as nervous as you are, and it all ends up working itself out.)

Manage your energy: This is a big one I never see anyone talk about but it's really important. Events are exhausting. Period. Between being "on" when you meet people to absorbing all the information that's flying at you, it can wear you out.

So it's important to know your limits and listen to your body. You don't have to be at every single networking opportunity. It's okay to skip a group lunch or dinner and get room service.

Everyone is going to have different limits and whatever that is, it's perfect for you and you should honour it. The last thing you want to do is wear yourself out so much that when that perfect client DOES show up on Day 3, you're not so drained you don't properly represent yourself (and end up losing the sale). There's one more thing I want you to do to make your event attendance as successful as possible, but this is SO important I'm going to devote an entire article about it. Stay tuned!

Why You Must Attend Events to Grow Your Biz

Look, I get it. Attending events can be a big deal. There's travel costs, time away from work, time away from the family, etc. etc. So why on earth should you bother? After all, between social networking and the telephone, you can meet all the people you want, right? And with all the classes and programs out there, you can get all the learning you need without leaving your house too. Right? Well that's not exactly true. You see, going to events is a lot bigger than the networking and the learning. I would go as far to say something magical happens when you start going to events. Here are 3 reasons why you MUST make attending events a part of your marketing tool kit. *Gets you out of your "day to day" rut.* It happens to the best of us. Between your huge to-do list and your commitments to your family, community, life etc., you have a lot going on. And sometimes it's all you can do to focus on the next thing you have to get done.

The problem is when you're in that mode (and trust me, I've been in that mode many times before) you can't see the forest for the trees. You're focused on the details, not the big picture. And when you get in that mindset, it's really easy to miss something — maybe it's a big opportunity, maybe it's a problem waiting to explode in your face.

Going to an event means a break in your routine. It gives you a chance to breathe, to see things you might not have seen when all those to-dos are staring you in the face. It can give you a perspective you never had. You could end up with an idea that could transform your business, add an additional income stream or stop a problem in the bud that could cost you thousands in money, time, energy and aggravation.

Keeps you from feeling lonely. There's no question about it — being an entrepreneur can be lonely. Chances are your friends, neighbors and family really don't "get" what you do to make money, much less what it means to be an entrepreneur — the responsibilities you have and the decisions you need to make. Who do you use for a sounding board? Who do you talk to when something goes wrong — maybe your web site goes down during a crucial launch or your assistant sends the wrong email to the wrong list and causes all sorts of confusion and complications. Your friends and family probably don't even understand the problem much less be able to give you any sort of help solving it.

But your entrepreneurial friends "get it." They know EXACTLY what you're going through because they're living it too. And it can be such a relief to be surrounded by your "tribe" (not to mention having the opportunity to brainstorm and bounce ideas off of other successful entrepreneurs to see what "pops" for your business.)

Gets you in front of people you would never be able to reach any other way. Are there people you'd love to connect with but think they're so "big" you'll never get their attention? People like Alex Mandossian or Ali Brown? Well, I can tell you from experience it's a heck of lot easier to connect with thought leaders at an event then it is to try to get them on the phone or through social networking. (And yes, one of the reasons why I got both of them as a client was I first met them at an event.) Over the years I've met nearly all my clients in person, and that has really helped me develop deeper relationships with them. And that doesn't even count all the joint ventures or other opportunities that have come up because I met great people in person at events.

I really believe one of the reasons why my business started taking off is because I started attending events several years ago. Events can be a great way to boost your business, especially if you know how to approach them. I'll cover some tips on getting the most out of your event attendance next week.

Event Hire Companies-Adding Life, Colour and Zest to Your Parties

Anyone who has ever held a party or any other event would certainly know the trouble that's associated with getting all the necessary equipment and to ensure everything runs seamlessly. Also, nowadays people would rather not go to a simple backyard barbecue party which offers nothing more than some barbecue, a few colourful balloons and drinks. This is where a good event hire company will add good value by peppering the event with lots of fashionable and attractive things. However, it's important to identify and hire only the best firms-best in terms of price and also in terms of services and equipment. Plenty of event hire firms today would offer things like classy martini glasses and breath-taking casino backdrops with fake GBP notes littered across the house. Hiring a top-notch firm means that they will get each and every detail looked into without you needing to break a sweat. Parties that replicate the sixties, the seventies and eighties are a big favourite among party enthusiasts and event hire firms alike. To help the people loosen up; the company could also use a projector to illuminate a section of the floor to make it look and feel like a dance floor. Nowadays, event hire companies will also throw in a few masked models that would portray certain childhood film characters and/or cartoons.

Additionally, you can also opt to lighten up your party by asking the event organisers to add a few game stalls-this would add a special zest, colour, joy and cheer to the party. To add further zest and cheer, consider asking for distorted mirrors to be hung up on some of the walls-also couple this with littering the entire place with multicoloured and eye-catching buntings. Another very popular idea among the event hire companies is to make the entire party feel like the discovery of the lost city of Atlantis. The team will make this happen via tactics such as installing a water effect projector and having the entire house littered with lost treasure and underwater gems.

Event hire companies have made parting even more fun. Everything and anything is possible-from fancy dress parties, clowns and bearded ladies to magicians and lion tamers. The job of these companies is to make your party a lifelong memorable event.

The Anatomy of a Successful Trade Show Exhibit

A trade show, also known as a merchandise show or market week, is an exhibition or a business gathering organized by companies that showcase and demonstrate their new products and services and also their latest offerings. Trade shows also provide opportunities for companies to meet their customers, to learn new trends and to identify new prospects.

Trade shows are not open to the public and can only be attended by company representatives, members of the trade and members of the press. One advantage of holding a trade show is that it shortens the time it takes for companies to look for prospective customers. But the major disadvantage is that customers and prospects pay little attention to the many exhibitors and their products due to the many distractions and the busy atmosphere inherent in trade shows. Exhibitors can make effective use of trade show displays in trade shows to direct visitors to their main display area. Trade show displays are used to give visitors a better understanding or appreciation of the products or services being marketed. Although exhibitors are only supposed to put their trade show displays within the confines of their designated trade show exhibit area, exhibitors also display items in strategic areas of the fair grounds. Trade show displays often used include banner stands, counters and cabinets, panel display etc. that clearly display the company logo, basic company information and company slogan. The trade show booth is an important component of the trade show display as it aims to enhance the brand and marketing experience for the visitor. It facilitates valuable direct face-to-face contact between the companies and their prospective customers. The whole booth set-up includes counters kiosks, lighting, flooring, literature racks, banner stands and high impact graphics, with the booth design, the staffing and the handouts the main factors to a successful trade show booth. Many companies prefer to rent pre-owned trade show exhibits and displays rather than to buy or to create them from scratch to save on the trade show booth construction costs and also on the expense of warehousing the displays after the trade show is over.

Trade shows demand a lot of work and effort, and exhibitors have to plan well in advance so as to make the trade show a success. It is because any successful trade show offers exhibitors with a very valuable opportunity to build relationships face-to-face with their clients and to close lucrative business deals.

The Importance of a Good Venue Finder

As companies seek to economise when it comes to corporate events, the importance of a good venue finder has never been greater. Cast your mind back to those heady pre credit crunch days of 2007. We were at the peak of the bubble. Britain had never been richer and our politicians were convinced they had finally solved boom and bust. In those days businesses could be as extravagant as they liked especially when it came to organising good corporate events. Only the best was good enough; the sky was the limit. Companies behaved as if they had limitless resources. As a result the best and most expensive corporate event locations quickly began to dominate the market. Places such as the NEC in Birmingham became a regular location for businesses of all types. However, as budgets come under control, every company-whether large or small-has to find a way to economise. In short we all have to be a little more savvy when searching for a good place to hold our event which is why companies are placing more importance than ever before on a good venue finder. A quick search online will present you with literally countless web based options. It can be tempting to simply go with the first venue finder you see, but quality, even when it comes to the internet, counts for a great deal. You want the best selection possible in order to give you the widest choice. It might seem like unnecessary extra work, but it will be worth the effort. Over the last two years the balance of power has moved away from larger, more established locations and swung towards smaller venues. Increasingly companies express themselves dissatisfied with the prices on offer and the relative lack of customer service.

If you opt instead for a small compact venue you get everything in the one place: less cost, better customer service and, most importantly of all, a higher efficiency when it comes to sales conversion. For proof we speak to members of the pet trade who recently found themselves presented with a couple of smaller shows in competition with established events. To the surprise of many they, even though these new events were smaller in scale, and attracted fewer visitors, they achieved similar sales as at the larger events. In terms of cost versus reward the analysis was simple. Smaller was better. More personal events offered much more in real benefits to companies of all sized.

So, when it comes to searching for your next corporate event, it pays to invest time and energy in the use of a good venue finder. The more choice you have the more likely it is that you can get the best bang for your buck.

Best Event Planning Tips

There are many people who don't have any idea about event planning. You might be someone who wants to know about event planning. Local functions are ordinary being a part of a community. Party planning is not only kept for specialized organizers. Local functions need volunteers to help in the planning process. You should not worry when you are tasked with organizing a company outing. This article is designed in such way so that you can easily plan an event. You need to just follow these simple tips.

You can come up to your local community for local projects to observe how they can help you. Keep in mind that you're not carrying out this professionally so any help that you can get a hold is welcome. You are in need of getting the help of experts. There are many areas to be able to leave to the experts. Normally, to promote a product, you go into party planning. It could be a launch of a product or service for your company. It could be for a business or a local celebrity in case of localfunctions. In order to optimize the event for the result, you need to do many things. It is always a great idea, when you get a host or speaker which is the most important part in function planning. The success or breakdown of an party can be dictated by a host or speaker. Getting the CEO of the company to speak during your organizations function is often a difficult but rewarding and crowd pleasing task. You have another option which is to get the professional of the service or product you're launching.

After the function, try to make a lasting impression, as an party will go for not more than a day or two. You need to give your guests and attendees a reminder of what took place at the event. Providing bobble heads as a giveaway or souvenir could be a popular way to carry out this job, because bobble heads are collectible dolls in having a bobbling outsized head. That's the answer to ensure that your event planning won't go to misuse. With the help of friends and experts, keep them fascinated with an amazingly organized event. You can make them pay concentration by having an excellent speaker. Never forget to pay attention to this advice. Hopefully, you will be happy after having these tips about event planning. You need to just follow the tips mentioned above.

All about Conference Planning

There are many things you need to take into consideration while being responsible for planning a conference. This article will provide you some important tips that will help you to plan. It is always a good idea to begin planning at least a year before the conference while having the luxury of time. Putting together a committee is very essential to assist for doing the planning. You will almost immediately be able to observe how much is occupied to making the conference run effortlessly. You need to select a date and time for the conference. Moreover, you also should check national calendars.

If you would like to hold the conference, you must find a suitable place. You have to confirm that the facility is big enough to seize the total number of people who plan on attending. You must have all the appropriate paper work in place (contracts, licenses, etc.), after you have come to a decision on a competence. You'll need to consider hotel accommodations, when you are hording a large group. Never forget to make arrangements for entertainment and foods. You can set up regular meetings with your committees. Committees must be following their time lines which need to be ensured. You make it clear who is executing what. You need to be in sound contact with the facility individual to go over menus, etc. Never forget to set the tone of the conference and make a decision with organizational heads what the conference plan will look like. There should be a deadline for their receiving or refuse to present at the conference. Initiating setting presentation schedules, workshops lectures, and social activities should be done once you have presenters.

Get in touch with each presenter with all related details in giving them an uncertain schedule. Supply the presenters the names of others who is going to be there and presenting at the convention. To make quality brochures, you need to work with a graphic design company. If you have one to sponsor the convention, try to make use of a website. You can also set one up simply for the conference to give permission for updated information, proposal submissions and on-line registration. Registration need to be set and orderly on the day of conference. Keeping a database of all who attend after handing out nametags to each attendee is a good idea. You never mistake keep track of your expenses. Moreover, at the end of the event, you need to do an expense sheet report.

When to Hire a Conference Planner

Conference planning may be difficult because it takes considerable planning, usually; you need a lot of time in planning the different details of the conference. The planner should be someone who is committed and disciplined enough in planning the conference. A successful conference planning needs the different factors such as, planning committee, budget planning, perfect venue, negotiating party agreements, event speaker, good planning and execution.

Conference planning may come have different types of purposes; it can be a training course, sales conference, incentive event, seminars or any kind of corporate gatherings that involves certain themes.

The very first thing that a planner must do is to assemble a planning committee and appoint the one who will be in charge with the committee or what you will call the conference coordinator. The number of members in the committee should be based upon how big the conference is going to be. A lot of times, the planner make a mistake when hiring large size of committee because it usually results in lack of coordination and indefiniteness. If you will hire members of your conference committee, make sure that the people have the essential traits such as dependable, experienced, and responsible, can effectively work well with other members of the group, a good leader and a good follower as well. The committee can appoint the conference coordinator, or he can also be someone hired based on his expertise and skills regarding the work.

The budget for the conference planning, should be given careful thought, it should be something that the sponsor, coordinator and planning committee both agreed on before it is even finalized. The conference coordinator is the one who is fully in charge of the budget. Certain payments should be approved by the conference coordinator before even paying certain parties, because he is accountable for the whole expenses of the conference planning. The expenses in planning the event is not considered as financial document, it is included in the planning management. It will serve as a list of expected expenses and sources of funds and revenue.

When it is time to choose your speaker, it is important that you find one that is appropriate with the theme of the conference. Make sure that the speaker is someone knowledgeable of the topic in the conference. Most event planner make a mistake in choosing the speaker, for most of them will choose someone popular, who do not have any knowledge of the topic at all. It is also important that you are organized during the event itself, make use of signs and orient everyone on what they will do on the conference itself, so that everyone will not get disoriented.

2

Planning and Policies

Mexican Priorities: Gaming, Tourism and Energy

Since early in January 2007 three issues have been highlighted as priorities, so that Mexico will be able to attract foreign investment and to create promised jobs that are currently nonexistent. First is a ruling on gaming permits that were granted by officials during prior administrations, the legality of which will depend on a forthcoming judgment by Mexico's Supreme Court. This ruling will relate to the validity of the 2004 Regulation of the Federal Gaming and Raffles Law, and whether or not permits issued under that authority in 2005 by former Secretary of Government, and now Senator Santiago Creel, are valid. Permits that well may have cost Creel the National Action Party (PAN) presidential candidacy.

According to most expectations, this proceeding — that is being handled by Justice Olga Sanchez Cordero, and that the Court as a whole must rule on — will favour and uphold the issuance of the permits. And by doing so, the Secretariat of Government will be able to grant future permits for Bingo-type numbers game parlours, remote betting centres called "Books," and electronic gaming machines.

Still, casinos per se, with gaming tables and the like, cannot be authorized until the 1947 law itself is amended. Yet if the aforementioned permits are allowed, surely reforms to the law will become more likely in the near term so that the next steps can be taken, as casinos and the gaming industry should be important development opportunities and attractions for many Mexican cities. The Mexican Congress can also be expected to take up this matter in the near future. And based on the agreement strategy on economic matters that has been reached by the National Action Party (PAN) and Institutional Revolutionary Party (PRI), advances could come about quickly on this issue that should not be allowed to lag behind.

The second matter, that has been the subject of considerable debate for years, deals with crude oil and its derivatives. It has been made clear that the privatization of Petroleos Mexicanos, PEMEX, will not be proposed due to difficulties in reaching agreements to change the Mexican Constitution in order to allow foreign investment in the state owned petroleum conglomerate. In other words, the exploration and exploitation of oil and gas will continue to be activities reserved for the state. Nonetheless, predictions are that advances will be made towards allowing private sector national and foreign investment in the refining or transformation of hydrocarbons, as well as in their storage and distribution. What will be important is to plan modifications based on the Mexican Constitution, and not to try to find novel interpretations of the Constitution that provoke opinion and debate but will not resolve the problem nor provide greater security for this investment. The subject of economic sovereignty in deciding amounts of exploitation of oil and gas fields, along with exploration, can continue to be safeguarded by the Constitution, but too new resources in the areas of oil and gas refining, storage and distribution should be promoted and empowered. By continuing an indiscriminate exploitation of crude oil in order to maintain exportation levels, and by not making investments needed in other development areas, in just a few years Mexico will be out of the oil export business. And soon thereafter it will become an importer, with the sovereignty over energy resources that is being defended today lost. Therefore this is an urgent matter.

The final subject that is to be a priority is tourism. Mexico has yet to take full advantage of its tourism opportunities and possibilities, and to thus become one of the leading tourist destinations in the world. Certainly it is an attractive destination, but it still comes up short in its potential for greater visitor industry income. During this sexennial tourism must become a true and stronger source of foreign exchange, on a par at least with crude oil exports and revenue from remittances sent home by Mexicans living abroad. And to do so, even more legal reforms will have to be made to allow outside capital in the tourist industry, part of which would be invested and brought to Mexico once casinos are authorized and opened. These three issues and areas are indeed important — and addressing them as immediate priorities is not only needed but also overdue.

Tourism Development Priorities in North East England

Understanding which niches, products and services are currently being developed and which areas of product development are being prioritised in the region, will help to identify whether a proposed project is likely to receive support and backing.

In North East England there are five organisations responsible for driving and developing sustainable tourism. They are One North East Tourism (the regional organisation) and the four Area Tourism Partnerships:

Visit County Durham, Northumberland Tourism, Tyne and Wear and visit Teesvalley. Collectively they are known as Tourism Network North East and they work together to provide a coherent set of services to promote and develop tourism in North East England. Through extensive research, the regional and area priorities for tourism have been identified, and strategies have been developed to meet these priorities.

Priority areas and current projects around the region are:

Northumberland Tourism

Priority areas/niches: Northumberland priorities for activity are divided into three overlapping – not mutually exclusive – approaches:

- Activity to realise plans for the key Destination Management Areas
- Delivery of the prioritised Capital Projects
- Actions delivering to agreed Programme Activities.

The priority Destination Management Areas for Northumberland are:

- Towns in the Market Town Welcome Programme (Berwick, Wooler, Seahouses, Alnwick, Amble, Haltwhistle, Morpeth & Hexham)
- Hadrian's Wall corridor
- Kielder Water and Forest Park
- Northumberland National Park
- The Northumberland Coast and North Pennines Areas of Outstanding Natural Beauty.

(Druridge Bay is also developing with potential to emerge as a future priority).

Priority Capital Projects are:

- Alnwick Garden (completion of cherry orchard)
- Hadrian's Wall Central programme projects (Vindolanda, Housesteads & The Sill)
- Kielder Water and Forest Park 'Big Picture'
- Seaton Delaval Hall acquisition
- Hexham Abbey Christian Heritage visitor facilities
- Market Town Welcome capital programme
- Northumberlandia at Blagdon.

A list of priority Programme Activities to develop the visitor economy of Northumberland – to improve the marketing and branding of the sub-region, the information available to visitors before, during and after their visit, and the whole visitor experience whilst they are in the area – is available in the Northumberland ATMaP.

Tourism Tyne & Wear

Priority areas:

- Business Tourism-supporting the development of an International Convention Centre and Exhibition Centre in Newcastle Gateshead
- Events-delivering a world class events programme
- Online and E-commerce-increasing the online visibility and capacity of tourism businesses
- Coastal Tourism-enabling coastal regeneration
- Visitor Information-transforming the provision of visitor information
- Quality-improving the quality of the tourism product
- Marketing-delivering effective marketing
- Attractions-providing great attractions and new reasons to visit
- Partnerships-strengthening tourism partnerships.

Priority projects:

- Convention Centre/events space in Newcastle Gateshead
- Wearmouth Jarrow World Heritage Site
- Development of visitor focussed coastal infrastructure
- Legible Cities projects.

Visit County Durham

Priority areas/niches:

- Optimise the potential of Durham city to attract visitors to the county and region, particularly through the development of Durham as a short stay destination and through investing in key attractions that will have a national profile and appeal.
- Improve the quality and service of visitor-facing businesses to improve the national appeal and attract higher-spending visitors.
- Develop local distinctiveness in line with the image and identity of the county utilising the name 'Durham' and its brand themes-history and innovation, people and location and connectivity.
- Tackle seasonality, particularly through focussing on high profile, off-peak events and on business tourism to increase visits in the shoulder season and mid-week.
- Raise the profile of the county regionally and nationally, particularly by developing the product. Specifically to grow events that have potential national pulling power.
- Extend the stay of visitors, particularly by helping rural town centres to develop services and facilities to draw visitors. Specifically develop destination development plans and ensure their implementation.

Visit Tees Valley

Priority areas/niches:

- Improve the physical product to local, national and international visitors. Our four key physical product elements are:
    - o The urban playground experience of Stockton and Middlesbrough
    - o The coastal stretch from Hartlepool to Redcar, Saltburn and onto Staithes
    - o The countryside and towns including Guisborough, Yarm, and Darlington and the outdoor experiences to be enjoyed there
    - o Heritage and innovation – a celebration of industrial heritage into the 21st century
- Develop and promote Tees Valley as an events destination of local, national and international significance

- Upskill the tourism and hospitality sector work force-the aim will be to give both visitors and residents a quality experience that meets and surpasses their expectations

Tourism and the Imperatives of Sustainable Development

Statement of the Committee for Sustainable Development

The Committee for Sustainable Development,

Recognising that the tourism industry has an increasingly important economic, social, cultural and environmental impact, both globally and on the national scale, and that the continuing growth of tourism and tourism-related activities has diverse implications for the achievement of sustainable development,

Recalling that issues of tourism were addressed by IPU on several occasions in recent years, such as the Inter-Parliamentary Conference on Tourism held in 1989 in The Hague and the two International Fora "Parliaments and Local Authorities: Tourism Policy-Makers" organised by the World Tourism Organization with the support of IPU respectively in Cadiz (Spain) in 1995 and Bali (Indonesia) in 1996,

Believing that the tourism sector is a major driving force behind the economic advancement of many countries, including developing ones, where it fosters job creation, stimulates economic diversification and boosts foreign exchange earnings,

Realising at the same time that over-reliance on tourism, especially mass tourism, entails significant risks for tourism-dependent economies,

Noting that demand for new forms of tourism, including ecotourism, is growing in many parts of the world and presents new challenges for the tourism industry, national governments, parliaments and the international community,

Recognising the important role played by the World Tourism Organization in shaping the future of the global tourism industry, and *recalling* in this regard the rich record of cooperation between IPU and this body,

1. *Believes* that projected sustained growth of the tourism industry will present serious challenges to environmental protection unless policy-makers develop effective regulatory policies and systems of economic incentives and disincentives and address the issue of promoting awareness of tourists, the tourism

industry and the public at large of the importance of safeguarding the natural and cultural environment;

2. *Emphasises* that linkages of tourism with other economic sectors necessitate its full integration into national development plans as well as the provision of adequate legislative support, for which parliaments bear primary responsibility, so that tourism develops in harmony with overall economic, social and environmental goals;
3. *Considers* that an integrated policy framework for sustainable tourism development should include a mechanism ensuring that investment, employment, operational and other business decisions of tourism enterprises take full account of the wider implications of these actions for the long-term development and economic sustainability of the destinations in which they operate and that the carrying capacity of sites visited by tourists should be respected even if this implies restricting access to sites at certain periods or seasons;
4. *Supports* the development of new and alternative forms of tourism, including ecotourism, which favour closer contact and understanding between tourists and receiving populations, respect cultural identity and preserve distinctive and original tourist products and facilities;
5. *Urges* the international community to enhance and strengthen international coordination and relevant monitoring systems through liaison among governments, parliaments, the private sector and concerned parties with a view to promoting the positive aspects and minimising the negative impacts of tourism;
6. *Is convinced* that national parliaments should show increased concern for tourism development and review existing laws on tourism, consolidate them into comprehensive legislation and codify national policy and priorities for tourism including such aspects as safety and security of tourists, spread of epidemic diseases such as AIDS, and elimination of terrorism, in particular by addressing its root causes;
7. *Energetically supports* the view that the promotion of ecotourism should be given priority within overall tourism development planning and that effective mechanisms should be introduced to prevent and control tourism-related abuse and exploitation of people, particularly women and children;

8. *Urges* national parliaments and other tourism policy-makers to support the objectives of the International Year of Ecotourism-2002;
9. With a view to deepening its reflection on the issue of tourism and sustainable development and in order to produce comprehensive recommendations for the Union's governing bodies in this regard, *resolves* to include a relevant item on the agenda of the session of the IPU Committee for Sustainable Development to be held in the year 2000.

Mekong Tourism Office Defines Priorities

The Mekong Tourism Office has announced its new marketing plan, 2008-2011.

The MTO's Senior Advisor, Mr. Peter Semone (pictured), told GMS member countries that the priorities would be to consolidate resources, build credibility and win the confidence of the private sector over three phases of activity. Addressing delegates of the GMS Tourism Working Group Ad-hoc Meeting in Vientiane on December 3, he recommended that phase I of the plan should include:

1. Appointing a country coordinator for Mekong activities in each member NTO
2. Upgrading the MTO's website
3. Creating a Mekong Travel Planner for travel agents
4. Presenting MTO at international events
5. Facilitating subregional networking activities
6. Enhancing the MTO member database
7. Improving monthly updates to all stakeholders
8. Holding regular private sector advisory meetings, and
9. Carrying out market research

Mr. Semone told the 35 delegates that it was important for the MTO to get the basics right. "Later phases should include GDS engagement, social website capabilities with search engine optimization, media familiarization trips, re-establishing the Mekong Tourism Forum, and a visit GMS year," he said.

About the Mekong Tourism Office

The MTO was established in February 2006. Its four key objectives are to:-

- Develop and promote the Mekong as a single destination, offering a diversity of good quality and high-yielding sub-regional products that help to distribute the benefits of tourism more widely
- Add to the tourism development efforts of each GMS country
- Contribute to poverty reduction, gender equality and the empowerment of women
- Promote sustainable development, while minimising adverse impacts.

Tourism bosses from national tourism agency Visit England were in the region yesterday (TUES) to meet with key businesses and organisations including Regional Development Agency One North East. Lady Cobham, chair of Visit England and James Berresford, chief Exec of Visit England, met with a number of tourism businesses to find out more about what the North East has to offer and how the region's public and private sector have worked together to help support tourism businesses in the region.

Businesses such as Hadrian's Wall Heritage, Newcastle International Airport and the Arts Council North East attended the event at Newcastle's Theatre Royal which was hosted by Geoff Hodgson, chairman of the North East Tourism Advisory Board and Stacy Hall, Director of Communications & Tourism at One North East.

Visit England was officially launched in April this year following consultation which identified the need for a distinct body responsible for tourism in England. It works in partnership with Visit Britain, the Regional Development Agencies, local authorities, and the private sector, creating a national tourism strategy, optimising marketing investment, and developing the visitor experience across England.

The visit was part of an England-wide tour by Visit England bosses to introduce the new organisation to businesses and discuss its key role and objectives.

Stacy said: "To continue to promote North East England as a major tourism destination we need to work in a co-ordinated way with national organisations such as Visit England and VisitBritain, as well as private and public organisations in the North East.

"Today's meeting has been vital in developing this relationship and has given the region a chance to share its priorities for tourism and to find out more about Visit England's future plans.

"Tourism is a major part of the region's economy, contributing almost £4bn and employing more than 60,000 people." This year the region has taken advantage of more people holidaying at home with occupancy levels for the first six months up on last year. And 63% of attractions have seen a rise in visitor numbers for the first six months of the year. Lady Cobham said: "It has been an absolute pleasure to be in North East England today. The region is a great example of partnerships working together to enhance the visitor experience and to provide a co-ordinated service for both visitors and businesses alike.

"Visit England looks forward to working closely with Regional Development Agencies such as One North East to drive forward the tourism strategy for England."

Tourism Planning

Tourism is one of many activities in a community or region that requires planning and coordination. This bulletin provides a simple structure and basic guidelines for comprehensive tourism planning at a community or regional level. Planning is the process of identifying objectives and defining and evaluating methods of achieving them. By comprehensive planning we mean planning which considers all of the tourism resources, organizations, markets, and programs within a region. Comprehensive planning also considers economic, environmental, social, and institutional aspects of tourism development.

Two Sides of Tourism Planning

Tourism planning has evolved from two related but distinct sets of planning philosophies and methods. On the one hand, tourism is one of many activities in an area that must be considered as part of physical, environmental, social, and economic planning. Therefore, it is common to find tourism addressed, at least partially, in a regional land use, transportation, recreation, economic development, or comprehensive plan. The degree to which tourism is addressed in such plans depends upon the relative importance of tourism to the community or region and how sensitive the planning authority is to tourism activities.

Tourism may also be viewed as a business in which a community or region chooses to engage. Individual tourism businesses conduct a variety of planning activities including feasibility, marketing, product development, promotion, forecasting, and strategic planning. If tourism is a significant component of an area's economy or development plans, regional or community-wide marketing plans are needed to coordinate the development and marketing activities of different tourism interests in the community.

A comprehensive approach integrates a strategic marketing plan with more traditional public planning activities. This ensures a balance between serving the needs and wants of the tourists versus the needs and wants of local residents. A formal tourism plan provides a vehicle for the various interests within a community to coordinate their activities and work toward common goals. It also is a means of coordinating tourism with other community activities.

Like any planning, tourism planning is goal-oriented, striving to achieve certain objectives by matching available resources and programs with the needs and wants of people. Comprehensive planning requires a systematic approach, usually involving a series of steps. The process is best viewed as an iterative and on-going one, with each step subject to modification and refinement at any stage of the planning process.

There are six steps in the planning process: 1. Define goals and objectives. 2. Identify the tourism system. a) Resources b) Organizations c) Markets 3. Generate alternatives. 4. Evaluate alternatives. 5. Select and implement. 6. Monitor and evaluate.

Step One: Defining Goals and objectives. Obtaining clear statements of goals and objectives is difficult, but important. Ideally, tourism development goals should flow from more general community goals and objectives. It is important to understand how a tourism plan serves these broader purposes. Is the community seeking a broader tax base, increased employment opportunities, expanded recreation facilities, better educational programs, a higher quality of life? How can tourism contribute to these objectives?

If tourism is identified as a means of serving broader community goals, it makes sense to develop plans with more specific tourism development objectives. These are generally defined through a continuing process in which various groups and organizations in a community work together toward common goals. A local planning authority, chamber of commerce, visitors bureau, or similar group should assume a leadership role to develop an initial plan and obtain broad involvement of tourism interests in the community. Public support for the planning process and plan is also important. Having a good understanding of tourism and the tourism system in your community is the first step toward defining goals and objectives for tourism development. The types of goals that are appropriate and the precision with which you are able to define them will depend upon how long your community has been involved in tourism and tourism planning. In the early stages of tourism development, goals may involve establishing organizational structures and collecting information to better identify the tourism system in the community. Later, more precise objectives can be formulated and more specific development and marketing strategies evaluated.

Step Two: Identifying Your Tourism System When planning for any type of activity, it is important to first define its scope and characteristics. Be clear about exactly what your plan encompasses. A good initial question is, "What do you mean by tourism?" Tourism is defined in many ways. Generally, tourism involves people travelling outside of their community for pleasure. Definitions differ on the specifics of how far people must travel, whether or not they must stay overnight, for how long, and what exactly is included under travelling for "pleasure". Do you want your tourism plan to include day visitors, conventioneers, business travellers, people visiting friends and relatives, people passing through, or seasonal residents?

Which community resources and organizations serve tourists or could serve tourists? Generally, tourists share community resources with local residents and businesses. Many organizations serve both tourists and locals. This complicates tourism planning and argues for a clear idea of what your tourism plan entails.

You can begin to clarify the tourism system by breaking it down into three subsystems: (1) tourism resources, (2) tourism organizations, and (3) tourism markets.

An initial task in developing a tourism plan is to identify, inventory, and classify the objects within each of these subsystems.

Tourism Resources are any (1) natural, (2) cultural, (3) human, or (4) capital resources that either are used or can be used to attract or serve tourists. A tourism resource inventory identifies and classifies the resources available that provide opportunities for tourism development. Conduct an objective and realistic assessment of the quality and quantity of resources you have to work with. A suggested classification to help obtain a broad and organized picture of your tourism resources.

Tourism Organizations combine resources in various proportions to provide products and services for the tourist. A partial list and classification of organizations that manage or coordinate tourism-related activities. It is important to recognize the diverse array of public and private organizations involved with tourism. The most difficult part of tourism planning is to get these groups to work toward common goals. You should develop a list of these organizations within your own community and obtain their input and cooperation in your tourism planning efforts. Setting up appropriate communication systems and institutional arrangements is a key part of community tourism planning.

Table: Tourism Resources

Natural Resources:

* Climate-seasons
* Water resources-lakes, streams, waterfalls
* Flora-forests, flowers, shrubs, wild edibles
* Fauna-fish & wildlife
* Geological resources-topography, soils, sand dunes, beaches, caves, rocks & minerals, fossils
* Scenery-combinations of all of the above.

Cultural Resources:

* Historic buildings, sites
* Monuments, shrines
* Cuisine
* Ethnic cultures
* Industry, government, religion, etc.
* Anthropological resources
* Local celebrities.

Human Resources:

* Hospitality skills
* Management skills
* Seasonal labour force
* Performing artists-music, drama, art, storytellers, etc.
* Craftsman and artisans
* Other labour skills from chefs to lawyers to researchers
* Local populations.

Capital:

* Availability of capital, financing
* Infrastructure-transportation roads, airports, railroads, harbors & marinas, trails & walkways
* Infrastructure: utilities water, power, waste treatment, communications.

Table: *Tourism Management Organizations and Services*

Off-site: Coordination, planning, technical assistance, research, regulation:

* Federal & state departments of commerce, transportation, & natural resources
* Federal, state, regional, & local tourism associations
* Educational organizations & consultants, e.g., Travel & Tourism Research Association; U.S. Travel Data Centre; Travel Reference Centre, Univ. of Colorado, Boulder; Travel, Tourism, & Recreation Resource Centre, Michigan State University.
* Travel information & reservation services.

On-Site: development, promotion and management, of tourism resources:

* Federal agencies, NB. departments of commerce, transportation, & land management agencies
* State agencies, NB. departments of commerce, transportation, & land/facility management agencies
* Local government organizations, e.g., visitor information, chamber of commerce, convention & visitor's bureaus, parks.
* Businesses:
    - Accommodations: Hotels, motels, Lodges, resorts, bed & breakfast cabins & cottages, Condominiums, second homes, Campgrounds
    - Food & Beverage: Restaurants, Grocery, Bars, nightclubs, Fast food, Catering services
    - Transportation: Air, rail, bus; Local transportation: taxi, limo, Auto, bicycle, boat rental; Local tour services
    - Information: Travel agencies, Information and reservation services, Automobile clubs
    - Recreation Facilities & Services: Winter sports: ski, skating, snowmobile areas; Golf courses, miniature golf; Swimming

pools, water slides, beaches; tennis, handball, racquetball courts, bowling alleys; Athletic clubs, health spas; Marinas, boat rentals and charters; hunting & fishing guides; Horseback enterprises; Sporting goods sales & rentals

- Entertainment: Nightclubs, amusement parks, spectator sport facilities; Gambling facilities: casinos, horse racing, bingo; video arcades; art galleries and studios, craft shops, studios, demonstrations; performing arts: theatre, dance, music, film; historic & prehistoric sites; museums: art, history, science, technology; arboreta, zoos, nature centres,
- Special festivals and events
- Support services: Auto repair, gasoline service stations; boat & recreation vehicle dealers and service; retail shops: sporting goods, specialities, souvenirs, clothing; health services: hospitals, clinics, pharmacies; laundry and dry cleaning; beauty & barber shops; babysitting services; pet care; communications: newspaper, telephone; banking and financial services.

Tourism Markets: Tourists make-up the third, and perhaps most important subsystem. Successful tourism programs require a strong market orientation. The needs and wants of the tourists you choose to attract and serve must be the focus of much of your marketing and development activity.

Therefore, it is important to clearly understand which tourism market segments you wish to attract and serve. Tourists fall into a very diverse set of categories with quite distinct needs and wants. You should identify the different types of tourists, or market segments that you presently serve or would like to serve. This may involve one or more tourism market surveys.

A visitor survey identifies the size and nature of the existing market and asks the following questions:

* What are the primary market segments you presently attract?
* Where do they come from?
* What local businesses and facilities do they use?
* What attracted them to the community?
* How did they find out about your community?
* How satisfied are they with your offerings?

A market survey (usually a telephone survey) also can be conducted among households in regions from which you wish to attract tourists. This type of study helps identify potential markets, and means of attracting tourists to your area.

Tourism market Segments

In a general tourism plan, some clear target tourism market segments should be identified. You might begin by defining the market area from which you will draw most of your visitors.

The size of your market area depends upon the uniqueness and quality of your "product", transportation systems, tastes and preferences of surrounding populations, and your competition. Identifying the market area will help target information and promotion and define transportation routes and modes, competition, and characteristics of your market.

Next, divide your travel market into the following trip length categories:

* day trips from a 50 mile radius,
* day trips from 50 to 200 miles away,
* pass-through travellers,
* overnight trips of 1 or 2 nights (most likely weekends), and
* extended overnight vacation trips.

After you have an idea of your market area and kinds of trips you will be serving, begin defining more specific market segments like vehicle campers, downhill skiers, sightseers, family vacationers, single weekenders, and the like. These segments can be more clearly tied to particular resources, businesses, and facilities in your community.

What kinds of products and services are likely to attract each of these groups? Tourist needs as well as their impact on the local community are quite different for day tourists versus overnight tourists.

Areas catering primarily to weekend traffic will experience large fluctuations in use. In deciding the relative importance of these different segments, communities need to assess both their ability to provide required services (do you have enough rooms?), as well as the demand for different types of trips relative to the supply and your competition.

The Environment: A tourism plan is significantly affected by many factors in the broader environment. Indeed, one of the complexities of tourism planning is the number of variables that are outside of the control of an individual tourism business or community. These include such things as tourism offerings and prices at competing destinations, federal and state policy and legislation, currency exchange rates, the state of the economy, and weather. These factors are discussed more fully in Extension bulletin E-1959 as part of the market environment analysis.

Local populations also must be considered in tourism planning. As they compete with tourists for resources, they can be significantly affected by tourism activity, and they are an important source of support in getting tourism plans implemented.

A survey of local residents can be conducted to assess community attitudes toward tourism development, identify impacts of tourism on the community, and obtain local input into tourism plans.

Public hearings, workshops, and advisory boards are other ways to obtain public involvement in tourism planning. Local support and cooperation is important to the success of tourism programs and should not be overlooked.

Table: *Tourism Market Segments*

I. Geographic market areas

II. Trip categories

Day Trips:

* short-within 50 miles
* long-up to 200 miles

Pass through traffic:

* day visitors
* overnight stays

Overnight Trips:

* weekend
* vacation

III. Activity or trip purpose

Outdoor Recreation:

* Water-based Activity:
    - Boating: sail, power, cruise, row, canoe, water ski
    - Swimming: pool, beach, sunbathing, scuba
    - Fishing: charter, sport, from pier, boat, shore, ice

* Land-based Activity:
  - Camping: back packing, primitive, developed
  - Hiking: climbing, beachcombing, spelunking
  - Hunting
  - Skiing: downhill, cross country
  - Snowmobiling
  - Bicycling
  - Horseback riding
  - Picnicking
* Air-based Activity:
  - Airplane rides, hang gliding, ballooning, parachuting
* General:
  - Nature study
  - Photography or landscape painting
  - Viewing natural scenery

Sightseeing & Entertainment:

* Visiting particular sites or areas:
  - historic or pre-historic
  - cultural
  - amusements
  - scenic
* Attending particular events, shows, or demonstrations:
  - ethnic festivals
  - sporting events
  - performances
  - agricultural fair or festival
  - boat show
  - shopping

Other Primary Purpose for Trip:

* Visiting Friends & Relatives
* Convention & Business/Pleasure

Step Three: Generating Alternatives. Generating alternative development and marketing options to meet your goals requires some creative thinking and brainstorming. The errors made at this stage are usually thinking too narrowly or screening out alternatives prematurely. It is wise to solicit a wide range of options from a diverse group of people. If tourism expertise is lacking in your community, seek help and advice outside the community.

Tourism planning involves a wide range of interrelated development and marketing decisions. The following development questions will get you started:

* How much importance should be assigned to tourism within a community or region?
* Which general community goals is tourism development designed to serve?
* Which organization(s) will provide the leadership and coordination necessary for community tourism planning? What are the relative roles of public and private sectors?

Tourism marketing decision questions include:

* Segments: Which market segments should be pursued; geographic markets, trip types, activity or demographic subgroups?
* Product: What kinds of tourism products and services should be provided? Who should provide what?
* Place: Where should tourism facilities be located?
* Promotion: What kinds of promotion should be used, by whom, in which media, how much, when? What community tourism theme or image should be established?
* Price: What prices should be charged for which products and services. Who should capture the revenue?

Step Four: Evaluating Alternatives. Tourism development and marketing options are evaluated by assessing the degree to which each option will be able to meet the stated goals and objectives. There are usually two parts to a systematic evaluation of tourism development and marketing alternatives: (1) Feasibility analysis, and (2) Impact assessment. These two tasks are interrelated, but think of them as trying to answer two basic questions: (1) Can it be done?, and (2) What are the consequences? A decision to take a specific action must be based both on feasibility and desirability.

Feasibility Analysis: First, screen alternatives and eliminate those that are not feasible due to economic, environmental, political, legal, or other factors. Evaluate the remaining set of alternatives in more detail, paying particular attention to the market potential and financial plan. Make a realistic assessment of your community's ability to attract and serve a market segment or segments. This requires a clear understanding of the tourism market in your area and how this market is changing. Also carefully identify your competition and evaluate your advantages and disadvantages compared to the competition.

Plan toward the future because it takes time to implement decisions and for your actions to take effect. Therefore, look at the likely market and competition for several years to come. Review forecasts for the travel market in your area, if available. Careful tracking of tourism trends in your own community can help identify changes in the market that you will have to adapt to.

Impact Assessment: When evaluating alternative development and marketing strategies it is important to understand the impacts, both positive and negative, of proposed actions. Table 4 presents a classification of economic, environmental, and social impacts associated with tourism development. The types of impacts and their importance vary across different communities and proposed actions. Generally, the size, extent, and nature of tourism impacts depend upon:

* volume of tourist activity relative to local activity
* length and nature of tourist contacts with the community
* degree of concentration/dispersal of tourist activity in the area
* similarities or differences between local populations and tourists
* stability/sensitivity of local economy, environment, and social structure
* how well tourism is planned, controlled, and managed.

Look at both the benefits and costs of any proposed actions. While tourism development can increase income, revenues, and employment, it also involves costs. Evaluate benefits and costs of tourism development from the perspectives of local government, businesses, and residents.

Table: *Impacts of Tourism*

Economic Impacts:

* Sales, revenue, and income
* Employment
* Fiscal impact-taxes, infrastructure costs

* Prices
* Economic base & structure

Environmental Impacts:

* Lands
* Waters
* Air
* Infrastructure
* Flora & fauna

Social Impacts:

* Population structure & distribution
* Values & attitudes
* Education
* Occupations
* Safety & security
* Congestion & crowding
* Community spirit & cohesion
* Quality of life

Impacts on Local Government Local government provides most of the infrastructure and many of the services essential to tourism development, including highways, public parks, law enforcement, water and sewer, garbage collection and disposal. Evaluate tourism decisions with a clear understanding of the capacity of the local infrastructure and services relative to anticipated needs, and take into account both the needs of local populations and tourists.

A fiscal impact analysis evaluates the impact of tourism on the community's tax base and local government costs. It entails predicting the additional infrastructure and service requirements of tourism development, estimating their costs, deciding who will pay for/provide them, and how. Will tourism generate increased local government revenue through fees and charges, local sales or use taxes, increased property values or property tax rates, or larger local shares of federal and state tax revenues?

Impacts on Business and Industry Businesses that are directly serving tourists benefit from sales to tourists. Through secondary impacts, tourism activity also benefits a wide range of businesses in a community. For example, a local textile industry may sell to a linen supply firm that serves hotels and motels catering primarily to tourists. A local forest products industry sells to a lumberyard where local woodcarvers or furniture makers buy their supplies. They in turn sell to tourists through various retail outlets. All of these businesses benefit from tourism. If most products and services for tourists are bought outside of the local area, much of the tourist spending "leaks" out of the local economy. The more a community is "self-sufficient" in serving tourists, the larger the local impact.

Impacts on Residents Local residents may experience a broad range of both positive and negative impacts from tourism development. Tourism development may provide increased employment and income for the community. Although tourism jobs are primarily in the service sectors and are often seasonal, part time, and low-paying, these characteristics, are neither universal nor always undesirable. Residents may value opportunities for part time and seasonal work. In particular, employment opportunities and work experiences for students or retirees may be desired. Residents may also benefit from local services that otherwise would not be available. Tourism development may mean a wider variety of retailers and restaurants, or a better community library. It may also mean more traffic, higher prices, and increases in property values and local taxes. The general quality of the environment and life in the community may go up or down due to tourism development. This depends on the nature of tourism development, the preferences and desires of local residents, and how well tourism is planned and managed.

Steps Five And Six: Implementation, and Monitoring and Evaluation. We will not attempt a complete discussion of decisionmaking, plan implementation, and monitoring, but these are critical steps in the success of a tourism plan. A set of specific actions should be prescribed with clearly defined responsibilities and timetables. Monitor progress in implementing the plan and evaluate the success of the plan in meeting its goals and objectives on a regular basis. Plans generally need to be adjusted over time due to changing goals, changing market conditions, and unanticipated impacts. It is a good idea to build monitoring and evaluation systems into your planning efforts.

Concluding Remarks

Successful tourism planning and development means serving both tourists and local residents. The bulletins in this series stress the importance of a market orientation for attracting and serving tourists.

This market orientation must be balanced with a clear view of how tourism serves the broader community interest and an understanding of the positive and negative impacts of tourism development. Remember, tourism should serve the community first and the tourist second. Tourism development must be compatible with other activities in the area and be supported by the local population. Therefore, the tourism plan should be closely coordinated with other local and regional planning efforts, if not an integral part of them

Abu Dhabi Races Ahead with Tourism Plans

With events such as The Formula One Grand Prix on the docket, Abu Dhabi is rapidly emerging as a world-class tourism destination and is threatening to overtake Dubai as the top tourism hot spot in the UAE. The capital of the UAE has long taken a back seat to Dubai on the tourist map, preferring to take a more low-key approach and focusing on business tourism rather than the leisure market.

However, in the wake of the global financial crisis the two emirates have seen the fortunes of their tourism industries go in opposite directions. Dubai's high-flying hotel sector, like much of the rest of the world, witnessed declines in occupancy and revenues throughout the downturn, while Abu Dhabi has risen to new heights. In the first half of 2009, average daily room rates in Dubai fell 24% while rates in Abu Dhabi rose 5% from the same period the year before, said a report by Hogg Robinson. And with room rates averaging $275 a night in the first half of the year, Abu Dhabi replaced Dubai as the most expensive major destination in the world, according to Hotels.com's hotel price index.

Detailed Strategy

Abu Dhabi's rise as a tourist destination is the by-product of a carefully thought-out strategy by the government that involves billions of dollars of investment in infrastructure, marketing, and tourism developments. In the immediate future, the emirate is expecting to receive a large influx of visitors for two high-profile events: the Abu Dhabi Grand Prix-the UAE's first-ever Formula One race-which will take place in the first week of November on Yas Island, and the FIFA Club World Cup UAE 2009, which will be held the following month. In addition to attracting race fans, the F1 event will also serve as a showcase for the $36bn island development, whose offerings when completed will include high-end resorts, golf courses, and a Ferrari theme park.

Seven new hotels will open this month on the island in time for the race, including the 500-room Yas Hotel from real estate developer Aldar, two Rotana-managed properties, two IHG hotels, a Radisson Blu by Rezidor, and the UAE's first Park Inn.

Diversified Growth

In addition to hosting the up coming sporting events, the capital is also hoping to gain a reputation as a cultural hub with the development of Saadiyat Island, which will be home to the Guggenheim and Louvre museums. The emirate's tourism efforts are being aided by the rapid growth of Abu Dhabi International Airport, which is now directly linked with 69 destinations and served by 32 airlines. Passenger traffic at the airport has grown significantly over the past five years, almost doubling from five million a year to nine million.

Abu Dhabi is on target to receive 1.5 million hotel guests in 2009, which would be on par with last year's performance, Ahmed Hussein, Deputy Director General, Abu Dhabi Tourism Authority (ADTA) told AME Info.com. 'Next year we are looking for a 10% increase with a 15% increase slated each for 2011 and 2012, so that by the end of 2012 we will reach our goal of receiving 2.3 million hotel guests,' he noted. To help meet these ambitious targets, approximately 10,000 rooms are under construction in the emirate to be delivered in the remainder of this year and through 2010, with a further 7,000 to come on line in 2011. Overall, the emirate hopes to have 24,000 available rooms by 2012.

Infrastructure Milestone

Last week Abu Dhabi achieved a milestone in its infrastructure with the opening of a bridge that links Saadiyat Island with the city for the first time. The city also opened a 27km expressway which stretches from Port Zayed on the Abu Dhabi mainland to the Shahama District, passing through Saadiyat and Yas islands. Abu Dhabi also recently launched a new hotel rating system aimed at raising hospitality standards in the emirate and providing accurate and consistent information for tourists. All hotels and hotel apartments in the emirate will have to display their rating by the end of October.

Two years in the making, the rating system will also give tour operators 'increasing confidence in selling the destination and being able to recommend suitable accommodation to their clients', Hussein said. 'Everyone will now know what to expect from hotels with specific star ratings-it gives us added product integrity.'

Oversupply Risk

Currently Abu Dhabi is very much undersupplied, hence the steep rise in price of its hotel rooms, said John Podaras, associate director at TRI Hospitality Consulting. 'Whereas a year ago people doing business in Dubai were staying in Abu Dhabi where hotels were cheaper, now the reverse is true,' he said. With so much supply coming on board, there is a risk that the emirate will be temporarily oversupplied, but since most of these projects are geared around major government initiatives, they should generate their own demand, he noted. 'Their master plans maps out a strategy for the future that is quite comprehensive and is very much vested in the development of Abu Dhabi as a capital city, with these various other developments all working with each other to provide a demand synergy which is not only targeting tourism but also the complete industrial and social framework of Abu Dhabi,' Podaras said.

Hotel room supply is rising much more rapidly in Dubai, where inventory is expected to reach 54,000 in 2010, up 40% from 2008. With so much being invested in the tourism industries in Abu Dhabi and Dubai, is it realistic to expect that both emirates, which are just one hour's drive apart, can sustain this growth? Podaras believes the answer is yes. 'Dubai and Abu Dhabi co-exist well because Dubai has chosen a different path. They are more focused on foreign investment and bringing private developers in to develop what it is going to actually be. And they are looking at a bigger market.' 'Abu Dhabi is looking at a much tighter integration between each of the districts they are developing across the whole of the emirate. It is a different strategy and the positioning is different, so they should complement each other very well,' he said.

Kerala Tourism plans 'Onam Road Show'

Kerala Tourism is teaming up with leading players in the tourism industry to organise a four-day road show covering Thiruvananthapuram and adjoining Kollam districts from Sunday.

This has been designed as a strategy to beat the 'recession blues' likely to get reflected in fall in tourist arrivals in the State during the peak season starting concurrently. According to sources, projections are that the beach destination of Kovalam stands to suffer the worst during the peak season kicking off in October, signalling at large the dire fortunes of centres of tourist importance in the southern districts. Titled 'Onam Road Show,' the event will feature at least 150 tour operators from across the country, including from Delhi, Mumbai, Kolkata, Hyderabad and Chennai, and second-tier cities such as Nagpur, Pune and Ahmedabad.

At least, 35 properties in Kollam and Thiruvananthapuram districts will be part of the four-day jamboree. Houseboat operators and homestay owners are also expected to pitch in.

Tourism Caravan

The South Kerala Hoteliers' Forum (SKHF) and the Association of Professionals in Tourism (APT) will combine with 'Incredible India' and Kerala Tourism to host the caravan that will travel from Thiruvananthapuram variously to Kovalam, Poovar, Chowara, Varkala and Kollam. Besides calling at the properties in Kovalam, Poovar, Chowara, Kollam and Varkala and taking time off for a backwater cruise in adjoining Kollam, the tour operators will sit down for business-to-business ('B-2-B') session. With the State Government-sponsored Onam celebrations set to roll out in Thiruvananthapuram city, the organisers have made arrangements to take the tour operators to the Kanakakkunnu Palace grounds, the hub of the celebrations, on Tuesday.

South African Tourism Plans to hold in-country Road Show in India in August 2009

South African Tourism (SAT) plans to hold an in-country road show in India in August this year and is planning to invite around 100 agents from India and South Africa. This was informed by Medha Sampat, Country Head India, South African Tourism, who said that the idea behind holding an in-country road show is to spread awareness about South African and Indian tourism's products mutually among agents of both countries. The in-country road show will be held in a five-star hotel; however, the exact venue and date are not yet decided.

SAT, last week, concluded its three-city road show in New Delhi. The other two cities were Mumbai and Ahmedabad. A delegation of 25 companies showcased their products to the travel trade in these three cities. The delegation companies comprised various travel and tour operators, game parks, hoteliers etc. from South Africa. "The response has been amazing and the delegates have been busy highlighting the products to the travel trade. This clearly shows that India is an important market for South Africa. The tourism board is looking at educating the travel trade through interactive workshops and presentations at our various events like road shows and Incountry Famil," said Sampat.

The tourism board will soon launch a luxury and indulgence guide and adventure sports guide as a supplement with a leading Indian magazine, which will act as a ready reckoner for travel agents and end consumers to plan their holidays. These guides will cover various aspects of Luxury Tourism and Adventure Sports Tourism. In addition to this, South Africa will host FIFA World Cup in 2010, which will further boost tourist arrivals to the country. This year, SAT has active promotional strategies wherein it will advertise on billboard, television and on the web. It will also advertise in children's magazines such as Robin Age published in Pune and Mumbai for special distribution in schools. Sampat believes that children can have greater influence in their families for building awareness about South Africa whereby the country will receive large number of tourist from India. Commenting on the total number of Indian tourists visiting South Africa, Sampat said about 60 per cent of travellers are form northern India while the remaining 40 per cent are from western India and southern regions of India.

CR-T1021: Tourism Plans and Investment Designs in Wild Protected Areas

Project Description: Out of the 10 Protected Areas benefited with the Program currently under development by the Bank, only 3 of them have Sustainable Tourism Plans with their corresponding priority investments identified. Furthermore, even for these three Areas, the priority investments are only listed and located on a map, while they lack a detailed design of the corresponding works. Since such detailed designs and environmental permits are required to execute the investments financed with the Loan, the present technical cooperation (TC) will help develop Sustainable Tourism Plans for the 7 Protected Areas that don't have such Plans and produce detailed designs and environmental assessments for the investments already identified in the three Sustainable Tourism Plans already finished. The implementation of this TC to develop the mentioned products will be carried out during the period before approval of the Loan Program by the Costa Rican parliament, and will be very useful to assure a fast start-up of the Program, to help execute the Loan within its scheduled execution period.

Tourism Plans Road Show in Middle East

Seychelles will host a road show around the Middle East countries in November to promote our archipelago as tourism destination.

Alain St Ange, the director of tourism marketing at the Seychelles Tourism Board (STB) said this on Monday after taking part in the Arabian Travel Market (ATM) tourism trade fair held in Dubai from May 5 to 8. He said the road show will help consolidate what his delegation launched during the fair.

"We will go with groups of people from the private sector here. The airlines flying to Seychelles will join us to go right round this part of the world to ensure Seychelles is perceived as a destination that is ready to receive clients. We will meet tour operators and the press," he said. He said STB will invite Vice-President Joseph Belmont who is the Minister for Tourism to launch the show, "so as to set the tone that it is an official event". Seychelles delegation at the ATM was headed by the STB chairman Maurice Lousteau-Lalanne.

Also present at the ATM were members of the local trade – 7°South, Creole Travel Services, Select Seychelles, Starwood Hotels in Seychelles, the Fisherman's Cove and the Barbarons Beach Hotel and Berjaya Hotels and Casino. Saying their mission was successful, the delegation said it is now evident the Middle East remains a potential market for Seychelles "with virtually daily flights coming to Seychelles from that region". "A large number of travel agents visited the Seychelles' stand, asked about our country and established contacts with our destination management companies. The delagates met with many tour operators including Emirates Holidays, Qatar Holidays and DNATA. They also met with the two major airlines flying to Seychelles from the Middle East – the Emirates Airline and Qatar Airways. "Our meetings with the media were attended by representatives of magazines, newspapers and radio stations who showed keen interest to learn about Seychelles and to feature it" said Mr. St Ange. "The trade fair reconfirmed what we knew about the possibilities existing for Seychelles in the Middle East. This part of the world remains the area with the biggest growth potential."

"We must not sit and wait for business to grow by itself because that will be a long process, we need to be proactive and the new STB will be spearheading a revamped marketing strategy for that market to ensure we get our fair share of that market."

Tourism Plans for Andamans go on, Tsunami Notwithstanding

The Andaman and Nicobar Islands are still seen as tourist havens, even after being ravaged by the tsunami in December 2004. The tourism policy of Andaman and Nicobar Island 2003 listed its objectives as large-scale, resource-intensive tourism, opening more islands for tourism, attracting private investment for high-end eco-tourist resorts and obtaining relaxation of the Coastal Regulation Zone (CRZ) rules. The model is still followed, with minor modifications, after the December 2004 disaster.

The question, however, is: can islands like the Andamans, vulnerable to tsunamis and other natural disasters, depend exclusively on tourism? In 1996, the Commission on Sustainable Development warned small island states in the Caribbean and Pacific about the perils of over-reliance on tourism. Their warnings ring true for the Andaman and Nicobar Islands as well. But the island's administration continues to milk dry the tourism cow. Of course, post-tsunami there were neither tour operators nor tourists. Souvenir, handicraft and small hotel businesses—the mainstays of an island economy dependant on tourism—were destroyed. Take Murugan's experience for instance. The tides devastated his hotel and house in Wandoor, a south Andaman island. The family of six adults and a child got refuge in a temporary shelter. The roadside coffee shop they built fetched them a pittance. "Only revival of tourism could save our living," were Murugan's mother's words back then. Tourism had admittedly become important for local communities. But Murugan's story also holds another lesson: in islands prone to natural disasters, the vulnerability of the tourism economy is several fold higher.

This is a lesson that's not yet been learnt. "The hotels here violate CRZ rules. It is only in some cases in Havelock that locally available materials have been used," says Samir Acharya of the Port Blair-based Society for Andaman and Nicobar Ecology (SANE).

Lip Service

Of course there is a master plan for the islands that speaks of enabling environmentally sustainable tourism. But it needs closer scrutiny. Consider one proposed by the Union ministry of tourism in association with the World Tourism Organisation. It envisages lowering the limits of coastal development prohibition zones in areas earmarked for development for tourism. The threshold will be down to 50 m behind the high-tide line (HTL) if this UN Environment Programme funded plan gets underway. It is currently 200 m behind HTL. The plan also calls for de-reserving forest lands in areas marked for tourism. All this contravenes the Supreme Court order of 2002 directing that tourism be low impact and sensitive to the ecological context of the islands. This master plan was, of course proposed before the tsunami, but continues to remain on the anvil. Plans to link Port Blair in the Andaman and Nicobar Islands with Phuket in Thailand is also on the anvil. This, despite the fact that tourism development in Phuket has cost the country its reefs, forests and subsistence agriculture dearly. Various tourism development plans for Andamans dating to the pre-tsunami days stress the need to improve air connectivity. Experiences from across the world have, however, shown that contrary to boosting the tourism industry, over-connectivity has deepened the tourism crisis during natural disasters and contributed to the rapid downfall of tourism dependant economies.

No Regulation

Post-tsunami, there is a sense of urgency to continue what was planned for the islands before the catastrophe. The Parliamentary Standing Committee on Home Affairs prepared a background note on developmental activities in the Andaman and Nicobar Islands. Among its objectives is: "Promotion of resorts preferably by private sector." It recommends that more islands with tourism potential need to be opened for investment by the private sector. Even as the islands struggle to recover from the devastation wrought by tsunami, the administration has selected 50 sites on 15 islands to set up "eco-friendly" hotels and resorts. SANE says these plans violate CRZ rules on Havelock and other islands. It has recommended banning backpackers during the revival stage. The tsunami showed how catastrophic the impacts of unplanned and unregulated development could be. But the lesson, obviously, has not yet been learnt.

Madhya Pradesh Lines up Big Tourism Plans

The Madhya Pradesh government is considering a proposal to launch 'Malwa Odyssey', a luxury train on the lines of 'Palace on Wheels' in Rajasthan, linking its tourist destinations with Bhopal. A suggestion in this regard was first made by the Indian Heritage Hotels Association which submitted a detailed report to Chief Minister Shivraj Singh Chouhan last week on ways to boost tourism in the state. The association has stressed on the need for running such a train, to attract domestic and foreign tourists, connecting Ujjain, Indore, Shivpuri, Gwalior, Satna, and Jabalpur with Bhopal. The association in its Annual General Meeting (AGM) held in Bhopal also submitted a list of heritage sites to be developed as hotels and resorts, saying it would open a huge tourism opportunity for the state.

Chouhan, who met Railway Minister Lalu Prasad and Tourism Minister Ambika Soni in New Delhi some time back, has sought Central assistance to boost tourism in Madhya Pradesh. He also requested the railway minister for a rail ink for the historical sites in the state to provide easy access to places of tourist importance in Madhya Pradesh which are either untapped or did not get prominence due to lack of connectivity. Chouhan, however said the state government was doing its best to connect the destinations through road to facilitate entry of tourists, both Indian and foreigners, by road. Efforts were also being made to connect major tourist attractions including Sanchi, Khajurao, Gwalior, Pachmarhi, Datia, Jabalpur, Rewa, Tikamgarh, Mandu and Maihar (Satna).The state government was also planning a Son-et-Lumiere (light and sound) show at Mandu fort, Ujjain temples, old Taj Mahal at Bhopal, Islam Nagar fort near Bhopal in conjuction with Indian National Trust for Art and Cultural Heritage (INTACH) or India Tourism Development Corporation.

Initiatives have also been taken to improve visitors' management system at Mandu Fort, as well as at Sanchi, Orchha, Bhimbetka, Gwalior on the lines of Ajanta and Ellora caves, the official said.

The state government was also considering to form a state level Tourism Advisory Board, consisting of government departments and tourism industry stake holders, to promote tourist destinations through marketing and publicity materials, tourism friendly literature and signages in different languages. The government also plans to establish better connectivity to these places through train and air, by air taxis and helicopter services. Apart from this, the state's tourism ministry has identified 16 private properties owned by the erstwhile royals to convert them into heritage tourism destinations. The objective is to promote tourism and protect the heritage sites, the official said. The list of 16 heritage sites were forwarded by the Indian Heritage Hotels Association to the chief minister in its recent meeting in Bhopal. These include assets at Berasia (Bhopal), Chhatarpur, Gwalior, Datia, Jabalpur, Mandu, Tikamgarh and Maihar (Satna). These sites were selected by the Madhya Pradesh Tourism Ministry after a survey to convert them into heritage hotels, lodges and resorts.

Association president Maharaja Gaj Singh told *PTI* that the chief minister has invited them in November for a detailed discussion on the development of these sites. The 16 sites identified by the state government are Alipura Garhi (Chhatarpur), Datia Qila, Pili Kothi and Narayan Singh Mahal (Datiua), Raja Gokul Ballabh Mahal

(Jabalpur), Jamnia Gaddi (Mandu), Tikamgarh Palace, and Maihar Qila (Maihar, Satna). At present, Welcome group has six heritage hotels at Bhopal, Jabalpur, Kanha, Bandhavgarh, Pachmarhi and Ujjain. Rakesh Mathur, President, ITC Welcome hotels group told *PTI* that we are looking at the proposals on whether these sites could be developed or not, as per our system but emphasised that the government should develop proper infrastructure first.

Madhya Pradesh has every thing except necessary infrastructure for the development of tourism in the state Maharaja Gaj Singh said. Pushparaj Singh, Maharaja of Rewa and a member of the Heritage Hotels Association told PTI that he was in favour of developing museum hotels besides adventure, health and educational tourism for foreigners and provide them detailed information and recreation with regard to India adventure, herbal healthcare and history.

Puerto Rico Tourism Plans Major European Expansion

The Executive Director of the Puerto Rico Tourism Company (PRTC), Terestella Gonzalez Denton, along with the Secretary of the Department of Economic and Commercial Development, Ricardo Rivera Cardona, recently travelled to Europe to launch an aggressive strategic plan aimed at further developing Puerto Rico's presence in Europe. Their visit initiated an agenda of meetings and presentations by PRTC representatives that included visits to six cities and four countries with very high potential for tourism and economic development in Puerto Rico.

"The development of the tourism industry is intricately linked to the economic progress that our people enjoy. In connection with the economic policies designated by our Governor, PRTC is working toward short- and long-term goals defined by our Strategic Tourism Plan to enhance Puerto Rico's tourism offering, providing substantial economic impact to the Island, said Gonzalez Denton. "One of our priorities is strengthening the Island's presence in Europe, a region which has the potential to increase visitors to Puerto Rico, and in turn economic growth to the Island."

PRTC meetings were held in London, Madrid, Naples, Rome, Genoa and Frankfurt with airlines, cruise lines, wholesalers and travel agents to grow relationships and establish partnerships between Puerto Rico and the European tourism industry to increase the number of European visitors and their length of stay on the Island. A key objective for Puerto Rico was to enhance air access and introduce direct flights from diverse European destinations, making Puerto Rico a more attractive vacation and business destination for Europeans. PRTC met with British Airways, Princess Cruises, Virgin Holidays, Delta Airlines, Iberia, MSC Cruises, Top Cruises and several wholesalers and travel agents, among others.

Gonzalez Denton explained that at the beginning of the current term, there existed a certain distance between the European and Puerto Rican markets. Consequently, PRTC has begun to implement a number of strategies to amplify the presence of the Island in this market by actively participating in tourism trade shows, investment forums and meetings with industry leaders to better understand their needs and to promote Puerto Rico's extensive tourism offering.

PRTC held a successful meeting with its long-term partner, Iberia, who reaffirmed its commitment to work together with PRTC to develop additional traffic on its San Juan route. The plan includes trying to attract European tourists to experience the Caribbean through multi-destination packages which would include a connection in San Juan as part of the roundtrip ticket.

Dubai World scraps most of its Rwanda Tourism Plans

According to the Rwanda Development Board (RDB), which promotes foreign investment in the east African state, Dubai World has pulled out of all but two of its ambitious tourism schemes, citing the impact of the global financial crisis. The planned portfolio had included a sprawling luxury hotel and golf course in the capital Kigali, and an eco-lodge in Akagera national park, but these projects have been shelved, said Clare Akamanzi, deputy CEO at RDB.

Banahaw Ecotourism Plans Studied

Research activities are now being conducted to boost the ecotourism potential of mystical Mt. Banahaw in the Southern Tagalog Region.

The studies are being done under the project "A Comprehensive Diagnostic Assessment to Enhance Eco-Tourism in Barangay Kinabuhayan and Taytay in Mt. Banahaw-San Cristobal Protected Landscape (MBSCPL)." The project is implemented by the Department of Environment and Natural Resources-Ecosystems Research and Development Bureau (DENR-ERDB) headed by Director Marcial Amaro Jr. Funding it is the Department of Science and Technology-Philippine Council for Agriculture, Forestry and Natural Resources Research and Development (DOST-PCARRD) headed by Executive

Director Patricio Faylon. Both DENR-ERDB and DOST-PCARRD are based in Los Banos. Supporting the project are the DENR-Region 4-A; DENR-Protected Area and Wildlife Bureau (PAWB); Quezon Provincial Government Environment and Natural Resources Office; South Luzon State University (SLSU) in Lucban, Quezon; the local government units of Dolores Quezon, Majayjay, Laguna, and San Pablo City; Department of Tourism – Region 4; and Laguna Lake Development Authority.

"Our goal is to provide scientific knowledge that will serve as a basis in establishing an eco-tourism management plan for the MBSCPL," said Dr. Lope Calanog, ERDB senior science research specialist who is project leader. "We also intend to encourage stakeholders to support and strengthen the project," he said. ERDB recognizes the area's vital role in the economy, religious belief, culture, and health of the people. It is also a habitat for plants and animals.

However, the ERDB research project team noted the alarming condition of the area. Tons of garbage have been dumped and left everywhere because of the increasing number of tourists and pilgrims, most especially during the Lenten season.

India: Sikkim to Expand Tourism Plans

The resurgence of the campaign for Gorkhaland in Darjeeling in the last few years has diminished tourism to Darjeeling but increased interest in the neighbouring state of Sikkim, which has seen so much tourism growth that it is embarking on a plan to become a year-round destination. The Himalayan state has many natural attractions to make it an adventure sports haven, including the world's third highest mountain, Kanchenjunga. Its mix of Buddhist and Hindu beliefs gives it strong cultural appeal as well. Earlier this year, general strikes in Darjeeling by Gorkhaland supporters kept tourists out of the area for long periods of time, which also affected travel to Sikkim because the road there from the plains passes through the Darjeeling hills. The Gorkhaland campaign remains active and could affect travel to Darjeeling for some time to come.

Confident of LTTE rout, Sri Lanka Draws Tourism Plans

The Sri Lankan government plans to turn the country's war-torn northeastern region, which boasts of some of the island's most scenic beaches, into a tourist attraction as the decades-old conflict with the Tamil Tigers seems to be nearing its end.

'The battle between the Sri Lankan forces and the LTTE (Liberation Tigers of Tamil Eelam) is nearing its end, paving way for long awaited peace and development in these areas. Against this backdrop, Sri Lanka Tourism is gearing up for a post conflict strategy focusing on development of the tourist potential in the northeast,' said an official statement issued here.

'The development of the east is of specific focus for the government as the beaches there are some of the best in the island. Arugam Bay is famous as one of the best surfing destinations in the world,' the statement said. The tourism department is making plans for development of other locations such as Passikudah and Trincomalee, which have excellent beaches for recreation. The strategies on the anvil include a marketing blitz for Sri Lanka Tourism, promoting the area as an 'off the beaten track' vacation, promotional activities with hotels and the national carrier Sri Lankan Airlines. The primary markets are the French, German and British tourists, the statement said. Nearly 250,000 post cards will also be distributed among visitors while a discount booklet will be distributed with over 50 discount offers for a range of hotels and shopping malls.

The statement said that in 2005, the LTTE had over 16,000 sq km under its control. But within two-and-a-half years of start of a military campaign in 2006, the government has managed to squeeze the rebels to 8 sq km area in the northeastern part of the country.

'As the conflict is drawing to an end in the north, there is a sense of relief among all citizens that peace, prosperity and development is close at hand.'

L.A. Port has Big Tourism Plans for Waterfront

The hulking container ships that ply the Port of Los Angeles already provide Southern California with a major source of revenue. Soon they could also provide the scenery for what port officials hope will be the region's newest tourist destination. Harbour commissioners are set to vote today on the port's $1.2 billion plan to remake the jumbled strip of parking lots, seafood stalls and ramshackle marinas into a seaside promenade bookended by passenger wharfs that could host the world's biggest cruise ships. Planners say the redevelopment would help sustain the gentrification of the adjacent community of San Pedro — where upscale bars and coffee shops share downtown streets with tattoo parlours — and diversify a maritime economy dominated by the shipping industry hit by the economic downturn.

"It gives the waterfront — a big section of the port — back to the people," said Geraldine Knatz, the port's executive director. "The view along our main channel, especially with ships coming in — it's majestic." But some San Pedro residents say the new cruise ship terminal envisioned, seen at least partly as a gambit to make Disney Cruise Line a long-term tenant at the port, would spoil the scenery at the area's beach, which feels a world away from the nation's busiest port complex. Others, meanwhile, wonder whether the industrial waterfront tableau of towering gantry cranes lifting containers off massive ships will be all that alluring to many visitors.

"It's a little bit of a hard sell," said Carl Winston, who directs San Diego State University's School of Hospitality and Tourism Management and serves on the Port of San Diego's cruise industry advisory committee. Officials intend to finance the renovations with about $900 million in port revenue and other public funds, with the rest coming from private developers.

The plan is the latest incarnation in a decade-long series of efforts to develop the port for walkers, bikers, diners and shoppers. The most recently scuttled version called for three hotels and a massive retail complex. It was dropped under pressure from activists in the nearby neighbourhood of modest single-story homes. Backers hope the current scaled-down project, including eight miles of waterside walking paths, will get the harbour commissioners' nod. If the port doesn't make space for the larger ships, cruise operators will take their business to other cities, such as San Diego and San Francisco where larger terminals are being built, Knatz said.

"We've been underdeveloped for years and the only chance to broaden our job base is to create a great attraction. It's the key to our future," said John Papadakis, who owns a popular Greek restaurant in downtown San Pedro and who supports the redevelopment plan.

Tourism as a Development Strategy

Since the Revelstoke Tourism Strategy was developed in 1997, the community has made extensive progress in promoting and marketing tourism opportunities in Revelstoke. The identification of the Chamber of Commerce as the lead tourism marketing and coordinating 'agency', the formation of the Revelstoke Tourism Advisory Committee, the hiring of a full-time Tourism Development Coordinator, and the commitment of the City of Revelstoke and the CSRD to provide long-term funding for tourism marketing activities have all been positive developments. The community has won awards for the quality of the electronic marketing initiatives which have been undertaken, and the quality, variety and distribution of the print-based promotional materials has also improved dramatically over the course of the past six years. The intent of the Revised Tourism Strategy is to identify the opportunities which will further enhance the tourism sector over the next 5 year period.

While the initial Tourism Strategy was prepared several years ago, many of the observations regarding the potential of Revelstoke to capitalize on its tourism assets are still valid today. The 1997 Strategy stated:

Revelstoke is very well positioned to take more effective advantage of the community and economic benefits associated with tourism. In addition to a very scenic location on a well travelled highway corridor, Revelstoke is unique among B.C. communities in terms of the range and quality of activity options, the uniqueness and visual appeal of the town itself, and the availability of related support services and infrastructure.

Since that time, the infrastructure to support tourism has expanded and the quality has improved, increasing the potential for further tourism related development.

Revised Strategy Format

The revised strategy identifies eleven (11) objectives that will set the framework for tourism development over the next five years. These objectives build on the work that has been done since 1997, and have been endorsed by the Tourism Advisory Committee and the tourism industry and wider community through their participation in the Tourism Forum held in October, 2003.

Tourism Strategy Objectives

This has been partially achieved. Following the 1997 strategy, the Chamber of Commerce was identified as the lead agency for tourism development. It is important that the Chamber of Commerce continues to inform the funding agencies and the wider community of the work that it does in coordinating and promoting tourism. The Tourism Advisory Committee and the Chamber of Commerce will work to secure consistent and stable long-term funding for the position. In addition, to raise the profile of the tourism promotional activities that are underway, the Chamber of Commerce will establish an identity exclusively for tourism promotion. The Tourism Advisory Committee functions as a communications body between the Chamber of Commerce, the Tourism Development Coordinator, and the community. The committee meets on a monthly basis. The Committee will organize an annual Tourism Forum to facilitate communication with, and to solicit input from, the wider tourism industry and the community. Articles by the Tourism Development Coordinator will also be included in the quarterly publication, Development News.

While several tourism businesses have participated in professional development activities such as the Superhost program since 1997, there is still room for improvement in the level of service offered to visitors. The Chamber of Commerce will initiate a Tourism Service Awards program. In addition, the Tourism Development Coordinator will work on a one-to-one basis to encourage tourism businesses to maintain or develop high levels of customer service.

Many of the recommendations and strategies identified in the 1997 study are still valid, and not all marketing and promotional activities have been undertaken. The role of the Tourism Development Coordinator will be to assist local operators and tourism companies to package and promote winter activities e.g. a weekend visit including cross-country skiing and snowshoeing; a 4-day package including downhill skiing and snowmobiling.

These packages (i.e., getaway and destination) can be marketed via:

- *Canadian, American and European tour wholesalers;*
- *Tour wholesaler fam tours;*
- *Direct advertising to Canadian, American and European winter sport clubs;*
- *Ongoing publication of travel articles; and*
- *The Internet.*

Revelstoke needs to do a better job of positioning and marketing itself as a summer destination.

The role of the Tourism Development Coordinator will be to assist local operators and tourism companies to package and promote summer activities e.g. hiking and kayaking; canoeing and bird-watching; trail-riding and visits to local museums; or a combination of any of the above. Marketing activities will be the same as Objective #4. Despite improvements to the appearance of the entrances to the community from the TCH, this remains a critical activity for the community to pursue. Further improvements to signage and to areas adjacent to the highway west of town are required to help entice more travellers to visit Revelstoke. In addition, new signs need to be developed to attract more visitors who stop at Woodenhead Park and the fast-food outlets into the community. The Tourism Advisory Committee will continue to provide support to the Enhancement Committee and the City in the highway revitalization efforts. The areas west of town (before the bridge, on either side of the highway) need to be developed and made more attractive.

A specific long-term strategy will be developed by the Tourism Development Coordinator with input from the Tourism Advisory Committee, the City of Revelstoke, and the community.

This objective was identified in the 1997 Tourism Strategy, and very little progress has been made over the past six years. The objective and rationale described in 1997 are still relevant today. An Events Committee was formed in 2003, and includes the Tourism Development Coordinator. The Events Committee will ensure that this important objective is pursued during the life of the strategy.

There are excellent opportunities to attract small and medium-sized conferences and conventions to Revelstoke. There are a number of high quality accommodation properties, and the community offers a wide range of recreational and cultural activities which can be packaged to enhance a conference program. The community needs to promote Revelstoke as a Conference Centre and aggressively pursue opportunities that arise.

According to the Tourism Activities and Motivations Study, the Visual Arts, Performing Arts and Heritage Tourism sectors are projected to be the fastest and greatest growth activities in tourism over the next 25 years. Revelstoke has a wealth of cultural and heritage tourism attractions which can be marketed further. A strategy will be developed to increase the promotion of this sector to the appropriate markets.

More initiatives should be undertaken to jointly market with regional and neighbouring communities. For example, preliminary discussions have begun with Nakusp to organize a Kayak the Columbia event, a recreational kayak/canoe race between Revelstoke and Nakusp. Similarly, and the idea of a Peddle the Pass bicycle race between Revelstoke and Golden is being considered. The Revelstoke Golf Club is examining the potential of a TCH golf tour, in partnership with other neighbouring communities on the TCH, Golden, Sicamous and Salmon Arm. These type of events increase the number of visitors to each community and help raise the profile of all communities involved. The Tourism Development Coordinator will also work with the Tourism Action Society of the Kootenays to seek opportunities for partnering with the Product Club initiative.

It is critical that some objective measures be developed and implemented to try and measure the success of the activities described above. Obviously, the primary measure of success will be increased tourism visitation, resulting in increased expenditures in the community and increased employment in the tourism sector. The Tourism Development Coordinator, with input from the Tourism Advisory Committee, will work to develop some indicators which can be used to measure success.

Tourism Development Strategy: 2001-2010

The Tourism Development Strategy for the Borough of Coleraine can be downloaded from the link below:

Tourism Development Strategy: The background and objectives of the report can be read here:

Background/ Objectives

The Coleraine Borough Council commissioned TTC/ Tourism & Leisure Partners to assist it in developing a strategy to develop the area's tourism into the 21st century. The key aims of Coleraine Borough Council in commissioning this study were:

- to review tourism's role as a vehicle for economic growth;
- to develop a strategy for the future, particularly identifying the constraints which need to be addressed; to set the priorities for the sector, including targets, product development and marketing strategies;
- to identify factors which would improve profitability of the sector and attract investment; and,
- to review the role of government and the commercial sector; to quantify the resources necessary, and support the case for public sector funding where appropriate.

The Terms of Reference for the Tourism Development Strategy clearly defines the key aim of the study as follows:

"To produce a Tourism Development Strategy for the Borough which is soundly market-based-identifies the opportunities and the needs of the Borough-attracts support from the private, public and community sectors; and,-provides a dynamic framework for action over the next ten years".

In meeting the key aim of the study the Council also specified the importance of:

- maximising sustainable economic benefits from tourism; and
- a clear and definite action plan to deliver the economic and social benefits.

The strategic framework is intended to assist a number of different stakeholders involved with tourism. These include policy makers, businesses engaged in tourism, financial institutions and professional advisors to the sector.

This report aims to provide information, guidance and direction to all involved in the future development of the industry within the area.

East London Tourism Development Strategy and Action Plan 2004-2006

The completed strategy and action plan for East London aims to support the growth of the east London tourism industry and ensure that the area is firmly on the visitor map. The strategy was launched on 28th September 2004. The plan will make the most of east London's diverse attractions and communities, its rich culture and history and its vibrant new businesses. The plan is an innovative joint venture between the LDA, Tour East London and Visit London and has been completed with input from all key stakeholders. The plan covers the London Boroughs of Barking and Dagenham, Bexley, Greenwich, Hackney, Havering, Lewisham, Newham, Redbridge and Tower Hamlets, plus the Corporation of the City of London.

The plan has a number of priority actions including research to quantify the benefits of tourism to each borough, specific research into the views of visitors to the area, target markets and product clusters in order that the area can be marketed more effectively in the future

Dcms Sustainable Development Strategy: Sectors Tourism

Tourism has a significant input to the economic strand of sustainable development; tourism in rural England alone supports

380,000 jobs and underpins 25,000 small and micro businesses. Sustainable tourism is about adopting a long-term perspective on quality, competitiveness, impacts on the environment and local distinctiveness.

Tourism's Potential as a Sustainable Development Strategy

This publication contains the proceedings of the 2004 WTO Tourism Policy Forum, organized by the WTO Education Council and held at the George Washington University in Washington, D.C. It includes over thirty speeches and academic papers from Tourism Ministers, development agency representatives, WTO officials, academics, and other tourism experts who presented at the main session of the conference. Also included are summaries of the parallel sessions in which case studies were presented. The Forum was organized with the aim of exchanging views with bilateral and multilateral donor organizations, as well as representative recipients; discussing sustainable tourism development policies in relation to the MDGs; reporting on WTO general initiatives in relation to sustainable tourism and development and particularly the WTO ST-EP program to bring sustainable tourism development into the service of poverty elimination; sharing promising practices for sustainable development and considering lessons learned from exemplary tourism projects supported by donors; and formulating recommendations for utilizing tourism as a sustainable development tool for achieving MDG outcomes.

Fifteen years ago, a group of university professors, professionals and public tourism officials gathered together at The George Washington University to attend the first Tourism Policy Forum (TFP), which was held at the initiative of Professor Donald Hawkins. Some of us in attendance were seriously concerned about the exhaustion of the tourism paradigm of the 1970s and 1980s, the so-called mass tourism model, which we later re-named Fordian tourism. The externalities of this tourism business paradigm were already threatening the very sustainability of tourism activity, and called into question tourism's capacity to contribute to development.

The 1990 TPF made it possible—I believe for the first time ever—to carry out a deep, collective reflection at the global level regarding (i) tourism scenarios in the 1990s (taking into account economic, technological, socio-cultural and environmental aspects), (ii) Tourism Policy objectives going beyond simply maximizing the number of tourists and/or tourism revenues, and (iii) the instruments of this sectoral policy. Using today's terminology, it could be said that 1990 TPF was an international exercise in knowledge management in tourism, which had a considerable influence on the development of tourism policy in the 1990s.

Indeed, some of the key tourism policy documents of the 1990s (e.g.: Australia's Passport to Growth: A National Tourism Strategy, 1992; Futures: Plan Marco de Competitividad del Turismo Espanol, 1992; or White Paper: Development and Promotion of Tourism in South Africa, 1996), it seems to me, show the impact of many of the concepts discussed at 1990 TPF, whether due to the direct participation of their authors in the TPF, or thanks to the dissemination of such concepts through the academic and governmental publications and forums of the time (e.g.: meetings of the International Academy for the Study of Tourism, academic activities and research work supported by the European Union's DGXXIII, General Assemblies and knowledge management activities of the WTO, etc).

In September 2003, on the occasion of the awarding of the WTO's Ulysses Prize to Professor Hawkins, and the tribute event held in his honour in Andorra by the WTO·Themis Foundation, the idea arose to revive the TPF, this time as a permanent programme of the WTO under its Department of Education and Knowledge Management (WTO.EKM) and in close collaboration with the WTO Education Council (WTO.EdC). As everybody knows, the WTO.EdC is composed of some fifty educational and research institutions from around the world, which have received the WTO's TedQual Certification through a quality audit. The WTO.EKM, for its part, carries out the Programme of Work of the WTO in the areas of research, education and training, and the application of knowledge to tourism policy and governance in tourism.

Introduction

For one thing, it was decided to make it a biannual event, thus allowing constant interaction with the WTO's deliberative bodies and decision-making organs (the Executive Council and the General Assembly). For another, the new WTO TPF was to place greater emphasis on practical results and encourage the active participation of public bodies, both national and international, as well as of civil society entities with the capacity to support and implement the conclusions reached by the forum.

It remained only to decide the subject areas to be tackled by this new WTO TPF, and this task was made relatively easy in view of the full integration of the WTO in the UN system in December 2003, and its consequent dedication to the Millennium Development Goals, and especially to the issue of development and poverty reduction (e.g., ST-EP Foundation, WTO. Scholars programmes in collaboration with the cooperation agencies of Italy and Mexico, etc.). Thus, the 2004 TPF took shape with a focus on the issue of tourism as an instrument of development.

This issue is both old and new at the same time. Tourism's capacity to generate income and wealth, to consolidate cultural and environmental assets and to transmit knowledge and information has been discussed and analysed from very diverse perspectives-academic, professional, and governmental-over the past several decades. And yet, actual tourism policies have paid much more attention to the purely promotional and microeconomic/entrepreneurial aspects of tourism. For this reason, the WTO, in organizing the 2004 TPF, had two great hopes from the outset: (i) that it would contribute to clarify the methods and instruments of tourism as a motor of development, and (ii) that it would lead to broad consensus among governments, institutions of the United Nations, development agencies, educational and knowledge management institutions, NGOs, and the private sector regarding best practices, initiatives and recommendations.

We believe that the results have lived up to expectations, although it is clear that we have a huge task ahead of us. The 2004 TPF, which was held at The George Washington University (Washington D.C.) in October 2004, drew some 200 participants representing the upper echelons of decision-making in tourism, plus another 200 highly qualified observers. In my view, the event constituted a milestone in the WTO's Programme of Work, and a high point in the effort to tackle the issue of tourism as an instrument of development. Someone once said that humanity's development has been a race between knowledge and chaos. I believe that the 2004 TPF has given a substantial lead to knowledge-and I trust in its concrete application as well.

Tourism Development Strategies

Recognising its importance, the Lao government has declared tourism to be one of the top three priority areas for socio-economic development, with a target of 1.2 million tourist arrivals by 2010. Significant investment has already been committed to the upgrading of the tourism infrastructure and plans are currently being prepared for the establishment of a tourism marketing and promotion board and the adoption of a master plan for tourism development. At the present time by far the greatest proportion of foreign tourists visiting Laos are those from neighbouring countries of the Asia Pacific region. In 2004 this group made up 81.59 per cent of the total number, incorporating the two largest visitor groups from Thailand (489,677, 54.72 per cent of the total) and ViCt Nam (130,816, 14.62 per cent of the total). Other major national groups visiting the country in 2004 included Americans (37,181, 4.16 per cent of the total), Chinese (33,019, 3.69 per cent of the total), French (27,806, 3.11 per cent of the total), British (27,402, 3.06 per cent of the total), Japanese (20,319, 2.27 per cent of the total), Australians (15,149, 1.69 per cent of the total) and Germans (14,009, 1.57 per cent of the total). At present few figures are available for domestic tourism, but this is also believed to be on the increase.

Market research of recent years has shown consistently that the cultural heritage scores highly amongst the country's visitor attractions – in 2004 56 per cent of the 1,417 international visitors surveyed at Wattay International Airport claimed to have been drawn to Laos mainly by its culture, 39 per cent by its temples and monuments, 54 per cent by its natural beauty and 23 per cent by its ethnic minorities. The consequence for tourism has been that to date around 80-90 per cent of all tourism has focused on relatively short visits to the country's two main cultural centres of Vientiane and Luang Prabang.

In practice, the main focus of cultural tourism to Laos has been the former royal capital of Luang Prabang, which was awarded World Heritage status in 1995 for its 'exceptional example of fusion' between traditional architecture, Lao urban design and the structures built by colonial authorities in the 19th and 20th centuries. In the years which followed that award the town's tourist infrastructure expanded exponentially. Many local people were displaced as hotels, guest houses, restaurants and souvenir shops sprang up everywhere, often in contravention of building regulations, while at the same time numerous historic buildings were renovated with little regard for authenticity.

Realising that urgent action was required to deal with the unplanned and inappropriate development in Luang Prabang, the government established a National Inter Ministerial Co-ordinating Committee for the Protection and Development of Cultural, Historic and Natural Heritage by Prime Ministerial Decree in 1996. This was followed in 1997 by the Presidential Decree on the Preservation of Cultural, Historic and Natural Heritage, which outlined regulations and measures for the management, conservation, preservation and use of the national heritage, including the upgrading of movable and immovable assets with historical or cultural or natural value into national heritage.

In Luang Prabang itself an inter-institutional body known as the Provincial Committee for the Protection and Development of Luang Prabang Heritage was also set up in 1996 with support from UNESCO to bring together the key stakeholders in the Luang Prabang World Heritage site, namely the Luang Prabang Provincial Government, the Luang Prabang Provincial Service of Information and Culture, the Luang Prabang Provincial Tourism Office and the Luang Prabang Service of Construction, Transport, Posts and Communication. Since that time all construction work carried out within the protected area-whether for new structures or for renovation of old buildings-has required its agreement. In the same year the Maison du patrimoine (Heritage House) was established under the auspices of the Luang Prabang-Chinon (France)-UNESCO World Heritage Centre Cooperation Project as a technical office within the Luang Prabang Provincial Service of Information and Culture; this now acts as the Committee's executive arm and secretariat, offering advice on all building permit requests and developing regulations and plans for safeguarding and developing the Luang Prabang World Heritage protected area and buffer/support zones. A parallel initiative, UNESCO's Cultural Survival and Revival in the Buddhist Sangha Project, is currently training monks in the traditional arts and crafts skills needed to properly care for, preserve and conserve their temples.

Similar measures are currently being implemented for the heritage sites of Wat Phu Champassak and the Plain of Jars, regulating construction and requiring all new buildings in those areas to conform with regulations in respect of size, style and building materials used.

However, with 105,513 foreigners and an unquantified but undoubtedly substantial number of Lao tourists visiting Luang Prabang (a tiny city of 30,000 inhabitants) in 2004 and visitor numbers at Wat Phu Champassak and the Plain of Jars also showing significant increases in recent years, the Lao authorities recognise the urgent need to diversify the tourism sector in order to take spread the load more evenly. As a result, the LNTA is currently placing the development of ecotourist attractions at the core of its official tourism development strategy. In 1993 the government identified and designated 20 locations as National Biodiversity Conservation Areas (NBCAs). These areas now fall under the jurisdiction of the Division for Resource and Development of the Ministry of Agriculture and Forestry's Department of Forests. Zoning, management and safeguarding guidelines and regulations for both the environment and people living within the protected areas are in the process of being created.

The LNTA's National Ecotourism Strategy and Action plan 2004-2010, produced with advice from the SNV Netherlands Development Organisation, sets out the framework for the development of ecotourism in Laos by: strengthening the institutional arrangements for planning and managing ecotourism growth; supporting training, capacity building and the promotion of good practice; supporting environmental protection and nature conservation; providing socio-economic development and cultural heritage protection for host communities; and developing ecotourism research and information.

One particular Lao ecotourism project has been operating with success for several years. The UNESCO Nam Ha Ecotourism Project in Luang Namtha Province is being implemented by the LNTA in cooperation with the Lao Ministry of Agriculture and Forestry, the Luang Namtha Provincial Service of Forestry Resource Conservation and the Luang Namtha Provincial Service of Information and Culture. The UNESCO Office of the Regional Advisor for Culture in Asia and the Pacific is the project's executing agency and provides technical assistance and monitoring. The project itself is funded by grants from the government of New Zealand and the International Finance Corporation (IFC).

The objectives of the project are: to ensure that tourism contributes to the conservation of Laos' natural and cultural heritage; to involve local communities in the development and management of tourism activities; to use tourism as a tool for integrated rural development; to provide training and human capacity building skills to tourism providers and local communities; to integrate public and private sector investment in culturally and environmentally sustainable tourism; and to assist communities to establish cultural and nature tourism activities in and around the Nam Ha National Biodiversity Conservation Area (NBCA). The UNESCO Nam Ha Ecotourism Project has received the UNDP Award for Poverty Alleviation and the British Airways Tourism for Tomorrow Award.

Promotion of community-based ecotourism is also an important focus of the four-year US$14.2 million Mekong Tourism Development Project, currently the LNTA's flagship programme, which was launched in 2003 in partnership with the Asian Development Bank. This project, which also covers Cambodia and Vietnam, seeks to improve tourism-related infrastructure, support pro-poor, community-based sustainable tourism in rural areas and strengthen sub-regional cooperation with a view to facilitating the flow of tourists in and between the three countries. An important component of the Mekong Tourism Development Project is the Pro-poor Community-based Tourism Development programme, which is similar in format to the Nam Ha project but covers four provinces-Luang Namtha, Luang Prabang, Khammouane and Champassak.

This programme aims to assist local communities with distinctive rural lifestyles or living in areas with pristine ecosystems to manage and determine their limits to tourism growth, to increase control over the selection of tourist types and modalities, and to equitably distribute tourism benefits. It is envisaged that it will develop pilot ecotourism and village-based tourism projects, foster the conservation and improvement of the cultural and environmental heritage of selected areas, monitor social impacts, promote the role of women, and establish mitigation measures to minimise negative impacts due to increased tourism.

Development Strategy to the Challenge of a "Plan de Excelencia"

The city of Cáceres is located in the mid western part of Spain, about 300 km from Madrid, at an altitude of 459 m. above sea level. It is the capital of its province, and belongs to the *Extremadura* region. According to the population services, the town counts 90.930 inhabitants, of which 60% is comprised between 20 and 60 years old, and 20% under 20. To these figures we have to add an extra population of 15.000 non-residents, most of them students.

The economy of the city has been traditionally based on the primary sector, though in the last half century Cáceres has evolved into a third sector city, with a small presence of textile and food industries. Nowadays it is the main commercial, economic and administrative centre of its province, and the most important tourism destination of the region.

Cáceres was founded as colony by the Romans in 25 B.C., with the name of Norbensis Caesarina (Home-page of the Municipality of Cáceres), close to an important way of communication that will be later known as "The Silver Route". The settlement is destroyed by the

Visigoths in the 5th Century, and the city remains abandoned until the arrival of the Muslims from the north of Africa in 8th Century. This population takes advantage of the strategic position and transforms the ruins into a military base to face the Christian kingdoms of the north during the first centuries of the reconquest.

Part of the walls are rebuilt under the rule of Almoarab leader Abu Ya'qub. In 1229 the town is definitively occupied by the troops of Alfonso IX, monarch of the Leon Kingdom. The city is granted a free status, and is ruled by 12 *Regidores* (Rulers) elected by the citizens. This status makes the city prosper, and new churches and palaces rise on the foundations of previous mosques and Muslim palaces. The 15th, 16th and 17th century are the most important centuries from the built heritage point of view, since the fortunes brought back from America by adventurers and emigrants transform the downtown into the monumental city we see nowadays. Palaces and sumptuous residences spread around two focuses:

Santa Maria Square and San Mateo Square. The most impressive palaces are built by the powerful families between the 15th and 16th century. In the following centuries Cáceres evolves into a quiet, forgotten province's capital. The situation essentially remains the same until the 1950's when immigration from the countryside starts to make its economy shift from the first to the third sector. In 1986, following a gradual growth of tourism, Cáceres was included in the list of World Heritage Cities.

Tourism Development Strategy: Plan de Excelencia (Excellence Plan)

The tourism vocation of the city has developed at the end of the 20th century: the number of beds grew of almost 50% in the last decade.

However, it is difficult to calculate the average number of tourists per year, since the indicators we have are partial or can't be compared between them. For example, the "Institute de Estudios Turisticos" of the Ministry of Industry Tourism and Commerce provide figures related to the whole region, and can vary from the first available estimation of 1.562.000 Spanish tourists in year 2001 to the 1.227.000 in year 2002. Other indicators, provided by the Municipality, are the number of visitors of different cultural attractors in Cáceres in the year 2003: 20.791 visitors to the Museo de Historia Cultura "Casa Pedrilla"; 34.677 to the Sala de Exposiciones permanente municipal

"Ciudad de Cáceres"; 28.505 to the Museo Vostell; and 68.813 to the Centre de Interpretacion "Torre de Bujaco". We will have to wait until the launch of the planned Tourism observatory before we have reliable estimations of the number of tourists that arrive to Cáceres every year. The offer of tourism in Cáceres has traditionally been related to Hunting, and thus concentrated in the autumn season. The progressive increase of city-breaks and of cultural tourism in general opened an interesting perspective of development. This lead the local authorities to try to develop a tourism of quality (in terms of purchasing power of the visitor), and improve the ratio of overnight stays rather than just the number of visitors.

However, in the late 1990's the lack of a defined strategy was evident: the offer was a monothematic, un-structured, and initiatives were taken mostly by private actors. The chance to put some order and to exploit the sector according to sustainable and also rational criteria came with the *Plan de Excelencia* started in 2000. In Spain this kind of plan comes out of a series of national framework plans for tourism competitivity: FUTURES (1992-1995) and PICTE (2000-2006), launched in the early nineties by the Ministry of Industry, Tourism and Commerce. The first framework plan was created to reduce and correct the negative impacts (mainly ecological and in terms of town planning) of thirty years of wild tourism development, and the second one was created after assessing the success of its predecessor, with the same goals. The *Planes de Excelencia* are the operative tools developed to accomplish these goals: they are addressed to "mature" destinations: mostly traditional "sun & beach" destinations, but also to cities of great historic value, where the main issue is to rise or control the tourism capacity. The investments, financed equally by a Collective Agreement of local, regional and national administrations, are distributed over three or four years. The objectives of the *Planes de Excelencia* are usually focused on the diversification of the tourism seasons and the development of a care for details in the offer: improvement of marketing strategies to attract tourists in low-season, embellishment of historical centres, renovations and reforms of infrastructures, and adaptation of hotels and restaurants to quality standards.

In the specific case of Cáceres, the *Plan de Excelencia* was launched by a collective agreement between the Ministry of Economy, the Region of Extremadura, the Municipality of Cáceres and the representatives of the private sector of the city. Its planned length was of three years, from 2000 to 2003, and the total budget amounted to 2,7 Millions of Euros. The generic goal of the *Plan* was to transform the city in a tourism benchmark at national and international level, but developing a tourism of quality, different from the mass-tourism models of the sun & beach offer.

Concrete Actions Within the Cultural Tourism Strategy

A series of objectives were defined, in order to achieve the generic goal source: Ministry of Industry, Tourism and Commerce):

- Urbanistic rehabilitation of the downtown.
- Improvement of the management.
- Recovery of the Historical built Heritage.
- Construction and development of infrastructures.
- Promotion.
- Equipment
- Definition and diversification of the tourist offer.

The objectives generated a series of actions, presented in a publication of the Municipality of Cáceres in 2003 and 2004. Regarding the urbanistic rehabilitation, it involved restoration of facades, from specific and isolated cases to whole districts in close cooperation with the urbanism councillor. This objective also lead to the creation of a limited traffic area in the downtown, equipped with sophisticated access monitoring systems. Another action issued from this objective was the creation of a pneumatic system for the automatic collection of the rubbish in the downtown area. Concerning the improvement of management, it meant the provision of the funds needed to have a full-time staff devoted to the accomplishment of the Plan, and development subventions to the tourism-related enterprises of the city. The Historical built Heritage recovery activities consist in the lighting of historical buildings, as well as the rehabilitation of representative places for its public use (for example, the transformation of Torre de Bujaco into a visitors centre with a viewpoint, and the enhancement, in different phases, of several stretches of the city walls). Regarding the construction and development of infrastructures, the actions undertaken have been the improvement of the streets of the downtown, and the construction of a bus parking area. The promotion actions, varied from the organisation of fairs and seminars, to the advertising of the city in newspapers and specialised magazines, as well as the publication of a *Plan de Excelencia* bulletin.

Concerning the equipment objective, it entailed the installation of street furniture, as well as urban and tourism signpost, and information panels on the facades of representative built heritage elements. Finally, the definition and diversification of the tourist offer entangled the preparation of strategic plans and the development of cultural tourism offer: the most relevant actions in this context were the preparation of tourism routes in cooperation with the Church administration, the inauguration of two visitor centres (in the Parking Galarza and in Torre de Bujaco), and the creation and/or promotion of events in low season, in order to increase the number of visitors (i.e., the medieval market, the "Semana Santa", theatre festival).

The *Plan de Excelencia* expired in 2003 but some actions have been achieved in the following years. In October of 2006 according to a press note released by the Municipality to *El periodico de Extremadura*, the *plan* isn't still fully accomplished (98%). Beside the concrete actions awaiting to be completed (mainly the enhancement of the Wall and a second tower for visit purposes), the strategic plans and the objectives fixed by the plan are still defining the policies of the municipality. For example, there is the idea, presented in the second issue of the Plan de Excelencia's publication, of launching a "Tourism Observatory", as the one in Avila, a platform devoted to the monitoring of Tourism flows, to visitor studies and to macroeconomic studies that will show the incidence of tourism in other productive sectors of the city. This will also analyse the offer of the sector and the national and foreign demand, in terms both quantitative and qualitative, providing info to establish coherent future strategies.

The Tourism Observatory, which hasn't been launched yet, is the result of a mature and professional approach to audiences management issue, and arrives in due time, since one of the gaps in the tourism policy of Cáceres detected by PICTURE surveys was precisely the absence of monitoring tools. In this sense, the Tourism Observatory, if organised as the one of Avila or the one of Cordoba, will probably be very close to the Cultural Offer Quality Monitoring Tool developed by the UAM team. The techniques and methodologies are different, but both tools are conceived as part of the whole process of management of cultural resources. They do not just complement the management process and strategies, they are integrated into it. The main difference between a Tourism Observatory and our (UAM) tool is that our tool provides more qualitative analysis of the city's cultural offer quality, while other Observatories aim more to statistical results. This is why the testing of our tool offers complementary information suitable to improve the cultural offer of the cities, and Cáceres in this particular case. The detailed survey and conclusions of our tool can be found in the final report.

However we would like to mention here the most remarkable outcomes in relation to the strategies of the *Plan de Excelencia.* Regarding the urbanistic rehabilitation of the downtown, and the recovery of the Historical built Heritage, the results proceed adequately, gathering the visitor's full appreciation of the value of the downtown's built heritage; however, there seems to be a problem with the promotion, because our tool has detected a mismatch in the perception of Cáceres between real and potential visitors. The first group is already aware of the rich tangible and intangible heritage of Cáceres, and comes to the city for that reason, while the second group has an idea of the city as a place with little or no cultural offer at all. This means that the efforts in promotion must continue and strengthen the image of Cáceres that the municipality wants to export.

Concluding Comments and Transferable Key Lessons

The experience of Cáceres is for many reasons a reference model in the management of Heritage cities. Here are the main keys that have contributed to its success.

- Holistic approach: understanding that the dynamics of Tourism are not separate from the dynamics of other domains (social, economical, environmental...), they all are interconnected parts of a system where any action may alter the inner balance;
- Existence of a strategic plan where the tourism policies are integrated into the general policies of the administration;
- Tight cooperation and coordination between different departments (Culture, Urbanism, Environment);
- Integration of assessment and evaluation tools in all the stages of the strategic plan;
- Investment of external funds (*Plan de Excelencia*) not only in short-term and isolated actions (i.e., built heritage conservation and embellishment) but also defining and launching development strategies that will survive after the aid is over.

National Sustainable Development Strategies

The United Nations Conference on Environment and Development (UNCED) held in Rio de Janeiro in 1992, recognised the pressing environment and development problems of the world and, through adoption of Agenda 21, produced a global programme of action for sustainable development into the 21st century.

Agenda 21 states that countries should adopt national strategies for sustainable development, which "should build upon and harmonize the various sectoral economic, social and environmental policies and plans that are operating in the country". The 1997 Special Session of the UN General Assembly set a target date of 2002, for "the formulation and elaboration of national strategies for sustainable development". It confirmed the approach and purpose of national sustainable development strategies as "important mechanisms for enhancing and linking national capacity so as to bring together priorities in social, economic and environmental policies". It also reaffirmed that "all sectors of the society should be involved in their development and implementation".

The Millennium Declaration was signed in September 2000. The associated Millennium Development Goals includes onerelating to environmental sustainability, to "integrate the principles of sustainable development into country policies and programmes and reverse the loss of environmental resources". Activities towards developing and implementing national sustainable development strategies will, thus, contribute to the achievement of this goal.

Finally, the World Summit for Sustainable Development (WSSD), held in August 2002, urged in its Plan of Implementation that "States should take immediate steps to make progress in the formulation and elaboration of national strategies for sustainable development and begin their implementation by 2005".

Since UNCED, governments have made extensive efforts to integrate environmental, economic and social objectives into decision-making by either elaborating new policies and strategies for sustainable development, or by adapting existing policies and plans.

To assist in this process, an International Forum on National Sustainable Development Strategies was held in Ghana in November 2001. The Forum adopted a guidance document containing a number of recommendations on approaches for integrating the principles of sustainable development into policies and programmes of both developed and developing countries. The Forum agreed that a national sustainable development strategy is a tool for informed decision-making that provides a framework for systematic thought across sectors and territory. It also helps to institutionalize processes for consultation, negotiation, mediation and consensus building on priority societal issues where interests differ. Development of a strategy empowers countries to address inter-related social and economic problems by helping them to build capacities, develop procedures and legislative frameworks, allocate limited resources rationally and present timetables for actions. It was strongly reiterated, that countries would benefit from formulating strategies both directly (as a result of making development more sustainable) and indirectly (from the process itself).

United Nations Department of Economic and Social Affairs Division for Sustainable Development

"The next 50 years could see a fourfold increase in the size of the global economy and significant reductions in poverty but only if governments act now to avert a growing risk of severe damage to the environment and profound social unrest. Without better policies and institutions, social and environmental strains may derail development progress, leading to higher poverty levels and a decline in the quality of life for everybody."

Tourism Development Strategy (2006 – 2010)

Vision

By 2010 Linden has become a tourist destination topping 10,000 visitors per year. More than 300 beds are offered by hotels and bed & breakfast providers. Linden and Region 10 offer attractive events and particularly Linden serves as a hub for tourists to other destinations in the interior. Tourism has developed into the third biggest industry in the Region after mining and forest production. The enterprises working in the tourism sector are well-trained and developed into hospitable entities serving satisfied clients. The Region 10 Tourism Development Association (RTTDA) offers professional services, avails of a well-functioning office and counts more than 100 members. The Region 10 tourism industry is well integrated into national efforts to attract even more tourists to Guyana.

Summary

The Tourism Development Strategy centres around three axes:

1. Development of Region 10 into a genuine tourist destination (identification of destinations, creation of events),

2. Improvement of services through local enterprises (training, information),
3. Institutional strengthening of the Region 10 Tourism Development Association (organisation, coordination).

The three axes are accompanied by an aggressive marketing of Region 10 as a tourist destination (external marketing) and of the RTTDA as the major platform for local enterprises earning their livelihood from tourism (internal marketing of the association). Logic of this strategy: the creation and identification of tourist events and destinations trigger a higher influx of visitors who will be professionally hosted and catered for by the local tourism industry to make them come back again in future. RTTDA is the institutional backbone ensuring organization, coordination, promotion and services to its members.

Target Market

Given the comparatively low attraction of Region 10 destinations and events to foreign tourists at present, focus will be laid on national and Caribbean visitors. Some potential for European and American tourists is identified in bird watching possibilities, Linden as a transition to more attractive destination in Region 9, and in linking Linden to other cities during flight hopper tours (such as Bartica – Linden– Georgetown on a day tour). Greatest market potential lies in the Diaspora Lindeners having keen interest in revisiting their birth town while some are expected to resettle and invest in Linden after retirement. The influence of this target market became clearly visible with the announcement of 300 Diaspora Lindeners visiting the Linden Town Week 2006 celebrations with the dedicated assistance of the Linden Fund/USA.

Tourist attractions (events + nature)

New tourist attractions will be created if the tourism industry is to grow. The starting point is the successful operation of singular events (such as the Kashif & Shanghai Football Tournament and the Linden Town Week). More events preferably stretched over several days will be identified to improve the influx of tourists. The Rockstone Fish Festival planned for August 2006 is the first step into this direction. Other ideas emitted so far are: Jazz Festival, Cycling race Georgetown – Linden with finish in Linden, extended carnival festivities (LICA = Linden Carnival), and regattas. It is evident that developed event ideas need to be marked by a great uniqueness.

Apart from the event attractions, other destinations and related services will be offered. Some have already been identified and will be further explored: bird watching and *Victoria Regia* on Gluck Island *(ecotourism niche for short one-day* visits, and possibilities of setting up larger tourist facilities such as a guest-house *or professional boat services*), museum, fishing and hunting tours around Rockstone, visits to reclamation activities in the mined-out areas with scientific guidance, regular weekend visits of the bauxite mine, etc.

Events and nature will be accompanied by a comprehensive signage system leading tourists to and guiding them in Linden. A huge signboard at the Soesdyke- Linden junction will indicate the way to Linden. Arriving in Linden a tourist signboard with map and important destinations of relevance for tourists in Linden will be established (another one for visitors coming from the South). In collaboration with the Town Council traffic signs will be placed in Linden and on the routes to Kwakwani, Ituni, Rockstone, Lethem and other destinations in Region 10. In Linden itself, buildings of relevance for tourists (such as the waterwheel, museum, etc.) will be indicated by special boards explaining the history in brief. Differently coloured sign posts will guide the tourists to these destinations.

Tourist services

Existing and new tourist attractions and events can only be marketed successfully if the clients' needs are satisfied. Hence, we favour competition and we welcome any investor in the tourism sector from abroad or from other areas in Guyana. Tourist services will be provided through the "Linden Office for Visitors" (LOV) as the most important entry point for client information and through individual service providers being members of the association.

a. The "Linden Office for Visitors" (LOV) is the executive branch of the association where contacts with clients are made. Hard copies of all promotion material are made available to incoming visitors. Email queries are answered and the association's activities are coordinated by an executive secretary. More personnel might be hired if the financial situation allows for that. The office is located in the museum; it is equipped with PC, printer, photocopier, display shelves. LOV serves as a facilitating and mediating agency linking customers to the Region 10 tourism service providers. It will concentrate on association members in the first place, hence creating a need for service providers to join.

b. Individual service providers: existing hotel accommodations in Linden, Ituni and Kwakwani will be inspected and rated according to existing standards. A four-tier categorization will be applied as this is currently done with the B&B providers.

The rating (stars for hotels and restaurants, diamonds for B&B providers) will be officially acknowledged through specifically designed signs (size: 1x1 ft) which can be fixed on the walls of the establishments. These signs carry high promotional value and may also attract other service providers to join the association. Assessments and inspections will be done on a yearly routine basis providing room for all members to improve their standards and services. Tourists can easily locate recommended establishments. While rating criteria exist for hotels and B&B providers, a similar rating system for restaurants will be elaborated and applied.

Service providers will be trained in areas common for all such as client reception, customer care, monitoring of customer satisfaction, pricing of services, importance of insurance systems, safety regulations and cleanliness issues. These training offers will be binding for the association's members in order to maintain and eventually improve their grades. Furthermore, there will be sector-specific training arrangements on a needs basis such as cooking of speciality dishes, accommodation standards and design, kitchen hygiene, etc. The needs of the different tourism sectors will be analysed during meetings with the committees to be established under the umbrella of the RTTDA.

Institutional Strengthening

RTTDA is a certified and recognized institution under the Friendly Societies Act. However, in the past the internal functioning was based entirely on the voluntary work of dedicated members who were never asked to pay any fees. The newly developed fees structure distinguishes between a general admission fee of $2,000 for all and sector-specific yearly fees which have been developed in accordance with income prospects. In future, only those individuals and enterprises are considered members who have paid their dues and will be eligible to vote and to decide during the internal meetings.

At the end of each fiscal year, RTTDA will conduct "Certificate Award Functions" during which members who provided excellent services and other personalities and institutions which contributed significantly to the tourism development in Region 10 will be awarded with certificates and plaques. These functions are also meant to enhance visibility of the association and the sector. Increase in (paid) membership will be achieved through the provision of services which consist primarily of marketing, training and lobbying. The services will be organized according to our members' needs and in cooperation with the regional and national bodies in which RTTDA is organized.

Sector-wise committees (for example: B&B providers, restaurant owners, etc.) will be established whenever desired by the members in order to make sure that specific questions can be professionally dealt with by the concerned business people. Chiefs of committees will be elected who report to the RTTDA General Assembly during its official meetings.

RTTDA will become a paying member of the Linden Chamber of Commerce, Industry and Development to ensure the best representation of its interest on the regional level. Interests on the national level will be defended through membership in THAG and close cooperation with the Ministry of Tourism, Industry and Commerce (MINTIC) and particularly the Guyana Tourism Authority (GTA). We will develop special relationships to identified sponsors and donor agencies because it is acknowledged that the membership fees will hardly suffice to pay for overhead costs and association staff. A particular relationship exists with the Linden Fund representing the largest tourism target group at the time being, GTIS and LEAP which provided valuable assistance in the past. Inputs in institutional strengthening are required in the following areas: preparing requests for external assistance, internal functioning of the association and membership care, linkage to potential visitors overseas, tourist product development, assistance in design of marketing devices.

Marketing

The printing of the "Discover Linden" glossy magazine will serve as a starter in Region 10 tourism marketing efforts. The Linden Town Week is the catalyst to get more diversified marketing efforts on stream.

The RTTDA Web Page is the central long-term marketing tool informing customers about tourist destinations and accommodation facilities. The office in the museum building is centrally located; it will be staffed with at least one competent person who answers questions on the telephone, replies to email inquiries, links visitors to accommodation facilities, distributes tourist brochures and sells tourism articles and literature.

Brochures on the following issues are circulated per hard copy: B&B facilities, hotel accommodation, restaurant and catering services, travel-, boat and fishing tours, Linden tourist map, other tourist services such as bars, taxi and other transport services, offer of handicraft products, and a general flyer summarizing key information of interest to tourists.

To attract visitors from Georgetown, regular ads are published in national newspapers, particularly in conjunction with the different events to be organized. On very special occasions, TV ads will be made on the national TV station. All published information material will also be accessible to interested persons at the "Tourism & Hospitality Association of Guyana" (THAG) of which RTTDA becomes a member. National seminars and workshops on tourism will be used as a platform to attract visitors and investors in the tourism industry to Region 10.

Tourism Development Strategy

In 1993, a detailed community survey of Revelstoke was conducted and a Vision Statement prepared. The Vision Statement, which provided direction and a statement of community values, is being used to guide Revelstoke's growth and development. In 1995, this vision statement served as the basis for the development of a Community Economic Development Strategy.

As recommended in this Strategy, a Tourism Development Strategy was prepared during 1996-97, and has served to guide the development of tourism over the past 6 years. In 2002, the members of the Revelstoke Tourism Advisory Committee recommended that the strategy should be revised to better reflect changing conditions in the local tourism industry. It was decided that revisions to the Tourism Development Strategy could be carried out 'in house' by the local Community Economic Development Department, and that the Revelstoke Tourism Advisory Committee would act as the Steering Committee for the development of the revised Tourism Development Strategy.

During 2000, as part of the development of a new Revelstoke Community Development Strategic Action Plan, an extensive community survey was undertaken to determine the priorities and concerns of Revelstoke residents. Over 68% of those surveyed identified tourism and hospitality as the highest priority sector of the economy for the community to develop. This was by far the most important sector for development identified by the community. The revision to the Revelstoke Tourism Development Strategy was undertaken during

2002-03. The Revelstoke Tourism Advisory Committee acted as the steering committee for the project. During this time, Revelstoke had undertaken an initiative to develop a strategy to determine how best to market the community to outside investors. As part of this initiative, external consultants reviewed the state of the local economy and met with several business and civic leaders to determine community economic priorities and the most effective ways of promoting the community to international investors. The consultants recommended a focus on tourism development as the best way of attracting investors and of improving the local economy. It was decided to utilize the same consulting team to interview local tourism operators to obtain their input regarding the state of the Revelstoke tourism industry. This information (included in Appendix I) was used to assist in determining tourism priorities for the next five year period.

Objectives

The overall goal of this study is to prepare a tourism strategy that provides the community of Revelstoke with clear direction relative to the development of the community's tourism industry for the period 2003 to 2008. The specific objectives of this project include preparing a tourism development strategy which supports the following:

- Achievement of a sustainable economy in keeping with the community's Vision Statement;
- Promotion of tourism growth and development to ensure economic stability;
- Enhancement of the growing tourism and outdoor recreation sector; and,
- Diversification of the local economy and creation of job opportunities.

Study Process

The steering committee felt that the existing (1997) strategy provided a solid base. The intent of the revised strategy project was to update the existing strategy i.e. identify what has been accomplished, what still needs to be done, and establish priorities for the next 5 years.

The following activities were carried out:

1. Update baseline data (including a review of strengths and weaknesses)
2. Identify gaps/ review tourism strategies from other communities

3. Consultation with the tourism industry
4. Compile information/ identify priorities
5. Prepare draft strategy/ circulate for comment
6. Prepare final strategy.

The Development Strategy For Ecotourism in Wolong

Wolong Natural Reserve (WNR), known as a shining pearl in the southwest China, is the largest national-level natural reserve specializing in protecting giant pandas and natural ecological system. With respect to protection and development, active efforts were made in the 1990s but failed. It was widely acknowledged that tourism should be given the top priority for the development and protection of WNR. Therefore it is of great necessity to re-consider the tourism development strategy so as to make it more efficient and more compliant with market rules.

Advantages in Resources & Marketing Orientation

Famed as the "Hometown of the Giant Panda" and with a total area of 2000 km2, WNR is located in the Aba Tibetan and Qiang Nationalities Autonomous Prefecture, and is just 120 km from Chengdu.

Advantages in Resources

Nature has richly endowed in tourism resources, including natural resources such as wild animals and plants, forests, mountains, lakes and pleasant weather conditions. WNR boasts abundant cultural resources from the religious traditions of Taoism & Buddhism, customs of Tibetan and Qiang nationality and local house styles. WNR accommodates over 100 Pandas in the wild, 10% of the total wild population, and 64 Pandas in its breeding centre. Moreover, WNR has a complicated land ecology system with 7 vertical ecology system belts resulting in tremondous biological diversity. There are 1989 higher plants varieties and 450 kinds of vertibra, of which 57 under key state protection. WNR has a world-class panda protection research centre, the only-one panda museum, and the largest trial park for training animals back to the wild. Wild animals and rare birds can be easily observed in various places within WNR. Flocks of blue sheep and Takins in Yinlonggu, thousands of swifts in Guanyingya and rare birds including the Tibetan Eared Pheasant, blood pheasants and Chinese Monals in Pengsheng Gaur Valley can all be seen in WNR. It has the largest primitive Davidia forest in China and two highland grasslands, Huangcaoping and Niupingzhi.

Market Orientation

The development of tourism in WNR should be aimed at an international, high-quality ecology tours oriented to domestic and foreign markets, featuring by giant pandas and the beautiful scenery of their natural habitats.

Products Patterns & Strategic Targets

Stress will be laid on the following four tour product patterns. 1. Forest holiday-making. With comfortable weather conditions, fresh air, and sufficient sunshine and, tour products such as forest recuperation, travels, conference tours, and health-making tours can be developed. Villas and hotels for holiday-seekers can be constructed accordingly. 2. Unique eco-tour. Its waters, large areas of virgin forests, wild animals, numerous snow-capped mountains and waterfalls are extremely suitable for eco-tours. 3. Panda image products. The image resources of pandas should be turned into actual resources by constructing a panda ecology valley where people can go directly to see pandas in the wild. This would allow WNR to produce tour souvenirs for tourists and videos of the giant pandas for tourists. 4. Ethnic culture products.

Generally, the development of tourism in WNR will concentrate on creating a world-class ecology tour attraction and China's national park by 2005; bidding for world heritage, serving as a model for sustainable development among national reserves and world natural heritages, and enjoying an important position among tour sites in Sichuan as well as in China.

Principles & Measures for Development

The following principles should be observed in the tourism development of WNR: 1. Protection of unique and irreplacable resources; 2. Market-oriented, sustainable development; Harmonious co-existence between humans and nature. Based on the ideas and development principles above, and practical experiences in developing eco-tour sites at home and abroad, the development of WNR must follow the principle of "Tour inside, lodge outside". A "For-ecology Moving-out" Project will be implemented, that will move all residents in Wolong Township to Gengda Township, merging Gengda and Wolong Township to create a new township with strong ethnic flavours so as to make it a reception centre for tourists. An ecology protection system that is much stricter than other reserve areas should be established and implemented in order to have ecology-friendly protection regulations.

Operation & Management Measures

The reserve should be strictly administered in accordance with the management rules of national park and natural heritage regulations. A new method of "Separation of Rights" will be introduced, namely separating the rights of ownership, management and operation. The ideas above have been included in the just-completed WNR General Plan of Ecotourism. By now the preparatory works for merchant-invitations and project-bidding have already been started. We firmly believe that in near future China's national Yellow Stone Park or a World-Class Eco-tour Attraction will emerge in southwest China.

2008 Economic Development Strategies-Agritourism Industry

With New Jersey farmers facing rising costs and stagnant commodity prices, agri-tourism offers an important opportunity to generate additional farm income and keep farms economically viable. Agri-tourism presents opportunities for New Jersey growers seeking to add value to their crops and/or capture more of the market price of their products by directly accessing consumers. Many residents consider agriculture a novelty and something to be explored and enjoyed. They desire to share the agricultural experience while increasing farm income at the same time. New Jersey's agri-tourism industry provides for a great introduction to the agriculture of the Garden State. The educational and economic contributions of agri-tourism to the state's agricultural economy are many.

A National Agricultural Statistics Survey (NASS) study conducted this year determined that the economic impact of agri-tourism upon New Jersey's economy was $91 million in 2006. This quantitative information confirms the qualitative recommendations of a 2005 Rutgers University study that examined farmers' and farm leaders' perceptions of the opportunities and challenges associated with agri-tourism. There are other states that have comprehensive agri-tourism programs and these will be studied as work moves forward to more closely cooperate with the various agencies that share a common interest in promoting tourism in New Jersey.

A new interactive, GIS-based, agri-tourism industry website, "visitnjfarms.org", allows for easy consumer mapping based on products, services and location, within a specified town or county, or within a specified driving radius of a user-defined beginning point. It also allows farmers password access to the site to provide updates to their own listing.

To assist in the development of the agri-tourism industry, the Department will be focusing on three major objectives: developing strategic partnerships, consumer promotion and industry education.

Develop Strategic Partners

Strategy – Continue to support the New Jersey Agri-Tourism Industry Advisory Council in their charge to develop, support, and market this sector of the agricultural community.

Strategy – Continue working with the N.J. Office of Travel & Tourism (T&T) to develop and market agri-tourism. Develop three agri-tourism based travel tours for each of the state's six tourism regions. Encourage T&T to integrate an agri-tourism press familiarization tour into their work. These tours acquaint the regional travel and tourism media with New Jersey agri-tourism. Encourage T&T to incorporate agri-tourism research into their established travel industry research program. Market agri-tourism to the travel and tourism trade through participation in the annual Governor's Conference on Tourism, cooperative advertising, and other industry opportunities.

Strategy –Publicize the National Agricultural Statistics Survey (NASS) study that assessed the economic impact of agri-tourism upon New Jersey's economy.

Consumer Promotion

Strategy – Produce and distribute an inexpensive agri-tourism brochure with industry websites and contact information. This brochure would promote seasonal events, special attractions, and direct farm marketing opportunities. Create and disseminate regular press releases promoting the agri-tourism industry and related websites. Work to expand the promotion of the agricultural fairs in New Jersey.

Strategy – Continue to develop and promote the "visitnjfarms.org " website.

Industry Education

Strategy-Coordinate an Agri-Tourism symposium to address common opportunities and challenges and to provide some basic tourism and hospitality industry training. Work with Rutgers Cooperative Extension to develop and implement this training. Strategy-Conduct tourism industry outreach activities for agri-tourism operators. Promote listings in the N.J. Office of Travel & Tourism's "Calendar of Events". Promote participation in "The 2007 New Jersey Governor's Conference on Tourism". Promote the use of the "Tourism Cooperative Grant Program" to organizations representing various facets of the New Jersey's agri-tourism industry.

Strategy – Continue to review, comment, and support work towards the adoption of agri-tourism Agricultural Management Practices (AMP's) as proposed by the State Agriculture Development Committee. Compliance with the agri-tourism AMP's will aid grower protection under the Right to Farm Act.

The success of tourism in Cambodia depends in Fart on the country's ability to develop a knowledgeable and skilled work force. Meeting the wide range of education and training needs must therefore be seen as essential for d l sectors of the industry. Failure to cmbrace all of the training issues will result in an imbalance within the travel product. Visitor satisfaction can diminish in a number of ways, and destinations that fail to recognize and address the needs and expectations of their tourists place the tourism industry at risk.

There are a number of different dimensions in beginning to understand a human resource development slrategy. It cannot be assumed that classrooms are the only settings for education aild training but rather that training and education can occur in a number of different ways. Given new technology and means of delivery, significant number of Cambodians can develop new skills and knowledge that are essential in ensuring the quality of the countrys tourism industry. There are a number of new providers in the country that have shown entrepreneurial skills in beginning to address some of the important training and education needs in tourism. It is essential that the public and private sectors come together and the research work behind the strategy clearly recognizes the importance of this partnership. The docuinent is divided into three parts: An assessment of public sector training and education needs.

The Ministry of Tourism

In assessing the training needs for each of the departments, there appears to be overlap in responsibilities. In many cases the tasks within a particular department would logically be the responsibility of other departments within the Ministry of 'Tourism. In some instances, the responsibility would be that or other government ministries where the appropriate expertise would be more readily available. As of October 2000, the registered number of staff at MOT based in Phnoin Penh is approximately 450. It is believed that 30%-

40% of the registered employees are actually active. This is derived from interviews as well as advice from consultants assigned to M01. Thc percentage of active staff to registered staff will serve as basic data necessary for determining the scale of staff training and capacity to perform daily duties. In other words we arc not dealing with 450 staff members who require training but rather a much sinaller subset that actually are working within the Ministry. A number of staff have participated in overseas training, a high percentage being university graduates which reflects the practice of' donors to impose requirements for overseas training such as the need to possess a University degree or equivalent qualifications, three years of' employment in a related field and language competener; (English) before training is provided. While there has been a satisfactory level of international training there has not been any formal evaluation from the point view 01' quality and relevance of that training. It is recommended that all international training exercises require baronial report both of the individual as well as of the individual supervisor.

Domestic Training

Domestic training carried out in the past five years can be categorized as "introductory training the training for tour guides", "basic training" (tourism development and management) "skill training" for MOT staff, and "hospitality training related to tourism awareness".

The majority *of* the training was related to % wiliness". Though this can appraised from the viewpoint of broadening the tourism base one cannot help but say that this activity only covers a small part of the training and education gap. There is no evidence that a needs survey was conducted before deciding on the content, hereby indicating that the is no assurance that the desirable level of training was necessarily provided.

Mot and other Ministries' Training Needs

Through a series of questionnaires and several meetings has identified a number of training requirements that need to be met if the government bureaucracy in Cambodia is to meet the country's tourism objectives. However, until staff is paid a living wage much of the training will not necessarily! increase the capacity of staff given their need to seek additional forms of livelihood.

A possible solution might be in job sharing where two persons share the responsibility for specific objectives and outputs. The working day could be split into two time units, with a handover period, e.g., 7.30 to 12.30 and 12.00, 17.00 hours. Staff would then be officially free to undertake secondary employment. This strategy relieves office space increases motivation, and allows employees to supplement their income until such time as the Government is in the position to enhance the Fasic wages of civil servants.

Ministry of Tourism

Introduction to Basic Tourism Planning and Development Concepts

There is an urgent need for staff at all levels to understand what is meant by 'tourism'; to appreciate that it is basically the sale of a shared experience, based on physical comfort, providing a visual experience and a service component. The expectations of the tourists need to be clearly understood, in order to create a positive growth environment. Within this context the Ministry can then embrace its responsibility to provide guidance and support to a growing industry.

Basic General Skills

The following training needs have been identified. Private sector training organizations offer courses covering all of these topics. Selected staff can be enrolled on an individual basis, or group rates can be negotiated for larger numbers.--

* Language skills-Basic, Intermediate and Advanced
* Report writing
* Keyboard skills
* Word processing
* Computer literacy
* Numeracy skills
* Basic accounting
* Database management
* Stock control

Statistical Analysis: In the report on the development of an economic base study for Cambodia carried out by the need for such training is well illustrated and discussed. A basic introduction to economic analysis should be included.

When the tourism law is enacted there will be an urgent need to train inspectors in a wide range of technical and jurisdictional issues if they arc to be effective in carrying out their important tasks.

Basics of Small and Medium-Sized Enterprise Creation

Staff must begin to understand how to support small and medium-sized enterprises if poverty reduction is to occur. It is important that staff move from the rhetoric that is now becoming common about the importance of small and medium-sized enterprises to actually beginning to understand the dynamics behind the creation of such initiatives.

Training Needs for MOT and Other It event Ministries

Information Officers

It is evident that the staff of various ministries interacting with tourists needs assistance to develop its tourist information services. Information should include communication and courtesy skills, care and presentation of information desks, collection and filing of' information display of promotional materials, etc. Interpretation, design of exhibits and publications and the development of multimedia presentations also need to be trained. This will have to be at various levels and directed at specific staff.

Marketing and Promotion

Staff should be exposed to the basics of market research and promotion in order to allow them to participate effectively in the research process and to interact with marketing and promotion professionals. There should be no attempt to train a large number of skilled people but it is clear that market research skills are an important need in Cambodia. Relevant Ministries: Ministry of Tourism. Ministry of Cultural and Fine Arts and Ministry of Environment. Managing Service Excellence in the Cambodian Tourism Industry Knowledgeable travellers are demanding the best quality the tourism industry can provide. A competitive hospitality or tourism organization or business requires employees who (a> arc committed to exceeding industry standards for quality service. (b) can perform effectively in a multicultural environment. and (c) can contribute creatively to addressing service challenges in the work place. Consistent, predictable service quality translates into customer satisfaction and increased revenues from positive referrals to potential customers and repeats visits. Quality service training can also heighten employment satisfaction and positively influence employee retention.

The Management of Ecotourism

Such a course would allow the participants to understand the basic elements of ecotourism, evaluate market trends, assess the?

potential of individual and group ecotourist speciality markets use green guidelines for operating a successful ecotourism business, analyze and address the special needs of ecotourists and local communities, establish an ecotourism planning process at the local and regional levels, develop trip circuits and travel packages that are safe and offer a wide variety of experiences and understand the vital role of interpretation and education in adding value.

Ecolodge Development

Such a course would allow the participants to assess the market demand for ecolodge types and the experiences they provide, estimate realistic cost projections/ revenue potential and develop pricing strategies, and understand how to find the best locations and evaluate site development opportunities and constraints.

Coastal & Marine Ecotourism

Such a course would allow the participant to integrate coastal zone management and mariners conservation into a sustainable tour ism development strategy identify the special characteristics of marine ecotourists, use innovative resource planning techniques and coastal zone management best practices, establish zoning and visitor tracking methods, educate visitors and staff about low-impact forms of recreation, monitor and assess more accurately the long-term effects of tourism on local resources and increase government's commitment in marine park protection and effective coastal management.

Historical Site Management

Observation of activities within the Angkor Wat complex would indicate that site management would need to be urgently improved. While the present ad-hoc arrangements may have been acceptable for love volume traffic, there is an urgent need for staff to be trained to deal with ever larger number of visitor numbers.

Project Management

Staff must be exposed to leading-edge project management skills and knowledge areas. It is becoming increasingly important, as transparency and good governance are required that team leaders and managers understand how to manage large-scale projects in a financially responsible manner. There is increasing concern within the donor community about the level of project management in Cambodia. It is clear that this is age skill and knowledge area that will be urgently required as donors and others become more demanding.

Poverty Reduction through Tourism

As we discover more and more about the role that sustainable tourism can play in alleviating poverty, staff must be provided with the opportunity of developing their skills and knowledge in poverty reduction initiatives. The training should range from simple awareness raising to sophisticated training for small numbers in developing policies and programs designed to deal with the poverty issue in a comprehensive manner. Relevant Ministries: All ministries dealing with tourism.

Recommendations for Travelling and Education For the Private Sector

The Private Sector is made up of a number of different organizations and activities. The challenge is to ensure. That the relevant actors are trained and educated to support the overall tourism development and management process. From the beginning it is important to stress that the Ministry of Tourism is only one of many government actors responsible for delivering:! quality tourism product. There are therefore a series of other ministries that require capacity building. The assessment used the following list of private sector occupational activities as a means of organizing its work:

* Adventured Outdoor Tourism Guide
* Advertising Manager/Assistant
* Amusement Park Employee
* Amusement Park
* Operation/Management
* Bartender
* Beverage Services Manager
* Campground Operator
* Casino Dealer
* Casino Slot Attendant
* Catering Manager
* Director of Salcs and Marketing
* Door Staff
* Food & Beverage Manager
* Food Sr. Beverage Server
* Food Service Counter Attendant

* Front Desk Agent
* Golf Club Manager
* Guest Services Attendant
* Housekeeping Room Attendant
* Human Resource Management
* Hunting Guide
* Kitchen Helper
* Leisure Centre Manager/Assistant
* Line Cook
* Marketing Manager/Assistant
* Promotion Manager/Assistant
* Reservations Sales Agent
* Retail First level Manager
* Retail Sales Associate
* Sales Manager
* Small Business Owner/Operator
* Special Events Coordinator
* Special Events Manager
* Taxicab Driver
* Tour Bus/Vaii Driver
* Tour Director
* 'Tour Guide
* Tour Operator
* Tourism Small Business Owner
* Tourism Trainer
* 'Travel Counsellor
* Wine Service.

Survey of Training Needs In 'the Cambodian Travel and Tourism Sector

In order to better understand the needs of the travel and tourism sector several initiatives were taken. In addition to the significant number of interviews and meetings with many members of the tourism industry, the project worked with Rege: it College in Thnoni Penh in a study that was intended to provide a snapshot of the current human resource capacity in the travel and tourism industry. This included not only the hospitality sector, but also related industries of international and domestic travel services and other support services. The key objectives were to provide a clear and relevant overview of the current level of skills among personnel working in the hospitality and travel industry and, by analysis of current recruitment practices, human resource and training policies, to identify clear areas where a skills gap exists. In addition the study aimed to assess the commitment and capacity of owners. Managers and currently existing training institutions 10 address these questions. To achieve these objectives. Primary data was collected from a Closs section of accommodation services restaurant and catering services, and travel and tour operators. Secondary data was provided by the hospitality. Travel and tourism sectors, the Ministry of Tourism and Ministry of Education. 'The project team wishes to thank Regent College for its cooperation and professionalism in completing the survey.

Methodology

Due to the necessarily limited nature of the time and financial resources available to carry out a survey. Three key sites were selected as representing the current focus of tourism activity in Cambodia. These were:

Phnom Penh, the capital city and principal port of entry for the Kingdom. Despite a significant decrease of growth in arrivals, a< a result of the government's Open Skies policy, 56.75% of all visitors to Cambodia in 2000 still arrived through Pochentong International Airport.

Siem Reap, home of Angkor Wat and the principal centre for tourism development. In 3,000, 18.66% of all visitors to the kingdom arrived through Siem Reap Airport. a figure that has shown an enormous increase in the year to date, with a 110.98% rise in the first quarter alone. Sihanoukville (formerly Kampong Som), Cambodia's principal seaside resort town located 230km south of Phnom Penh. one of four international border checkpoints and a popular destination for domestic holidaymakers.

Primary research in each of these locales consisted of questionnaires, scheduled interviews and, in the case of Phnom Penh, follow-up felcus group discussions (FGD's). Potential respondents were drawn from PADECO's comprehensive listings of hotels, guesthouses, restaurants and travel and tour operators. PA1 IECO's categories were further subdivided based on considerations of price. Facilities, site, ownership and location. Subsets in each locale were identified using these four criteria, md from these subsets a random sample was made, proportionate to the size/ number of each location. A total of one hundred respondents were selected across the three locations.

Questionnaires focused on current recruitment and HR policy, the current educational and skill levels of management and staff, recent experience of, or participation in internal or externally conducted training, management commitment to staff development perceived constraints or obstacles to the provision of training and the prioritization of specific skills for enhancement or development. In addition to the quantitative data obtained, the questionnaires contained a qualitative component in the form of brief interviews based on a set of prospected questions. 'The questionnaires were administered in face-to-face interviews with owners or managers of hotels, restaurants or travel and tour operators. Questionnaires were available in English or Khmer as required and each interview team consisted of one native speaker and one Khmer interviewer to minimize problems of comprehension. Secondary information sources consisted primarily of the Ministry of Tourism Statistical Report for 7000. The 1999 MPDF report on Developing SMEs in the Tourism Industry and the 1996 National Human Resource Strategy developed by WTO/UNDP.

Immediately following completion of the formal questionnaires, respondents were invited to colour issues which had atisen in the course of the interviews in an informal setting, and to provide a more personalized insight into the topics covered. Following completion of all primary data collection, two focus group discussions were conducted to further explore the issues raised by the study, involving respondents from the training and education field, and owners and mangers from the private sector. 'This report provides information on the most important findings.

3

Market Plan of Travel Business

Tourism is one of many activities in a community or region that requires planning and coordination. This bulletin provides a simple structure and basic guidelines for comprehensive tourism planning at a community or regional level. Planning is the process of identifying objectives and defining and evaluating methods of achieving them. By comprehensive planning we mean planning which considers all of the tourism resources, organizations, markets, and programs within a region. Comprehensive planning also considers economic, environmental, social, and institutional aspects of tourism development.

Two Sides of Tourism Planning

Tourism planning has evolved from two related but distinct sets of planning philosophies and methods. On the one hand, tourism is one of many activities in an area that must be considered as part of physical, environmental, social, and economic planning. Therefore, it is common to find tourism addressed, at least partially, in a regional land use, transportation, recreation, economic development, or comprehensive plan.

The degree to which tourism is addressed in such plans depends upon the relative importance of tourism to the community or region and how sensitive the planning authority is to tourism activities.

Tourism may also be viewed as a business in which a community or region chooses to engage. Individual tourism businesses conduct a variety of planning activities including feasibility, marketing, product development, promotion, forecasting, and strategic planning. If tourism is a significant component of an area's economy or development plans, regional or community-wide marketing plans are needed to coordinate the development and marketing activities of different tourism interests in the community. A comprehensive approach integrates a strategic marketing plan with more traditional public planning activities. This ensures a balance between serving the needs and wants of the tourists versus the needs and wants of local residents. A formal tourism plan provides a vehicle for the various interests within a community to coordinate their activities and work toward common goals. It also is a means of coordinating tourism with other community activities.

Steps in the Planning Process

Like any planning, tourism planning is goal-oriented, striving to achieve certain objectives by matching available resources and programs with the needs and wants of people. Comprehensive planning requires a systematic approach, usually involving a series of steps. The process is best viewed as an iterative and nagging one, with each step subject to modification and refinement at any stage of the planning process. There are six steps in the planning process:

1. Define goals and objectives.
2. Identify the tourism system.
   a) Resources
   b) Organizations
   c) Markets
3. Generate alternatives.
4. Evaluate alternatives.
5. Select and implement.
6. Monitor and evaluate.

Step One: Defining Goals and objectives. Obtaining clear statements of goals and objectives is difficult, but important. Ideally, tourism development goals should flow from more general community goals and objectives. It is important to understand how a tourism plan serves these broader purposes. Is the community seeking a broader tax base, increased employment opportunities, expanded recreation facilities, better educational programs, a higher quality of life? How can tourism contribute to these objectives?

If tourism is identified as a means of serving broader community goals, it makes sense to develop plans with more specific tourism development objectives. These are generally defined through a continuing process in which various groups and organizations in a community work together toward common goals. A local planning authority, chamber of commerce, visitors bureau, or similar group should assume a leadership role to develop an initial plan and obtain broad involvement of tourism interests in the community. Public support for the planning process and plan is also important. Having a good understanding of tourism and the tourism system in your community is the first step toward defining goals and objectives for tourism development. The types of goals that are appropriate and the precision with which you are able to define them will depend upon how long your community has been involved in tourism and tourism planning.

In the early stages of tourism development, goals may involve establishing organizational structures and collecting information to better identify the tourism system in the community. Later, more precise objectives can be formulated and more specific development and marketing strategies evaluated.

Step Two: Identifying Your Tourism System When planning for any type of activity, it is important to first define its scope and characteristics. Be clear about exactly what your plan encompasses. A good initial question is, "What do you mean by tourism?" Tourism is defined in many ways. Generally, tourism involves people travelling outside of their community for pleasure.

Definitions differ on the specifics of how far people must travel, whether or not they must stay overnight, for how long, and what exactly is included under travelling for "pleasure". Do you want your tourism plan to include day visitors, conventioneers, business travellers, people visiting friends and relatives, people passing through, or seasonal residents?

Which community resources and organizations serve tourists or could serve tourists? Generally, tourists share community resources with local residents and businesses. Many organizations serve both tourists and locals. This complicates tourism planning and argues for a clear idea of what your tourism plan entails.

You can begin to clarify the tourism system by breaking it down into three subsystems:

(1) tourism resources,

(2) tourism organizations, and

(3) tourism markets.

An initial task in developing a tourism plan is to identify, inventory, and classify the objects within each of these subsystems.

Tourism Resources are any (1) natural, (2) cultural, (3) human, or (4) capital resources that either are used or can be used to attract or serve tourists. A tourism resource inventory identifies and classifies the resources available that provide opportunities for tourism development. Conduct an objective and realistic assessment of the quality and quantity of resources you have to work with.

Tourism Organizations combine resources in various proportions to provide products and services for the tourist. It is important to recognize the diverse array of public and private organizations involved with tourism. The most difficult part of tourism planning is to get these groups to work toward common goals. You should develop a list of these organizations within your own community and obtain their input and cooperation in your tourism planning efforts. Setting up appropriate communication systems and institutional arrangements is a key part of community tourism planning.

Natural Resources

* Climate-seasons
* Water resources-lakes, streams, waterfalls
* Flora-forests, flowers, shrubs, wild edibles
* Fauna-fish & wildlife
* Geological resources-topography, soils, sand dunes, beaches, caves, rocks & minerals, fossils
* Scenery-combinations of all of the above

Cultural Resources

* Historic buildings, sites
* Monuments, shrines
* Cuisine
* Ethnic cultures
* Industry, government, religion, etc.
* Anthropological resources
* Local celebrities

Human Resources

* Hospitality skills
* Management skills

* Seasonal labor force
* Performing artists-music, drama, art, storytellers.
* Craftsman and artisans
* Other labour skills from chefs to lawyers to researchers
* Local populations

Capital

* Availability of capital, financing
* Infrastructure-transportation roads, airports, railroads, harbors & marinas, trails & walkways
* Infrastructure: utilities water, power, waste treatment, communications

Tourism Management Organizations and Services

Off-Site: Coordination, planning, technical assistance, research, regulation:

* Federal & state departments of commerce, transportation, & natural resources
* Federal, state, regional, & local tourism associations
* Educational organizations & consultants, e.g., Travel &
* Tourism Research Association; U.S. Travel Data Centre; Travel Reference Centre, Univ. of Colorado, Boulder; Travel, Tourism, & Recreation Resource Centre, Michigan State University.
* Travel information & reservation services On-Site: development, promotion and management, of tourism resources:
* Federal agencies, NB. departments of commerce, transportation, & land management agencies
* State agencies, NB. departments of commerce, transportation, & land/facility management agencies
* Local government organizations, e.g., visitor information, chamber of commerce, convention & visitor's bureaus, parks
* Businesses: -Accommodations: Hotels, motels, Lodges, resorts, bed & breakfast cabins & cottages, Condominiums, second homes, Campgrounds -Food & Beverage: Restaurants, Grocery, Bars, nightclubs,

Fast Food, Catering Services

- Transportation: Air, rail, bus; Local transportation: taxi, limo, Auto, bicycle, boat rental; Local tour services

- Information: Travel agencies, Information and reservation services, Automobile clubs
- Recreation Facilities & Services: Winter sports: ski, skating, snow mobile areas; Golf courses, miniature golf; Swimming pools, water slides, beaches; tennis, handball, racquetball courts, bowling alleys; Athletic clubs, health spas; Marinas, boat rentals and charters; hunting & fishing guides; Horseback enterprises; Sporting goods sales & rentals
- Entertainment: Nightclubs, amusement parks, spectator sport facilities; Gambling facilities: casinos, horse racing, bingo; video arcades; art galleries and studios, craft shops, studios, demonstrations; performing arts: theatre, dance, music, film; historic & prehistoric sites; museums: art, history, science, technology; arboreta, zoos, nature centres,
- Special festivals and events -Support services: Auto repair, gasoline service stations; boat & recreation vehicle dealers and service; retail shops: sporting goods, specialties, souvenirs, clothing; health services: hospitals, clinics, pharmacies; laundry and dry cleaning; beauty & barber shops; babysitting services; pet care; communications: newspaper, telephone; banking and financial services.

Tourism Markets: Tourists makeup the third, and perhaps most important subsystem. Successful tourism programs require a strong market orientation. The needs and wants of the tourists you choose to attract and serve must be the focus of much of your marketing and development activity. Therefore, it is important to clearly understand which tourism market segments you wish to attract and serve. Tourists fall into a very diverse set of categories with quite distinct needs and wants. You should identify the different types of tourists, or market segments that you presently serve or would like to serve. This may involve one or more tourism market surveys.

A visitor survey identifies the size and nature of the existing market and asks the following questions:

* What are the primary market segments you presently attract?
* Where do they come from?
* What local businesses and facilities do they use?
* What attracted them to the community?
* How did they find out about your community?
* How satisfied are they with your offerings?

A market survey (usually a telephone survey) also can be conducted among households in regions from which you wish to attract tourists. This type of study helps identify potential markets, and means of attracting tourists to your area.

Tourism Market Segments

In a general tourism plan, some clear target tourism market segments should be identified. You might begin by defining the market area from which you will draw most of your visitors. The size of your market area depends upon the uniqueness and quality of your "product", transportation systems, tastes and preferences of surrounding populations, and your competition. Identifying the market area will help target information and promotion and define transportation routes and modes, competition, and characteristics of your market. Next, divide your travel market into the following trip length categories:

* day trips from a 50 mile radius,
* day trips from 50 to 200 miles away,
* pass-through travellers,
* overnight trips of 1 or 2 nights (most likely weekends), and
* extended overnight vacation trips.

After you have an idea of your market area and kinds of trips you will be serving, begin defining more specific market segments like vehicle campers, downhill skiers, sightseers, family vacationers, single weekenders, and the like. These segments can be more clearly tied to particular resources, businesses, and facilities in your community.

What kinds of products and services are likely to attract each of these groups? Tourist needs as well as their impact on the local community are quite different for day tourists versus overnight tourists. Areas catering primarily to weekend traffic will experience large fluctuations in use. In deciding the relative importance of these different segments, communities need to assess both their ability to provide required services (do you have enough rooms?), as well as the demand for different types of trips relative to the supply and your competition.

The Environment: A tourism plan is significantly affected by many factors in the broader environment. Indeed, one of the complexities of tourism planning is the number of variables that are outside of the control of an individual tourism business or community. These include such things as tourism offerings and prices at competing destinations, federal and state policy and legislation, currency exchange rates, the state of the economy, and weather. These factors are discussed more fully in Extension bulletin E-1959 as part of the market environment analysis.

Local populations also must be considered in tourism planning. As they compete with tourists for resources, they can be significantly affected by tourism activity, and they are an important source of support in getting tourism plans implemented. A survey of local residents can be conducted to assess community attitudes toward tourism development, identify impacts of tourism on the community, and obtain local input into tourism plans.

Public hearings, workshops, and advisory boards are other ways to obtain public involvement in tourism planning.

Local support and cooperation is important to the success of tourism programs and should not be overlooked.

Tourism Market Segments

I. Geographic market areas

II. Trip categories

Day Trips:

* short-within 50 miles
* long-up to 200 miles

Pass through traffic:

* day visitors
* overnight stays

Overnight Trips:

* weekend
* vacation

III. Activity or trip purpose Outdoor Recreation:

* Water-based Activity:
  - Boating: sail, power, cruise, row, canoe, water ski
  - Swimming: pool, beach, sunbathing, scuba
  - Fishing: charter, sport, from pier, boat, shore, ice
* Land-based Activity:
  - Camping: back packing, primitive, developed
  - Hiking: climbing, beachcombing, spelunking
  - Hunting

- Skiing: downhill, cross country
- Snowmobiling
- Bicycling
- Horseback riding
- Picnicking

* Air-based Activity:

- Airplane rides, hang gliding, ballooning, parachuting

* General:

- Nature study
- Photography or landscape painting
- Viewing natural scenery

Sightseeing & Entertainment:

* Visiting particular sites or areas:

- historic or pre-historic
- cultural
- amusements
- scenic

* Attending particular events, shows, or demonstrations:

- ethnic festivals
- sporting events
- performances
- agricultural fair or festival
- boat show
- shopping

Other Primary Purpose for Trip:

* Visiting Friends & Relatives

* Convention & Business/Pleasure

Step Three: Generating Alternatives. Generating alternative development and marketing options to meet your goals requires some creative thinking and brainstorming.

The errors made at this stage are usually thinking too narrowly or screening out alternatives prematurely. It is wise to solicit a wide range of options from a diverse group of people. If tourism expertise is lacking in your community, seek help and advice outside the community. Tourism planning involves a wide range of interrelated development and marketing decisions. The following development questions will get you started:

* How much importance should be assigned to tourism within a community or region?
* Which general community goals is tourism development designed to serve?
* Which organization(s) will provide the leadership and coordination necessary for community tourism planning?

What are the relative roles of public and private sectors? Tourism marketing decision questions include:

* Segments: Which market segments should be pursued; geographic markets, trip types, activity or demographic subgroups?
* Product: What kinds of tourism products and services should be provided? Who should provide what?
* Place: Where should tourism facilities be located?
* Promotion: What kinds of promotion should be used, by whom, in which media, how much, when? What community tourism theme or image should be established?
* Price: What prices should be charged for which products and services. Who should capture the revenue?

Step Four: Evaluating Alternatives. Tourism development and marketing options are evaluated by assessing the degree to which each option will be able to meet the stated goals and objectives. There are usually two parts to a systematic evaluation of tourism development and marketing alternatives: (1) Feasibility analysis, and (2) Impact assessment. These two tasks are interrelated, but think of them as trying to answer two basic questions: (1) Can it be done?, and (2) What are the consequences? A decision to take a specific action must be based both on feasibility and desirability.

Feasibility Analysis: First, screen alternatives and eliminate those that are not feasible due to economic, environmental, political, legal, or other factors. Evaluate the remaining set of alternatives in more detail, paying particular attention to the market potential and financial plan. Make a realistic assessment of your community's ability to attract and serve a market segment or segments. This requires a clear understanding of the tourism market in your area and how this market is changing. Also carefully identify your competition and evaluate your advantages and disadvantages compared to the competition. Plan toward the future because it takes time to implement decisions and for your actions to take effect. Therefore, look at the likely market and competition for several years to come. Review forecasts for the travel market in your area, if available. Careful tracking of tourism trends in your own community can help identify changes in the market that you will have to adapt to.

Impact Assessment: When evaluating alternative development and marketing strategies it is important to understand the impacts, both positive and negative, of proposed actions. A classification of economic, environmental, and social impacts associated with tourism development. The types of impacts and their importance vary across different communities and proposed actions. Generally, the size, extent, and nature of tourism impacts depend upon:

* volume of tourist activity relative to local activity
* length and nature of tourist contacts with the community
* degree of concentration/dispersal of tourist activity in the area
* similarities or differences between local populations and tourists
* stability/sensitivity of local economy, environment, and social structure
* how well tourism is planned, controlled, and managed.

Look at both the benefits and costs of any proposed actions. While tourism development can increase income, revenues, and employment, it also involves costs. Evaluate benefits and costs of tourism development from the perspectives of local government, businesses, and residents.

Impacts of Tourism

Economic Impacts:

* Sales, revenue, and income
* Employment
* Fiscal impact-taxes, infrastructure costs
* Prices
* Economic base & structure

Environmental Impacts:

* Lands
* Waters

* Air
* Infrastructure
* Flora & fauna

Social Impacts:

* Population structure & distribution
* Values & attitudes
* Education
* Occupations
* Safety & security
* Congestion & crowding
* Community spirit & cohesion
* Quality of life

Impacts on Local Government Local government provides most of the infrastructure and many of the services essential to tourism development, including highways, public parks, law enforcement, water and sewer, garbage collection and disposal. Evaluate tourism decisions with a clear understanding of the capacity of the local infrastructure and services relative to anticipated needs, and take into account both the needs of local populations and tourists.

A fiscal impact analysis evaluates the impact of tourism on the community's tax base and local government costs. It entails predicting the additional infrastructure and service requirements of tourism development, estimating their costs, deciding who will pay for/provide them, and how. Will tourism generate increased local government revenue through fees and charges, local sales or use taxes, increased property values or property tax rates, or larger local shares of federal and state tax revenues? Impacts on Business and Industry Businesses that are directly serving tourists benefit from sales to tourists. Through secondary impacts, tourism activity also benefits a wide range of businesses in a community. For example, a local textile industry may sell to a linen supply firm that serves hotels and motels catering primarily to tourists. A local forest products industry sells to a lumberyard where local woodcarvers or furniture makers buy their supplies. They in turn sell to tourists through various retail outlets. All of these businesses benefit from tourism. If most products and services for tourists are bought outside of the local area, much of the tourist spending "leaks" out of the local economy. The more a community is "self-sufficient" in serving tourists, the larger the local impact.

Impacts on Residents

Local residents may experience a broad range of both positive and negative impacts from tourism development.

Tourism development may provide increased employment and income for the community. Although tourism jobs are primarily in the service sectors and are often seasonal, part time, and low-paying, these characteristics, are neither universal nor always undesirable. Residents may value opportunities for part time and seasonal work. In particular, employment opportunities and work experiences for students or retirees may be desired. Residents may also benefit from local services that otherwise would not be available. Tourism development may mean a wider variety of retailers and restaurants, or a better community library. It may also mean more traffic, higher prices, and increases in property values and local taxes. The general quality of the environment and life in the community may go up or down due to tourism development. This depends on the nature of tourism development, the preferences and desires of local residents, and how well tourism is planned and managed.

Steps Five and Six

Implementation, and Monitoring and Evaluation. We will not attempt a complete discussion of decisionmaking, plan implementation, and monitoring, but these are critical steps in the success of a tourism plan. A set of specific actions should be prescribed with clearly defined responsibilities and timetables. Monitor progress in implementing the plan and evaluate the success of the plan in meeting its goals and objectives on a regular basis. Plans generally need to be adjusted over time due to changing goals, changing market conditions, and unanticipated impacts. It is a good idea to build monitoring and evaluation systems into your planning efforts.

Concluding Remarks

Successful tourism planning and development means serving both tourists and local residents. The bulletins in this series stress the importance of a market orientation for attracting and serving tourists. This market orientation must be balanced with a clear view of how tourism serves the broader community interest and an understanding of the positive and negative impacts of tourism development. Remember, tourism should serve the community first and the tourist second. Tourism development must be compatible with other activities in the area and be supported by the local population. Therefore, the tourism plan should be closely coordinated with other local and regional planning efforts, if not an integral part of them.

Strategic Framework for Tourism

Juneau needs a vision and framework for carrying out tourism. The vision defines what Juneau wants to achieve from the tourism sector and the framework specifies how, when and where the various professional and community discussions and actions about tourism take place. The framework also needs to define roles among the various public and private sector entities involved in tourism. It needs to lay out where tourism is going so that both businesses and residents can make plans with a common understanding of direction and scale. And it needs to prescribe the actions that move Juneau toward its tourism goals. When building a new strategic framework, which is happening through the adoption and implementation of this plan, transitions must be incorporated into the planning process. Roles need to be handed off at appropriate times, dictated either by funding cycles or tourism seasons.

Vision and Objectives

Juneau intends to succeed at both cruise tourism and destination travel – with success being defined on Juneau's terms. That success entails maximizing the benefits of tourism in Juneau, while minimizing the costs and impacts. Juneau looks to tourism, expecting social, economic, and environmental benefits. Juneau seeks a more positive image among its neighbors in Alaska, and with its visitors and travel industry partners. Juneau intends tourism to help create a more diverse economic base. To that end, Juneau will work to create a positive atmosphere for business investment and operations, especially those businesses that are locally owned and operated.

Juneau wants, through tourism, to bolster its commitment to its heritage and cultural values. Juneau intends to be a high quality destination, providing rich and positive experiences for its visitors. It intends to make those visitors feel warmly welcomed.

Overall Guiding Principles for the Tourism Plan

This tourism plan is based on the development and management of a partnership between the people of Juneau, local tourism businesses, and the international cruise tourism industry. In the sections that follow, relationships of that partnership are described, responsibilities outlined, and venues for working out issues among the partners are laid out in considerable detail. In a partnership approach, all partners invest to achieve results that cannot be achieved outside that partnership. In this case, investment ranges from financial, to time, to energy, to the sharing of Juneau with outsiders. A true partnership plan recognizes and values all these levels of investment.

This plan is based on the principles of sustainable tourism development. That means that social, economic, and environmental resources must be utilized in such a way that they keep their integrity, and at such a pace that they can withstand the impacts of use. Our guideline in building this plan is to assume that at the start of each season social, economic, and environmental resources should be in as good or better shape than at the start of the previous season.

Strategic Directions – Tourism Positioning

The market and product analysis conducted as part of this tourism management planning process revealed that Juneau has a superb opportunity to strengthen its destination tourism sector. The combination of an outstanding natural resource base, diverse history and culture, and coastal community location make it attractive to the growing nature, adventure, heritage, and Eco-tourism travellers. This potential notwithstanding, it is clear that Juneau will have to establish leadership in realizing this potential.

Industry cannot make Juneau a successful destination by itself – it needs a partnership with government, particularly in marketing and training areas. Juneau's competitive position in the Alaska cruise market is already strong.

The cruise industry indicates its continued desire to bring its customers to Juneau. There is general agreement that the volume of visitors (about 700,000 in 2001) represents a near-capacity situation for Juneau harbor. Industry advises that they will be allocating an additional ten percent capacity for 2002, although there is no guarantee they will be able to fill that capacity with customers given the September terrorism events.

Beyond that, they expect growth to settle down to about four percent per year. The most appropriate course of action for Juneau to assume in the cruise sector involves maintenance of its current competitive position, but to prepare for the possibility of continued vigorous growth.

Juneau has not realized success in the development of a meetings and convention market in southeast Alaska, in spite of its stature as a state capital. However, with general improvements in tourism product quality and greater attention to both destination and waterfront development, we believe that this situation can be reversed. Based on the technical product and market analysis prepared for this tourism management plan, the recommended strategic directions for Juneau tourism are as follows:

1. Premier destination, combining nature, adventure, heritage, and cultural experiences Attracting high value customers Focusing on guided experiences
2. Maintain and strengthen Juneau's competitive position in the Alaska cruise tourism market Build on current strong tour product mix Significantly enhance visitor experience in downtown Juneau
3. Position Juneau as a small meetings and convention host in Alaska, the Pacific Northwest, and matched niche markets.

Rationalize and Modernize Juneau's Approach to Tourism

Unlike most communities throughout North America, Juneau experiences annual tourism visitation well in excess of its population. In 2001, Juneau hosted over 800,000 visitors, of which about 700,000 were cruise arrivals.

The cruise industry is a major contributor to Juneau's economy, generating estimated economic benefits in 1999 of about $90 million and 750 jobs. Clearly, Juneau is in the tourism business and must organize itself to respond to the opportunities, challenges and issues it faces in ensuring that tourism sector activities enhances, rather than comprises, the community's quality of life.

Current Management Approach

Juneau's approach to tourism management has largely been delegated to semi- independent boards and agencies as shown below.

* Agency
* Role and Responsibility
* Docks and Harbors Board
* All matters related to Juneau's port including primary interaction with the cruise ship industry
* Juneau Convention and Visitor Bureau

* Primarily focusing on destination marketing and responsible for attracting meetings and conventions to Juneau
* In 2000, Juneau created a Tourism Planning Manager position within the City staff organization, reporting to the Deputy City Manager. The primary purpose for this position was to respond to tourism issues raised by the community. Juneau also decided to proceed to prepare a tourism management plan to provide a blueprint for appropriate tourism sector management.

Alternative Models for Tourism Management

There is a range of potential models the CBJ could implement for its tourism management function. Tourism management can take a lassies faire approach at one extreme, or it can extend to a full partnership approach with the tourism industry, guided by a tourism management plan. In some regions of the world, government assumes a more controlling role, directing the path and nature of tourism development and tightly holding access to operation, development, and marketing rights. In light of the scope and scale of Juneau's tourism sector, the opportunity for growth in the destination market segment, and the need to better manage community impacts, we recommend a much more proactive approach to tourism sector management and Juneau's current position. This is illustrated in the chart below. McDowell Group, October 2000, The Economic Impacts of the Cruise Industry in Southeast Alaska. The recommended position for Juneau in establishing itself as a full partner with the tourism sector is premised on two initiatives:

- This Tourism Management Plan, approved by the Assembly and establishing the framework for CBJ policy and program support for tourism.
- The creation of an appropriate agency or tourism entity – responsible for implementation of the Tourism Management Plan on behalf of the CBJ and all stakeholders.

Update the Comprehensive Plan

The CBJ adopted a position on tourism in its Comprehensive Plan to guide its actions related to the tourism sector. With the adoption of this Tourism Management Plan that position should be updated to achieve consistency. The adopted tourism policy in the Comprehensive Plan CBJ is aimed at encouraging tourism in a collaborative manner: Policy 2.12. It is the policy of the CBJ to encourage tourism, convention and other visitor-related activities through the development of appropriate facilities and services, while protecting Juneau's natural and cultural attractions for local citizens and visitors alike, and to participate in the accommodation of the future growth of tourism in a manner that addresses both community and industry concerns.

Included in the plan are a number of implementing actions to carry out the intent of this policy. Both the policy and the implementing actions are now superseded by the formal development of a tourism management plan by the CBJ. Given the proposed adoption of this plan by the CBJ, the Comprehensive Plan will need to be updated accordingly. The recommended amendments to the Comprehensive Plan are structured to recognize the Tourism Management Plan as the mechanism by which the CBJ will promote and manage tourism. In this way the Comprehensive Plan recognizes by reference the (adopted) Tourism Management Plan as the "Implementing Actions" of the CBJ position on tourism.

The Comprehensive Plan amendments are recommended as follows: Delete Policy 2.12 and the "Implementing Actions" pursuant to this policy and substitute the following amendments

1. Policy 2.12. The promotion and management of tourism by the CBJ shall be governed by the following vision for tourism:
2. Policy 2.12.1 The CBJ shall encourage tourism in accordance with the Tourism Management Plan, adopted on [insert date] by the Assembly.
3. Policy 2.12.2 The CBJ shall re-confirm the Tourism Management Plan including any amendments consistent with the vision and objectives for tourism, annually, based on the recommendations of the Juneau Tourism Partnership and the CBJ staff.

Motivation of Nature Tourism

In the following essay through a behavioural perspective, which means not considering external factors, we try to understand why nature tourism is one of the fastest growing segments of world tourism. To understand why this is happening is to comprehend the intrinsic motivation "nature tourists" have to pursue this type of tourism. To recognize this motivation we must search for clues in the theories of travel motivation proposed throughout the travel research literature, and try to see if these diverse theories can actually help us identify the motivation of nature tourists and hence the growth of this tourism segment. The following essay is able to draw from several authors and their theories important conclusion on whether the models or frameworks presented can be useful to understand nature tourism and if so conclude why they are valuable. We firstly define what nature tourism is and from there we review several travel motivation theories that are applicable to this type of tourism.

To know what nature tourism is we must understand a broader classification of tourism that includes nature tourism, and that is alternative tourism. "Alternative tourism can be broadly defined as forms of tourism that set out to be consistent with natural, social and community values and which allow both hosts and guests to enjoy positive and worthwhile interaction and shared experiences".

Newsome, Moore & Dowling, 2002). Under alternative tourism we can see the presence of natural, cultural, event and other types of tourism. Nature tourism, called by Newsome & et al. (2002) "natural area tourism", is in short "tourism in natural settings".

The proposed classification of Newsome, Moore and Dowling (2002) and theirconception of nature tourism is confirmed by Ceballos-Lascuráin (1996) when he defines it as "all tourism directly dependent on the use of natural resources in a relatively undeveloped state, including scenery, topography, water features, vegetation and wildlife."

Newsome, Moore & Dowling (2002) include under nature tourism: adventure, nature- based, wildlife and Eco-tourism. McKerchner (1998) expands the scope of nature tourism including: adventure tourism, Eco-tourism, alternative tourism, educational tourism, anti-tourism, sustainable tourism, responsible tourism and many other forms of outdoor-oriented, non-mass tourism. These two views of what nature tourism includes and overlap, agree, but also contradict themselves. To better understand, and conclude, what nature tourism is (for the purpose of this essay) we must understand the three relations that can occur between the natural setting and the visitor which are: in, about and for the environment. So any tourism based in a natural setting and experienced in, about or for the environment will be considered 'nature tourism'.

Tourist motivation can be defined "as the global integrating network of biological and cultural forces which gives value and direction to travel choices, behaviour and experience". The general motives underlined by research of why nature tourism is the fastest growing segment internationally in tourism are: widespread changing environmental attitude, development of environmental education, development of environmental mass media. Pearce, Morrison and Rutledge (1998) present ten trends which represent important issues of content in describing tourist motives, we can mention four which are related to nature tourism motivation: motive to experience the environment, motive to rest and relax in pleasant settings, motive to pursue special interests and skills (scuba- diving, fishing), and motive to be healthy and fit. These motives are good starting points to discuss motivation of nature tourism, but some appear to be just social changes or reasons that have affected in some way the motives of the tourist. These motives do not give us clues in how to identify human motivation towards travel, for that reason it cannot be applied to further studies. So it is necessary to undertake an analysis of travel motivation theories.

When assessing a theory of tourist motivation and deciding if it is good for our purpose we must identify seven requirements: it functions as a true theory, it appeals to different users, it is easy to communicate, it suggests ways to measure motivation, it allows for many motives, it is dynamic and, it accounts for intrinsic and extrinsic motivation. This essay will not review all theories of motivation and afterwards decide if they are pertinent to our purpose, which is to understand the motivation of nature tourism. The scope of this essay will only include theories, which have been reviewed and might have relevance to our purpose. In the reviewing process of motivation theories applied to nature tourism we searched for the seven requirements proposed by Pearce, Morrison and Rutledge (1998), and also took into consideration if they were applicable to understand nature tourism motivation.

People who live in cities, for example, are motivated to travel as tourists to wilderness areas because they need to escape from an artificial, monotonous environment. Gray's travel-motivation theory, although an oversimplification of motivation as noted by Mansfeld (1992), gives us two motives which can help explain why people go to natural settings. The first motive is the desire to go from a known to an unknown place, called in Gray's theory 'wanderlust'.

Secondly, a place "which can provide the traveller with specific facilities that do not exist in his or her own place of residence", referred in Gray's theory as 'sunlust'. It appears that the wanderlust-sunlust motives do help us understand why nature tourists search for settings which are different from the city-work-home routine and that enable the nature tourist to participate in activities in unknown territory and that are possible in those natural settings and not at home.

The problem with this theory is that it "represents a confusion between person-specific motivations and resort-specific attributes". For this same reason we will not consider 'Push & Pull' factors as relevant to the study of motivation. For this reason Gray's model only partially might help us understand what motivates a person to participate in nature tourism. Several other theories such as Crompton's nine motives and Iso-Ahola personal-interpersonal motives also work under these 'Push and Pull' factors which means that they focus not only in the intrinsic motivation to travel to natural settings, but also in the characteristics and benefits these settings might appear to offer (pull factors) to satisfy a need. For this reason of not focusing purely on the motivation of tourists, we will not consider them relevant to understand nature tourism motivation.

An interesting finding, while not considered a theory, is the one by Krippendorf after analyzing eight theories of travel motivation found in the literature on tourism. Through his research he saw a common place in these theories. "Firstly, travel is motivated by 'going away from' rather than 'going towards' something; secondly travellers' motives and behaviour are markedly self-oriented". So it seems that the pull factors are not so important, hence the benefits offered by the natural settings and their operators are of second importance in deciding to travel. There is more power in the intrinsic motive of self-indulgence and personal care, physically and psychologically, and by the so called 'escape' motive, than by pull factors considered in the mentioned motivation theories.

So if this 'Push and Pull' approach does not succeed in understanding motivation maybe we can try another approach, for example focusing in factors that influence motivation such as 'needs'. Pearce presents a hierarchy of travel motives based on

Maslow's theory of motivation combined with the idea of a career ladder. "The career ladder emphasizes that people have a range of motives for seeking out holiday experiences". The travel career ladder with its different levels allows for many motives, it is dynamic and to sum up it covers the seven requirements presented before. On the other hand analyzing the different levels, especially the relationship needs, self-esteem/development needs, and fulfillment needs presents possible clues to understand the motivation of nature tourism.

By comparing the needs described in different levels of the career ladder such as 'need for achievement', for example, and then consider nature tourism activities like hiking, tramping and mountaineering where the tourist proves its competence and if successful achieves a goal, it can be concluded that the travel career ladder is a helpful theory to understand nature tourism motivation. Another comparison can be drawn from the self- esteem needs level. The "need for mastery, control and competence" can be a motivation for a nature tourism activity such as scuba diving. Where mastery is required to undergo the activity successfully and safely, as well as competence, and control is basic in case of extreme scenarios underwater conditions. So can the 'Travel Career Ladder' be the most appropriate theory to understand nature tourism motivation? If we consider the vast use of Maslow's Theory and sometimes overestimated usefulness considering it only concentrates in needs as the only driving forces to understand motivation, as well as its origin from a study of neurotic people, the answer is no. "Maslow's theory of needs largely ignores more recent developments in motivation theory" and only concentrates on needs it is a work considered a partial theory, which "tend[s] to concentrate in one particular aspect of motivation".

Travel motivation cannot be understood by concentrating on one of the factors as mentioned before in the case of needs. It requires a complete knowledge of "the processes whereby these needs are transformed into motivated behaviour and, in particular, of the way in which people's expectations give motivated behaviour its direction". Witt and Wright (1992) present a very complete and interesting "Expectancy Theory" applied to tourist motivation, based on Vroom's theory of work motivation. It is a theory that finally is able to include all the concepts involved in the motivation process by creating a theoretical framework. It includes the needs which are important to understand motivation, but also the "decision making involved in choosing whether to go on holiday". Together with this it is able to consider 'push and pull' factors, as well as reasons of travel. In conclusion the expectancy theory provides a framework for the analysis of tourist motivation. With all this good points taken into consideration the expectancy theory fails one of the requirements set by Pearce, Morrison and Rutledge (1998) when deciding on a good motivation theory and that requirement is it must be "easy to communicate". This is concluded as well by Witt and Wright when they say "the complexity of expectancy theory also makes it difficult to use the model to predict individual behaviour", and so complex that they suggest using the framework in training travel advisers to ask the proper questions to deliver the information best suited for a customer.

Taking into account the positive attributes of this framework, as well as the negative, let us use the framework to understand nature tourism motivation. Vroom proposes two equations; the first can be used to understand the motivation of travel or not to travel and the second formula to know why a tourist has chosen a certain destination. For our purpose we will concentrate on the first equation, which states that an individual's behaviour is determined by his/her belief that the attractiveness and valence of an outcome (a type of holiday taken) is useful to attain another outcome (e.g.., relaxation, spiritual growth, knowledge) with greater attractiveness and valence. In other words the need of a person will be searched for depending on the value attached to that need, maybe Maslow's hierarchy of needs is useful here, and its attractiveness, through the lived experience of the instrumental outcome considered as a chosen holiday. The belief that going to a natural setting to experience the environment is seen as an outcome with certain intrinsic value and attractiveness, but above all useful (instrumental) to attain physical and psychological recovery from stress. This framework includes important variables to understand motivation: needs, values, and beliefs. The equation is also able to tell us that a tourist to natural setting does not go only to have an encounter with nature, but also to achieve a further self-indulgent goal. Vroom's Expectancy Theory has proven its value, but there is another interesting concept to consider such as intention influencing behaviour, that according to Ajzen and Fishbein (1980) is influenced by attitudes and subjective norms. This model was called the 'Theory of Reasoned Action'. Ten years later they updated their model including 'perceived behavioral control' as another element influencing intention, calling this new model 'Theory of Planned Behaviour'. According to this theory changing beliefs will produce a change in behaviour, but this might not be enough if attitudes and/or subjective norms do not change. Attitudes "can be viewed as enduring general evaluations of people".

Subjective norms are what we expect other people will think of us if we carried out a certain action, in other words social pressure. The model states that beliefs influence attitudes and the perception of subjective norms, at the same time these attitudes and subjective norms influence intention, and intention determines behaviour. How does this model become useful to understand nature tourism motivation? It becomes relevant and useful if we relate it to the New Environmental Paradigm and also to the general motives presented at the beginning of essay of why nature tourism has become so popular. The New Environmental Paradigm presents a new set of beliefs and values, including the desirability of restricting growth, of protecting the integrity of ecosystems, and of securing more harmonious relationships between man and nature. Relating the Theory of Reasoned Action with the New Environmental Paradigm can be a clue to understand how this change of beliefs in society are affecting the motivation of people in their travel habits resulting in a desire to visit natural areas.

The general motives presented by Lindberg, Wood and Engeldrum (1998): widespread changing environmental attitude, development of environmental education, and development of environmental mass media, seem more like reasons rather than motives, but are good reasons to understand this shift to a New Environmental Paradigm. If we include this new paradigm as a new set of beliefs rising in our post-modern world, which are influencing, according to Theory of Reasoned Action, the attitudes and subjective norms then we can understand why the intention of practicing nature tourism has become such an important trend worldwide.

Through the combination of the New Environmental Paradigm and the Theory of Reasoned Action we have found a framework that includes several components of how behaviour is constructed together with actual contemporary trends in environmental beliefs. It also succeeds in covering all the requirements set beforehand to consider a theory a good travel motivation theory. For these reasons we can conclude that these combinations of perspectives are useful to understand nature tourism motivation. Another conclusion to this approach of combining the theory and the paradigm can be that motivation, while it is an intrinsic process, when influenced by beliefs and these beliefs are a product of a social shared Environmental Paradigm then motivation becomes a socio-psychological process, influenced by external factors. The revision of different theories under a scheme of requirements to find a proper one, we have come across a needs-oriented theory (Travel Career Ladder), we have disregarded any push and pull factors-based models, interpreted an all-inclusive framework of motivation (Expectancy Theory), and ended with a simple but comprehensive interpretation of the motivation of nature tourism through the complementation of the New Environmental Paradigm and the Theory of Reasoned Action. In conclusion we can say that a proper revision of travel motivation theories can help us understand what motivation is, and what elements must be considered to understand it, and then interpret the different findings to understand the motivation of a certain type of tourist.

One important consideration is that when investigating what motivates a person to travel in a certain type of way we must concentrate on finding the intrinsic motivation while not distracting our attention to the "pull factors" of a specific destination. On the other hand we must say, as found while combining the Theory of Reasoned Action and the New Environmental Paradigm, that the trend of nature tourism becoming more popular can be better understood through a socio-psychological perspective, taking into account the influence of external factors, such as a new set of beliefs constructed by our post-modern western society. It is then proved that the behavioral perspective might not be enough and a psycho-sociological perspective gives us a better understanding.

Tourism Marketing

The marketing mix-the 4 Ps-target audience-segmentation-objectives-evaluation. These and other terms are all used in the process of "marketing." In tourism and tourism related industries, success means understanding this process. This bulletin is designed for those in the tourism industry who may not be completely familiar with marketing or who may simply wish to refresh their basic marketing skills. Covered will be important concepts used in marketing, the relationship of marketing to tourism, and a process for developing a marketing plan for tourism/recreation businesses and/or communities. It will be impossible to cover in detail all the aspects of marketing within the scope of this bulletin. There are, however, other bulletins in this series that will provide more in-depth information on the different components of a marketing plan.

What is Marketing

People hold a variety of misconceptions about marketing. Most common is its confusion with selling and advertising. Selling and advertising are actually types of promotion which is only a component of marketing.

Marketing involves much more, including product/service development, place (location and distribution), and pricing. It requires information about people, especially those interested in what you have to offer (your "market"), such as what they like, where they buy and how much they spend. Its role is to match the right product or service with the right market or audience. Marketing, as you will see, is an art and a science. According to the American Marketing Association, marketing is "the process of planning and executing the conception, pricing, promotion, and distribution of ideas, goods, and services to create exchanges that satisfy individual and organizational objectives." Simply stated it is creating and promoting a product (ideas, goods or services) that satisfies a customer's need or desire and is available at a desirable price and place. Modern marketing is a way of doing business, heavily based on the "marketing concept" which holds that businesses and organizations should:

(1) design their products/services to meet customer needs and wants;
(2) focus on those people most likely to buy their product rather than the entire mass market; and
(3) develop marketing efforts that fit into their overall business objectives.

By adopting this concept you not only provide your customers with better products, you will avoid wasting valuable time and money developing and promoting a product or service nobody wants.

Recreation and Tourism Marketing

Earlier it was mentioned that a product can be "ideas, goods, or services." Since tourism is primarily a service based industry, the principal products provided by recreation/tourism (R/T) businesses are recreational experiences and hospitality. These are intangible products and more difficult to market than tangible products such as automobiles. The intangible nature of services makes quality control difficult but crucial. It also makes it more difficult for potential customers to evaluate and compare service offerings. In addition, instead of moving the product to the customer, the customer must travel to the product (area/community). Travel is a significant portion of the time and money spent in association with recreational and tourism experiences and is a major factor in people's decisions on whether or not to visit your business or community.

As an industry, tourism has many components comprising the overall "travel experience." Along with transportation, it includes such things as accommodations, food and beverage services, shops, entertainment, aesthetics and special events. It is rare for one business to provide the variety of activities or facilities tourists need or desire. This adds to the difficulty of maintaining and controlling the quality of the experience. To overcome this hurdle, tourism related businesses, agencies, and organizations need to work together to package and promote tourism opportunities in their areas and align their efforts to assure consistency in product quality.

The Marketing Plan

One of the most important steps a business or community can take to improve the effectiveness and efficiency of their marketing efforts is to develop a written marketing plan. This plan will guide their marketing decisions and assist them in allocating marketing resources such as money and personnel time. The plan should include:

(1) the overall business objectives—what you want to accomplish;

(2) an assessment of the market environment—what factors may affect your marketing efforts;

(3) a business/community profile—what resources are available,

(4) market identification (segmentation)—the specific groups or clientele most interested in your product;

(5) the marketing objectives for each segment;

(6) the marketing strategies (or mixes) for different markets you target—the best combination of the 4 Ps (product, price, place, promotion) for each segment;

(7) an implementation plan—how to "make it work;"

(8) the marketing budget-how much you have to spend; and

(9) a method for evaluation and change.

A framework which can be used to develop a marketing plan. Each component will be briefly discussed in the remainder of the bulletin. For more information regarding different components of the plan be sure to consult other bulletins in this series.

Overall Business Objectives

Businesses, agencies, and communities should develop overall objectives and regularly monitor their progress. The objectives should provide guidance for all decisions including finances, personnel and marketing. They should be quantitative and measurable statements of what the business or community wants to accomplish over a specified period of time. Business objectives are often stated in terms of sales, profits, market shares and/or occupancy rates.

Communities frequently establish objectives relating to such things as increasing the number of tourists, developing or changing their image, facility and activity development, cooperation among tourism related businesses and increasing length of stay and local expenditures. It is important that the objectives be reasonable given the market conditions and the firm's or organization's resources. Establish a few reasonable objectives instead of a long, unrealistic "wish list." This is especially true for new businesses or communities which do not have much experience in tourism development and/or marketing.

Market Environment Analysis

The next step in developing a marketing plan is to assess the impact of environmental factors (such as economic, social and political) on present and future markets. Changes in these factors can create marketing opportunities as well as problems.

Demographic and Lifestyle Trends

Changing demographics and lifestyles are having a major impact on R/T participation. An assessment of these trends is important to understand how they will likely affect your business or community. Some of the important trends that bear watching:

(1) population growth and movement;

(2) rural community growth compared to metropolitan areas;

(3) number of adult women employed outside the home;

(4) the number of households is growing, especially non family and single parent households, but family size is decreasing;

(5) the impact of two wage earner households on real family income;

(6) the number of retired persons with the financial ability to travel;

(7) better health to an older age; and

(8) continued aging of the population (we are becoming a middle aged society).

Economic Conditions

Overall economic conditions can have significant impacts on recreation and tourism markets. A marketing strategy that is effective during periods of low unemployment rates may have to be significantly adjusted if unemployment increases. Businesses and communities should monitor and assess the likely impact of factors such as unemployment rates, real family income, rate of inflation, credit availability, terms and interest rates. Consideration should also be given to the prices of complementary products, such as lodging, gasoline and recreation equipment.

Laws and Government Actions

As a complex industry, tourism is significantly affected both positively and negatively by laws and by actions of governmental agencies. For instance, rulings on such things as liability issues or decisions regarding building and health codes may change or possibly prevent the construction of a proposed facility. If a public facility changes the prices of its services, this could affect the service offerings of associated private businesses. These actions may have both positive and negative effects on the marketing efforts of the business and community. To avoid wasting valuable resources it is important that R/T businesses, agencies, and communities continually monitor and evaluate governmental actions.

Technology

Technological developments are increasing rapidly. New recreation products, such as all-terrain vehicles and wind surfers, provide new ways for people to satisfy their recreational preferences. New production technologies and materials offer recreation and tourism businesses ways to reduce costs and improve the quality of their products/services. Advances in telecommunications have and will continue to create new promotional opportunities. Technological innovations, in relation to jobs and the home, have resulted in increased leisure time for many people.

Competition

Businesses and communities must identify and analyze existing and potential competitors. The objective of the analysis is to determine the strengths and weaknesses of the competition's marketing strategies. The analysis should include the competition's:

(1) product/service features and quality;
(2) location relative to different geographic markets;
(3) promotional themes and messages;
(4) prices; and
(5) type of customer they are attracting.

Business and Community Profiles

Too many communities attempt to market themselves as tourist destinations without accurate information about their resources (facilities, services, staff), image (projected vs. Actual), and how well their customers are satisfied. Without this information, it is difficult to make other decisions in the planning process. Included should be such things as recreational and entertainment facilities, cultural and historic sites, overnight accommodations, restaurants, shopping opportunities, special events and activities, staff size, and transportation. Each item of the "inventory" should also be assessed in terms of quality and availability.

Market Segmentation (Identification)

Recreation and tourism businesses and communities often make the mistake of attempting to be all things to all people. It is difficult, and risky, to develop marketing strategies for the mass market. Strategies designed for the "average" customer often result in unappealing products, prices, and promotional messages.

For example, it would be difficult to develop a campground that would be equally attractive to recreational vehicle campers and backpackers or promote a property to serve both snow mobilers and nature oriented cross country skiers.

Marketing is strongly based on market segmentation and target marketing. Market segmentation is the process of:

(1) taking existing and/or potential customers/visitors (market) and categorizing them into groups with similar preferences referred to as "market segments;"
(2) selecting the most promising segments as "target markets;" and
(3) designing "marketing mixes," or strategies (combination of the 4 Ps), which satisfy the special needs, desires and behaviour of the target markets.

There is no unique or best way to segment markets, but ways in which customers can be grouped are:

(1) location of residence—instate, out-of-state, local;

(2) demographics—age, income, family status, education;

(3) equipment ownership/use—RV's, sailboats, canoes, tents, snowmobiles;

(4) important product attributes—price, quality, quantity; and

(5) lifestyle attributes—activities, interests, opinions.

To be useful, the segment identification process should result in segments that suggest marketing efforts that will be effective in attracting them and at least one segment large enough to justify specialized marketing efforts.

After segments have been identified, the business or community must select the "target markets," those segments which offer them the greatest opportunity. When determining target markets, consideration should be given to:

(1) existing and future sales potential of each segment;

(2) the amount and strength of competition for each segment;

(3) the ability to offer a marketing mix which will be successful in attracting each segment;

(4) the cost of servicing each segment; and

(5) each segment's contribution to accomplishing overall business/community objectives. It is often wiser to target smaller segments that are presently not being served, or served inadequately, than to go after larger segments for which there is a great deal of competition.

Marketing Objectives for each Segment

Marketing objectives which contribute to the accomplishment of the overall business objectives should be established for each target market. Objectives serve a number of functions including:

(1) guidance for developing marketing mixes for different target markets;

(2) information for allocating the marketing budget between target markets;

(3) a basis for objectively evaluating the effectiveness of the marketing mixes (setting standards); and

(4) a framework for integrating the different marketing mixes into the overall marketing plan.

The target market objectives should:

(1) be expressed in quantitative terms;

(2) be measurable;

(3) specify the target market; and

(4) indicate the time period in which the objective is to be accomplished.

For example, increase the number of overnight stays by people from the Chicago market over the next two years by five percent.

Remember, rank objectives by priority and carefully evaluate them to ensure that they are reasonable given the strength of the competition and resources available for marketing.

Marketing Strategy (Mix)

The marketing strategy, or mix, should be viewed as a package of offerings designed to attract and serve the customer or visitor. Recreation and tourism businesses and communities should develop both external and internal marketing mixes for different target markets.

External Mix

The external marketing mix includes product/service, price, place/location, and promotion.

Product

Earlier we said the principal products that recreation and tourism businesses provide are recreational experiences and hospitality. The factors that create a quality recreational experience often differ among people. A quality experience for one skier might include an uncrowded, steep slope. To another it might be a good restaurant and a chance to socialize. Decisions on what facilities, programs and services to provide should be based on the needs and desires of the target market(s). They should not be based on the preferences of the owner/manager or necessarily on what the competition is providing.

Recognize that a recreational/tourism experience includes five elements: trip planning and anticipation; travel to the site/area; the experience at the site; travel back home; and recollection. Businesses should look for ways to enhance the quality of the overall experience during all phases of the trip. This could be accomplished by providing trip planning packages which include maps, attractions en route and on site, and information regarding lodging, food and quality souvenirs and mementos.

Recreation and tourism businesses should also view their service/ product in generic terms. Thinking of products/services in this manner helps focus more attention on the experiences desired by customers and also the facilities, programs and services that will produce those experiences. For example, campgrounds are the business of providing recreational "lodging" not just campsites to park an RV or set up a tent. Marinas should provide recreational "boating" experiences, not just slippage.

Location and Accessibility—Place

Too many tourism businesses and communities fail to recognize their role in improving travel to and from their areas. They focus instead on servicing the customer once they arrive at the site/ community. A bad experience getting to or leaving an R/T site can adversely affect a person's travel experience. Ways to help prevent this include:

(1) providing directions and maps;

(2) providing estimates of travel time and distances from different market areas;

(3) recommending direct and scenic travel routes;

(4) identifying attractions and support facilities along different travel routes; and

(5) informing potential customers of alternative travel methods to the area such as airlines and railroads.

Potential businesses should also carefully assess alternative locations for:

(1) distance and accessibility to target markets;

(2) location of competitors with respect to target markets;

(3) modes of travel serving the area; and

(4) other attractions and activities that might induce travel to the area.

Pricing Price is one of the most important and visible elements of the marketing mix. When setting prices it is important to take into consideration all of the following:

(1) business and target market objectives;
(2) the full cost of producing, delivering and promoting the product;
(3) the willingness of the target market to pay for the product or service you provide;
(4) prices charged by competitors offering a similar product/service to the same target market(s);
(5) the availability and prices of substitute products/services;
(6) the economic climate (local and national); and
(7) the possibility of stimulating high profit products/services (such as boats) by offering related services (such as maintenance) at or below cost.

When establishing prices, R/T businesses should give attention to pricing strategies which may encourage off season and non-peak period sales, longer stays, group business, and the sale of package plans (combination of room, meals, and recreational facilities). For additional information on pricing, see Extension bulletin E-1999.

Promotion

Promotion provides target audiences with accurate and timely information to help them decide whether to visit your community or business. The information should be of importance and practical use to the potential or existing visitor and also accurate. Misrepresentation often leads to dissatisfied customers and poor recommendations.

Don't make claims you cannot live up to. Developing a promotional campaign is not a science with hard and fast rules. Making decisions regarding which type or combination of promotion types to use (personal selling, advertising, sales promotions, or publicity) is not always easy. If, however, you follow a logical process and do the necessary research, chances for success will be improved. It will be necessary to make decisions regarding:

(1) Target audience—the group you are aiming at;
(2) Image—that which your community or business wants to create or reinforce;
(3) Objectives—those of the promotional campaign;
(4) Budget—the amount of money available for your promotion;
(5) Timing—when and how often should your promotions appear;
(6) Media—which methods (television, radio, newspaper, magazine) will most effectively and efficiently communicate your message to the target audience; and

(7) Evaluation—how can the effectiveness of the promotional campaign be determined.

More detailed information on tourism promotion is contained in Extension bulletins E-1939, E-1957, and E-2005.

Internal Mix

As stated, marketing services such as recreation and tourism differ from marketing tangible products. Recreation and tourism businesses must direct as much attention at marketing to customers on site as they do to attracting them. In this respect, internal marketing is important because dissatisfied customers can effectively cancel out an otherwise effective marketing strategy.

The success of internal marketing is dependent on creating an atmosphere in which employees desire to give good service and sell the business/community to visitors. To create such an atmosphere requires the following four important elements:

(1) Hospitality and Guest Relations—An organization wide emphasis on hospitality and guest relations, including a customer oriented attitude on the part of the owners and managers as well as the employees. If the owner/manager is not customer sensitive, it is unlikely the lower paid employees will be.

(2) Quality Control—A program which focuses on improving both the technical quality (the standards associated with what the customer receives) and the functional quality (the standards associated with how the customer receives the service). All employees who come into contact with customers should receive hospitality training.

(3) Personal Selling—Training the staff in the selling aspects of the property (business) or community. This also includes rewarding them for their efforts. By being informed about the marketing objectives, and their role in accomplishing those objectives, they can help increase sales.

(4) Employee Morale—Programs and incentives aimed at maintaining employee morale. The incentives can be both monetary and non-monetary.

A customer oriented atmosphere usually results in customers that are more satisfied, do less complaining and are more pleasant to serve. This helps build employee morale, their desire to provide good service and their efficiency.

Marketing Budget

Successful marketing requires that sufficient money and personnel time be made available to implement activities comprising the marketing strategy. A marketing budget is a financial plan which shows the total amount to be spent on marketing during different times of the year and how it is to be allocated among alternative activities. Separate marketing budgets should be developed for each marketing mix strategy. The separate budgets should then be aggregated to develop an overall marketing budget. If the total amount is too great it will be necessary to modify the overall objectives and the target market objectives, narrow down or drop target markets, or adjust marketing mixes.

The final budget should be realistic given your objectives. When deciding on a marketing budget, consideration should be given to the job that needs to be done as defined by the objectives. Basing marketing budgets on some percent of sales or what the competition spends usually leads to over spending or under spending. Decisions should also be based on the \costs, projected revenues, and desired profitability of different activities, not just costs alone. Successful marketing activities will generate additional revenues which can be projected based on the marketing objectives (such as increase off season stay by 5%).

Although budgets should be viewed as flexible plans, every effort should be made to adhere to them. Revisions in the budget should only be made after careful consideration of the likely impact of the change on the marketing mix and accomplishment of your objectives.

Implementation

Many well designed marketing plans fail because they are poorly executed. Businesses, agencies, and communities can increase the likelihood of successful implementation if they:

(1) identify specific tasks which must be accomplished;

(2) assign people or departments specific responsibility for different tasks;

(3) provide employees with information on the marketing plan (rationale, objectives, strategies);

(4) develop time lines and deadlines;

(5) adhere as much as possible to the budget; and

(6) regularly monitor and evaluate progress.

Evaluation

It is important that marketing efforts be continually evaluated. This will improve the effectiveness of marketing strategies by quickly identifying differences between actual results and expected performance and determining likely reasons for the success or failure to realize objectives.

A framework for evaluation would include:

(1) determining which elements of the different marketing mixes are most important to evaluate.——It is rarely possible or cost effective to evaluate all elements;

(2) establishing performance standards to compare against actual results.—Marketing objectives, if properly formulated, should serve as performance standards;

(3) development of formal and informal methods for collecting data on actual results.—There are many ways different elements of the marketing mix can be evaluated. For example, promotions can be evaluated with money off coupons. Special information request forms, telephone numbers to call or post office box numbers to write to can identify the area the request is coming from. Also, formal (written) and informal (face-to-face) surveys can be used to determine the promotional material the customer used in planning the trip;

(4) comparison of results with objectives;

(5) determination of needed change(s).

Conclusion

Customer satisfaction in tourism is greatly influenced by the way in which the service (hospitality) is delivered and the physical appearance and personality of the business. It is critical that these elements be communicated in the best possible manner to convince people to come and experience what your business or community has to offer. Equally important is the ability to generate repeat business because of your efforts.

Thus, marketing becomes the method to reach potential visitors. It is a vital part of tourism management and can be done effectively and well, with sophistication and tact, or it can be done poorly in a loud, crass and intrusive manner. Hopefully, this bulletin has given you the basics for the former rather than the latter. Remember that to do an effective job at marketing:

(1) adopt a strong customer orientation which includes regular research and assessment of their needs, wants and attitudes;
(2) allocate sufficient resources and time to marketing;
(3) assign formal responsibility for marketing to one person or department; and
(4) develop and regularly update a marketing plan.

Information Supply in Tourism Management

Operators in tourism management, compared to other management sectors, are confronted with a vast field of complex aims, requiring different plans of action. The special working requirements of the services sector are a result of its business peculiarities. Problems instrategic, and frequently operational planning, are characterized by their complexity, often being intermingled, non-transparent, individualistically dynamic and requiring the achievement of multiple goals. The vast amount of information or complex weighting of the different sectors can present an insurmountable problem for human resources. As are sult there are high expectations of decision-makers' trouble-shooting abilities.

In order to solve complex problems, decision-makers need to have a factual knowledge of the industry (declarative knowledge) and the methodology used (procedural knowledge). The wealth of knowledge is drawn from two pools; that obtained from the "storage" of already existing experiences, and by generating knowledge in the respective field. Com-bining these two pools creates an arena for problem solving.

Declarative Knowledge – Decision Basis in Tourism Planning

Currently, information gains more and more importance, leading legitimately to the development of a fourth economic sector – the information sector. Information also plays a vital role in tourism for entrepreneurs and managers who spend the whole day involved in information processing.

In the tourism industry there is no lack of market research data, on the contrary, there is a rather uncontrolled growth of various data sources, each having different survey purposes and survey designs. Tourism surveys of national and international market research institutes are published in ever shorter intervals and the level of itemization of market data increases rapidly. Information collected by these means has indicated data which can be organized into the following groups:

1. Information on markets and environment,
2. Information on customer behaviour,
3. Information on competition in the industry, and
4. Internal information for executive boards.

The first three information groups are predominantly non-discretionary from a manager's point of view as the information can very rarely be directly influenced by an individual company. Information from these groups are similar in nature and scope for most sectors represented in the tourism industry (hotel trade, restaurant trade, tour operators, travel agents, common carriers, pressure groups, etc.).

In the fourth group however, there is a larger scope for variety. Due to high costs for primary market research many tourism managers abandon market research in general. Even the larger businesses and tourism organizations lack market research departments and employees rarely work exclusively on market research items. This results again in an inconsistent development of marketing aims and strategies, as businesses as often as not grope in the dark for their direction.

In Europe the most frequent or highly recognized of the commissioned tourism studies are either publicly financed, directly by national or local authorities, or indirectly by government agencies. This method of procuring market research, is important and often a condition for its development, as the expensive primary studies cannot be financed by the numerous small or medium-scale businesses. The resulting obligation to pass on information, created by the above mentioned research financing, has lead to a wider search-inregional tourism organizations, and other bodies representing tourism-to find means of successfully sharing and communicating information.

Traditional data resources in tourism market research are reports, records and statistics which may be presented either in printed format or are electronically driven (CD-ROM). Computer-based information systems (databases) are currently a rarity, but usually can be found either in connection with the official statistical data of a country or a region or international institutions. The information available by this method is rarely used since it ignores the special information requirements of the end-user (managers), or is simply inaccessible due to high fees, complicated application procedures or is simply not user friendly.

The lack of practical relevance, of these information systems, can be explained by their bias toward representing the economic interest of the sponsors and data collectors and/or by the universal requirements the systems have to meet in the collection, storage and search of statistical data from other industries. Market research results are mainly available in print and they can be obtained either in bookshops, online or directly from the author. From the consumer's perspective this way of passing on secondary information has a number of disadvantages:

- Due to the complex design of market research reports the surveyed data is not up to date any more.
- Data from different sources cannot be easily compared especially if it has been surveyed for different purposes.
- Information contained in reports is often of limited relevance for the particular problem.
- Presentation of data is either not detailed enough, not significant enough, or supplementary information is missing which prevents a faultless interpretation of results.
- Often only very specific data from a more comprehensive study is required and thus the cost-benefit-ratio becomes unattractive.

There is usually an overabundance of available information leaving managers to cope with determining which is the best source. Often the entrepreneur has to rely on external consultants and market research specialists resulting in additional costs.

Procedural Knowledge – Decision Basis in Tourism Planning

"The big problem with management science models is that managers practically never used them." More than 20 years ago John Little described the discrepancy between the scientific development of planning instruments, models, level of itemization and the fact that, when available, the knowledge gathered is rarely put into practice. This is caused by the numerous, often poorly documented assumptions of model architects, which was denoted as model plutonism by Hans Albert. As a response to this problem Little suggested that the manager is included in the model. He postulated in his article on the Decision Calculus, aniline models with the following features: robustness, ease of control, simplicity, completeness of relevant detail and suitability for communication. The communication problem is of vital importance in the every day life of managers' daily events. It is still common practice to employ various levels of change rather than continue- ally observe the changes in market share and volume. Many entrepreneurs do not even know terms such as market segmentation or market positioning and they do not regard them as essential. They keep on looking for measures to expand seasonal business but lack knowledge of methods that will measure their success. Corporate planning only takes place if external financing is required and supporting documents have to be submitted to the lender. Heuristic forecasting methods are hardly ever used, accordingly quantitative methods are never used. Models of strategic market plan- ningportfolio analyses and analyses of the lifestyle of a product-employed in other in- dustries are hardly ever used in tourism management. The grounds for the poor employment of methodological processes in tourism management can be divided into two groups; technological development and insufficient training. Issues related to the technological development of existing information processing and transmission systems are:

- Data required for the application of tourism models is either not up-to-date or unsuitable.
- Standard software is not able to support the relatively complex tasks in tourism management.
- Specially developed software is too expensive for single tourism businesses. Issues related to the insufficient training of tourism managers are:
- Managers have little knowledge of existing methods or available data.
- Managers are confronted with various data sources and different results and they do not know how to cope with this situation.
- Managers do not know which data sources and models are suitable.

The Transmission of Market Research Data in the Internet

Due to the vital role of tourism in many countries and regions in Europe a number of programs concerning tourism promotion have been installed. Government and private tourism organizations have been established in order to strengthen a tourism destination. Usually the aim is to increase the added value of a region. The major tasks of these bodies are:

- to provide consumers with information about the destination,
- to coordinate and implement sales promotion measures,
- tourism advertising,

- support in sales and distribution, and
- to coordinate and implement market research projects.

For most of their tasks (except the coordination and implementation of market research projects) these tourism promoting bodies provide efficient methods. The actual effect of the last item mentioned has been lost in the past due to inefficient instruments relating to the transmission and utilization of declarative and procedural knowledge. Now with the development of cheaper hard- and software many tourism organizations are reconsidering their promotion policy.

In almost all industries systems are being developed in order to support investment and marketing planning. Also the tourism industry has de- veloped decision support systems and the most important applications are: (1) systems supporting marketing decisions in national tourism organizations, (2) travel counselling systems for shipping clerks, (3) systems supporting regional planning regarding the optimal selection of locations in which to invest (4) systems providing tourism portfolio analyses, (5) simulation tools for forecasting travel behaviour in certain regions. In Austria in 1982 the Austrian Society of Applied Research in Tourism (ASART) started a project aiming at the development of a marketing information system for the national tourism organization in Austria (Austrian National Tourist Office).

The first version of the tourism marketing information system (TourMIS) consisted of a database installed in a host system of the Scientific Computer Centre Vienna and an optimization programme for the advertising budget of the Austrian National Tourist Office.

Though the programmes were adapted in 1991 in favour of PC-software, and hence became accessible for a greater number of people (mainly employees of tourism organizations in the federal provinces), the area-wide information supply for top managers in the tourism industry did not begin until 1999 when the internet version was introduced.

4

Event Marketing Strategies: Public Relations

In your event planning marketing, getting the word out to a mass audience is the goal... and established public realtion channels can be very effective way to promote your event. This is particularly true if you do it yourself. Paying a PR person can be expensive and often times won't pull enough responses to justify the costs of this event marketing strategy. There are three pieces to the publicity puzzle as it relates to your semi-nars. First, you want to get the coverage. Second, you want to do the best job you can once you're in front of the media. Lastly, you want to sell a lot of seminar seats with this opportunity. To generate publicity, you'll need a hook. This is what causes the media to want to cover your event. You'll also want to formulate your message. This is what you say once you're in front of the media. An important thing to remember is that there are tons of people who are trying to get in front of the media to help promote their seminar or event. The media gets bombarded with requests for coverage from seminar promoters. This means that you must have something news-worthy or unusual to get their attention. In many cases, you'll be doing the publicity yourself. This is nothing to be ashamed of. Many people do their own publicity and promo-tion. If you understand the process, you can be very successful. Who can be a better advocate for your seminar or event than you?

Media Coaching Can Help

Before you start getting in front of the media, it's a good idea to under-stand how the process works. This will allow you to optimize your opportunities. I'd recommend that you go to a seminar by Joel Roberts to find out exactly how to maximize your chances for success. I have spent some time with Joel and attended his seminars. He does a great job in this area. Contact either Joel or his assistant Nancy. Let him know I sent you. You'll be glad you did. (His contact information is in the Million-Dollar Rolodex in Appendix A.)

Using Outside Publicity Experts

There are many people who present themselves as publicity experts who will be happy to take your money in exchange for claiming to help you promote your event. Be suspicious. If a publicity person is confident he or she can get you publicity, I suggest you compensate them differently than they might prefer. Offer to give them a piece of all of the registrations that come in from their efforts. Let's say the seminar is priced at $300. Let's also assume that the marginal cost for each attendee is $25. This means that every registration is worth $275 (net) to you.

Offer your publicity person a minimum of a 50-50 split on the regis-tration dollars for every person that their efforts generate. (This assumes that you can track the responses.)

I would even consider giving them more. If necessary, I'll give a PR person $200 for each person their efforts can generate. I'll still make $75 on the front end and have the opportunity to sell them products and other services while I build a larger database.

Most PR people will balk at this deal. Fine. Only use people who are willing to bite at this arrangement. If they are really good, they'll actually make a lot more money.

Persistence Pays

The key to getting media coverage is to be persistent. Don't expect to make one call and have them asking you to sit down for an interview and a photo shoot. As with all things where you're relying on some-one else to do something that's higher on your list than it is on theirs, persistence is the key here. Without being a pest, regular and polite call-backs are in order. If you've left several messages and none are being returned, a final message that simply says, "I assume you're not interested and I don't want to keep pestering you, so I'm not going to call again. But if you are interested and just busy right now, please do call me as soon as you can and let's talk about how we can help each other" is definitely appropriate.

If you're easily discouraged when people seem to ignore you, you'll find the PR route tough sledding. Editors are not only busy people, they are suspicious as well.

Press releases tend not to get the kind of atten-tion that the people who send them think they deserve. But if you are gently persistent in your follow-up, you can often get a reporter or editor on the phone to talk to you about your story. It's more often that conversation, rather than the release itself, that will lead to coverage.

So don't give up and don't get discouraged!

Don't Be Hurt When They Don't Cover You.

When, despite your patience and persistence, you don't get coverage by the media, don't be discouraged and don't take it personally. These folks are just doing their jobs.

Your goal is to make your event so enticing that they are compelled to give you coverage. Sometimes you just don't have a newsworthy event. It's not likely any major metropolitan daily newspaper or TV outlet or radio show is going to cover your seminar unless it has a hook and is something they haven't seen before (or at least recently). No hook, no coverage, even on a slow news day.

The Hook

The hook is what causes the media to stop what they're doing and take notice of your event. If there has just been an earthquake in San Francisco and you're doing a seminar on how to earthquake-proof your house, you've got a relatively easy sell.

In most cases, things won't be this easy.

You can also take a specific portion of your seminar and try to create a hook. In order for your hook to be effective you'll want to try and tie it to some current event or trend in the field.

TV Publicity (Empty)

We live in a time that is dominated by television. It's only natural that you would be eager to get yourself some good TV publicity. Don't bother.

As good as seeing your face on TV may be for your ego, stations rarely let you put up an 800 number or a Web site URL. This makes TV appearances just about worthless for product promotion unless you're already known and people can find you easily. I recommend that you not pursue TV unless you know someone.

Radio

To learn how to get your event covered on radio, I suggest you learn from the master of the radio interview, Alex Carroll. He has done more interviews for one book than virtually anyone on the planet. Go to his site, www.radiopublicity.com, to learn more about him and some of the materials that he has to offer. His information is backed by real-life experience as the interviewee in well over 1,000 radio interviews.

Print

The master of print publicity is another friend of mine, Paul Hartunian. Paul has generated the equivalent of well over $6 million in space advertising in magazines and newspapers. I suggest you obtain his materials before you start promoting your own events.

Give me a call and we'll get you a set of his materials.

Online

There are a number of sources for you to generate on-line publicity.

Some of these depend on your topic. If you're giving a seminar of interest to the building trades industry, for example, you should use your favourite search engine (my technical colleague Dan Shafer, who's a real guru in this field, currently recommends www.google.com) and look up building trades sites. Some, particularly associations and eZines devoted to your space, will be happy to list your seminar free.

You can also post notices about your seminars and workshops on the email lists, listservs, and discussion boards you belong to and contribute to regularly. Be careful here; spam is not appreciated and can have a severe negative side effect. But if you're a regular member of and contributor to some online communities in your space, and if you're careful about how you promote your seminar (avoiding blatant, obvious promotions but perhaps including a line about your

Project Managing for a Special Event

As the project manager of a special event, conference, or other major event you will most likely be faced with managing a team of people who will help to carry out the needs for the day. If you have recently found out you will be managing an event, planning your wedding, or planning an office event you should quickly try to find out who is going to be helping you. Evaluate the needs of the event, the number of guests, and how many team members you'll need to pull it all off. Once the team members have been identified, set up a time when everyone is available to meet together. As soon as you find out about the event that is coming in your future, find out who your team is going to be. Whether it is an assembled group of co-workers, hired professionals, or volunteers you need to know your team. Gather the team together early on, even if it too early for them to begin their planning. This will help everyone on the team to feel like they are involved and have an equal part in the planning process.

After you have explained the vision and brainstormed about some elements of the day, list of your needs and what jobs should be filled by members of the team. If you have an idea already of who would be good at a particular position, go ahead and ask/recommend that they take that job. For others positions, let people express what their strengths are and what jobs they wouldn't feel comfortable with. Its always important to be sure everyone enjoys to some degree and wants to be doing their part on the team. Lastly, as the planning process continues into the weeks or even months ahead, be available to your team. For each of them to be successful in their roles they must know that they can check with you about areas they are uncertain of or have questions regarding. Always keep the team updated about any changes that have been implemented or other elements that have been added. Try to avoid making major changes to an area that someone has been putting a lot of work into as this can be very discouraging. Always encourage the team by letting them know they are valuable to the success of the event and appreciated by you as the leader. If you're trying to find the best Chicago wedding reception venue for your reception, don't miss the unique European Crystal Banquet Hall. This gorgeous, award-winning banquet hall in chicago guarantees a beautiful, enjoyable and stress-free event for you and your guests.

Event Promotion Tip: Using the Seminar to Sell Your Consulting Services

Conventions are a way to trade your clients up to consulting. For some folk, your convention will be the 1st product they have purchased from you. Others will have bought other products before attending your event. In both cases, the convention gives you an opportunity to showcase both your talking talents and your content information.

There are more models for generating consulting business, but doing conventions is one of the simplest I know about. The keys to generating consulting business are like those which can lead to a great convention experience. First, you have to give folk a phenomenal quantity of helpful info. This could persuade them of your understanding of the subject and your eagerness to share it. 2nd, you should never withhold info. If you give folks the impression that you aren't giving them the straight scoop (i.e, that you are holding back to lure them to use you as a consultant), they won't reply well.

In turn, they'll be far less likely to offer you consulting work. Some convention leaders/speakers think that if you keep a tiny bit of info in your back pocket folk will pay more for you to show your cards. Nothing could be farther from the truth.

Folk are more likely to offer you consulting business when you give them everything you know and reply to all questions completely and forthrightly. If you do this, folk will be rather more likely to ask you to come and give them individual help. Irrespective of how much info you provide, they'll think you've more to give. When you purposely and glaringly hold back info, you risk having them feel taken by some sort of a ploy to get you to give them more cash. When a person asks you a query during your convention and you reply with : Well, hire me as an advisor and I'll give you all the info that you would like you are dead in the water.

People will feel exploited. (The exception to this and a fantastic opportunity to sell your consulting in the convention is if an attendee asks a question that's so specific to their company or situation that it is apparent that no-one else will need to hear the solution..) You have to be 100 pc prepared to share everything you know in the convention.

You owe it to your partakers. Behave this way and you will get plenty of consulting work.

Marketing Workshops Success: The Mental Side of the Product Sales Game

You can't get up in front of a bunch of folk and become successful selling your products unless you have one hundred percent confidence in the materials you're selling. In your even planning and management, you should always be thinking about your product, and you'd better feel GREAT about other folks achieving success with them! Part of your talking business is a promotions business and your product line is your pride and joy to present to them! For me, this has 2 elements. First, you want to form superb content. Second, you want to package your products attractively. Doing both will drastically increase your confidence when you get up in front of people and do your product display. You've got to have products you are pleased with. That does not necessarily mean that you have got to have them packed in fancy four-colour packing. It suggests that you have got to feel that your materials are worth many times more than the price you are charging. You need to also feel that your products will assist in making a serious change in folk's lives. Let me give you an example. I was just at a Peter Lowe Success event (an one day event which showcases a range of speakers) to critique a customer of mine who was one of the speakers. I was impressed with his talking capability. He is an excellent spokesman. He was sincere and packed his shows with content. Also he is terribly funny. Here's his problem. He feels uncomfortable SELLING up in front of a group. My query to him was : WHY?He told me it was as he felt a little bit uncomfortable with the full sales process. He felt a bit strange asking folks to buy his materials.

I asked him if his products truly worked. He shot back powerful and intensely : Yes, naturally they work! he had got many glowing testimonials from folks pronouncing a similar thing. I told him that with a product that works that well, he should feel guilty if each person in his audience doesn't buy. His products are so useful to folk he should approach the sale of his materials with a virtually non secular zealotry. Of course, in several cases, he was saving lives. His product sales have since increased significantly as a consequence of this change. In his case, a change of attitude. I believe he currently gets it. It has significantly modified the forcefulness of his product show.

Seminar Marketing Advantage: Know What You MUST Know about the Competition!

When marketing seminars, As with every business, you'll have competition. If you don't have any, you should be worried. This would mean that there may not be any demand for the kind or type of event you're thinking of promoting. Since you have some competition, it's a good idea to learn all you can about them. Your event marketing strategies should include this research!

Start your search on-line. If you're doing a marketing seminar for chiropractors, go to your favourite search engines and enter in the words: "marketing seminar for chiropractors." You'll also want to search for variations on these terms as well. Look everywhere you can on-line and you'll find what you're looking for. (If you want help with this, buy my friend and colleague Dan Shafer's amazing eBook, How to Find Anything on the Web in Less Than 10 Minutes, which is being published at the same time as this book. It's available through our joint Web site, www.publishingprofit.com.) You'll also want to approach trade associations. Act like a naïve "newbie" and tell them you're looking for a certain kind of event and ask who offers them. As soon as you decide to do seminars in a given topic or area, attend every seminar that anyone else offers that is remotely related. Take extensive notes at these events. Monitor them not just for the infor-mation, but for how they present the content. Take what you can from their events and make changes where you feel they're appropriate.

Talk to attendees. Ask them what they liked the most and least about the event. You can learn a lot by surveying the people who are there. Remember, their perspective will be very different from yours. They will be your future customers. While you're at it, collect business cards for your database. They will be ideal prospects for your events.

Make sure that you are on the mailing lists for all of your competitors. Do this both on and offline. If they take you off their lists because they identify you, just ask a friend to get on their list and send you their promotions. (When competitors find their way onto my mailing lists, I don't try and make it difficult for them. It actually takes too much work to ferret out a competitor.)

After attending their events, assess where their strengths and weak-nesses lie. Assess your own skill and knowledge base and see where you can provide a different approach or where you can fill in the gaps and do some coaching work.

An example from the publishing industry may help to illustrate my point. I help small to medium sized publishers make more money. There are two or three people who do something related. When I started this business, I attended their events.

My assessment turned up that although the individuals sponsoring these events were intelligent and knowledgeable, their content and presentation were lacking. I came in and quickly gained huge market share at their expense by providing a much better seminar with a slightly different slant.

As soon as you identify your competition, you'll want to see if they are amenable to a joint venture. In this case, a "joint venture" is a relationship in which they let you mail a promotion about your event to their customer base and you cut them in for 50% of what you make from their customers who attend. In many cases, you'll be met by immediate hostility. Very few people can see the positive benefits to them of a joint venture for your seminar. They may or may not be right. Here's how I see it. If I'm really good at what I do, I won't be scared to let my customers know about a seminar from one of my competi-tors. Why? Because they will inevitably be disappointed. I might as well get paid 50% by them to let them know about an event they will probably find on their own. Another thing to remember about people and seminars. Many people will hop from guru to guru looking for the next greatest idea in a field. Still others just want to listen to everyone's perspective on a given topic. Understanding these realities, it behooves you to make some money from your database in exchange for introducing them to the other gurus in the field. After all, they are highly likely to find them anyway. If they find them on their own, you won't make a dime!

Event Promotion Tip: 5 Things You MUST do to get people to Come to your Next Event

I know a guy who is in the communication field, and does conference promotion for his specialty. He's got extremely high rankings in Google due to his SEO efforts. When we got together not long ago, I was quizzing him about his business and what he does to promote events. One of the first questions I asked him was: "How Many of the people who use your services come back for a second helping?" I was SHOCKED by his answer! Virtually NONE of them. Holy Crap!

With stellar SEO rankings for a service that is IN DEMAND, he's doing just fine. For mere mortals like you and me, this would be DEADLY. Whenever I do a seminar or other event, I'm EXTREMELY conscious of doing a great job so that people will come back for more. I don't have and I suspect you're in the same position) an endless supply of people who will attend my events. If you're in the general field of "weight loss" or "making money", this article may not apply to you. If you ARE in those fields, I'd suggest you TARGET your market a bit more carefully, so this article SHOULD apply to you!

Deliver a LOT of High Quality Content

The problem with most people who do seminars is that they are obsessed with trying to sell their NEXT event. In doing so, there seminars and workshops turn into a sales presentation for next month's "big event."

To say this is misguided would be a dramatic understatement of the facts.

Like you, want 100% of the people who attend THIS event to come back to my next and every other subsequent event that I hold. To make this happen I want to make sure I deliver on the promises I made at THIS event. If I do that, everything will fall neatly into place.

Provide People with a ROADMAP

People don't want to just know WHAT to do. They want to know HOW to do it. Scared of telling people because you won't get any coaching or consulting work? Your fears are misguided. My mentor, Howard Shenson, used to tell me to "give them everything you got!" IF I did that, he told me they would come back to me for more. They were right.

IF you give people the exact/precise way to do something, they will be thinking two things. First, that you haven't told them EVERYTHING they need to know. It may not be the case, but their perception is their reality. Also, once you tell people how to "make the sausages" they may not want to make it. Many will ask you to do it for them.

Be Approachable

There are MANY seminar leaders who set themselves up as the "guru on the hill." A number of high profile marketing types pride themselves on this posture. Their thinking is: If I'm not accessible, people will have to pay me for my services to get access. In my opinion, this is FOOLISH.

You should be approachable but draw the line at where general helping ends and individual coaching or consulting begins. At an event I will fully answer any and all questions on general concepts. The specifics will not be germane to the entire group and will NOT help me sell future services. I leave those out.

Ask them to Attend Your Next Event

People won't come back to your next event if you don't ASK them! It may be an ADVANCED version of the seminar you just did. It may be tangentially related to what you just finished. Both of those are logical choices when asking people to sign up for your next event. But, they won't know about it unless you ASK them to do so. Have a date and venue set before you pitch it to them as a group.

You'll also want to provide them with an incentive for making their decision NOW! Give them a substantial price break for signing up before they leave your current event. Make it a GOOD deal. Put a deadline on your offer. Limit the number of spaces you have based on what makes good sense.

Be Yourself

Don't try and be someone you're not. People will SMELL the insincerity. Make sure that you are the best YOU you can be. Do this and some people may not like you. Don't do this and many more won't like you. You'll also end up attacting the "right" kind of people. The people that you get along with naturally. The people you'll like and who like you as you really are. This will make any additional work you do with them simple and easy.

I know what you're thinking. What about your choice of hotel or the food you serve? Meaningless to getting people to attend your next event! Follow the above 5 steps and your chances for having people come back to your future seminars and events will go WAY up. Do it differently than I've described and you're on your own. Over the more than 25 years I've been doing seminars, workshops and other events, this has worked very well for me!

Project Management Using Event Chain Methodology

There are large number of risks or event chains and project activities create an impact in the different phases of a project. Project management using event chain methodology is the uncertainty modeling approach practiced by project managers today to identify and eradicate such events.

Event Chain Methodology Objectives

Uncertainties can occur at any phase of the entire project lifecycle, and in turn, lead to project mishaps. At times, project managers ignore the risks which lay outside of the project scope. The key objective of event chain methodology is to identify the risks or event chains affecting processes or project outcomes.

By identifying these event chains, project managers gain as follows:

- Simplify schedule network analysis models
- Ameliorate project planning accuracies and meet deadlines appropriately
- Diminish the impact of known or unknown project planning prejudices

- Create error-free project schedules by providing flexible layouts
- Increase the ability in project managers to visualize chain of events disturbing project outcomes
- Give a way to lot of quantitative analysis models that are very accurate to identify potential events affecting projects.

As an essence, event chain methodology helps project managers to identify and avoid project delays, revenue losses and overall project failures.

Event Chain Methodology Principles

There are six principles practiced in project management using event chain methodology. Below you'll learn more on event chain methodology principles along with in depth information about each one of the principles.

Ground States and Excited States

Be it a real project or a virtual project, the procedures in projects are not always designed in a uniformed manner or as a continuous process. Both external or internal events change these processes from one state to another.

The ground state is nothing but the original state or how the activity was initially planned. Event chain methodology defines the changed state as an excited state.

The event chains sometimes create significant changes in project activities which can lead to project closure or failures. To avoid such scenarios, event chain methodology is used to analyze the project activities and the risk chains are identified. Monte Carlo simulation or statistical distribution are the widely used methods in event chain methodology to identify such event chains.

Chain of Events

Occasionally, a ripple effect is created when one event leads project activities to a chain of events and in turn, develops positivity or negativity in project objectives. Please see the below example to understand how the chain of events create an impact on the project deliverables:

- A key member *X* in *project activity A* goes on medical leave suddenly for an indefinite period
- Project manager pulls another key resource *Y* from *project activity B* to handle the responsibilities of *X*

- Resource *Y* is put in a situation to handle many different responsibilities at the same time
- Resource Y has to hand over or train a new resource to take care of *Y*'s role and learn the activities *X* was already performing.

How is the project affected due to above situation?

- Resource *Y* struggles and loses motivation which can spread among the team
- Delay in both the *project activities A* and *B* subsequently affects the interrelated or interconnected activities
- Project failure or closure due to inability of completing project activities on time.

How can Event Chain Methodology help in such a Situation?

- As a first step, the *new human resource requirement* in *project activity A* changes the ground state to an excited state. The *sourcing completed* state changes to *resource required* state.
- As a second step, a new resource is replaced in *project activity A* from *project activity B.* This process changes the ground state of *project activity B* to an excited state as *resource required.* If the state is not changed, appropriate resource utilization for project *B* may not occur.
- If *project activity B* proceeds with less number of resources, the excited state is further changed to *the extended lead time* to complete *project activity B*
- Once the responsibility of resource *Y* in *project activity A* is stabilized, he/she will be able to either train a new resource or manage both *A* and *B* activities. The extended period in *project activity B* will not delay the overall project.

In such methods, a project manager will be able to avoid project closure or failure by completing the chain of activities appropriately. According to Project Management Institute (PMI), there are four strategies such as risk acceptance, risk mitigation, risk transfer and risk avoidance used greatly in the chain of event principle.

Event State Tables and Chain Diagrams

In the case of complex chain of events, Gantt charts are used to simplify the events and identify solutions. Event chain diagrams and state tables are the visualizations used to clarify the relationship between chain of events and how they affect project activities. Such diagrams are used to simplify the risk analysis methods and find out uncertainties in advance.

Event Chains Related to Duration and Cost

The uncertainties related to duration and cost are common in real time and virtual projects. These uncertainties cause major problems in projects and can lead to project failures. The Monte Carlo simulation is used to identify such fluctuations in projects.

The events are identified and the moments are calculated by using statistical distribution methods. The quantitative analysis through the Monte Carlo method is used to calculate the cumulative consequences of the events.

The results normally include statistical distributions of event chains or a single event such as project duration, costs and in turn, the success of each activity in the project.

Performance Measurement Related to Event and Event Chains

There are different performance measurement system models used in projects. Normally, historical data is used to measure the performance of any project. By using historical data, project managers decide whether any particular event or event chain can have an impact on the project outcomes or not. However, it is not easy to understand which historical data is appropriate to identify such events.

Remember, projects differ from each other a lot and variations are more than common in project activities. In such scenarios, event chain methodology using the Bayesian belief network analysis method helps the project manager. Additionally, project managers also use events that occur based on the actual project.

Critical Event Chains

At times, there is a single event or a chain of events that causes major project issues. Such crucial events or event chains are known as critical event chains. To avoid the occurrence of such project issues, it is important for project managers to identify these critical event chains and mitigate them.

The sensitivity analysis is used widely in event chain methodology to find out these critical event chains. This method helps to identify events, variations, responses and project activity changes occurring under different conditions. Remember, even a single critical event can create an impact on multiple project activities.

Event Chain Methodology Facts

Project management using event chain methodology is a great model to identify an event or event chains that are affecting projects. Occasionally, these methodologies also create interesting situations. The closed or completed activity in a project gets started again or new activities that are not planned originally get triggered suddenly. However, a very well developed mathematical models in event chain methodology helps project managers to get rid of events causing issues in the projects.

Event Management-Corporate and Personal Events

In this age of consumerism, the events have become the normal parts of the corporate world where they require a platform or marketing tools to spread the products directly to the consumers. Event Management includes many services for leisure events that include leisure sport, music, recreation; cultural events under its broad category of ceremonial, religious, art, heritage and folklore; Personal events that comprised of weddings, birthdays, anniversaries and organizational events under the various categories of commercial, political, charitable, sales, product launch etc.

When you think to organize any event, first you need to investigate its feasibility, you have to start putting a plan together, as an Event Planner. There are many factors that have to be taken into account when planning even the simplest event, there are staff to arrange, venues to find, equipment to source and tickets or invitations to send out. There are different type of special events. Each has its own purpose and importance. Confusing the type of event can result in disaster.

Plan your Event

Decide the venue, decide about food and drinks, book entertainment or speakers, look after details like parking, coat check, security, and washrooms. Most important based on your budged adjust all the things. Prepare a detailed checklist of everything you will need – invitations, RSVP, who orders what and do it well in advance. Make a timeline working back from the day of the event and mark the deadlines for getting invitations out, placing ads in media, payments of deposits, to suppliers and entertainers, and when the RSVP must be received. Venue should be easy to search, comfortable to enter with enough space of front gate, enough space based on the number of invitees. Most comfortable arrangement of sitting.

Promote Your Event

Make a good promotion of your event. Even if it is a relatively small event, a unique name, slogan and logo can help to sell the event. A special website should be there for branding the event, with a link from your organization's website. A unique URL can help to brand the event and this can also make tracking registrations easier. If you are sending invitations to your mailing list, usually about six weeks to a month is an appropriate time to mail invitations. Use email lists and email invitations and have people register for the event on your website. If the event is open to the public, advertise in the media, using the media that will target your audience. Make press releases about your event, promote your event on social media websites, you can also arrange road shows for promotion of your event.

Event Management of Conferences

Event management of conferences: Conferences are among the most important events that professional event managers organize. The term "conferences" can apply to a variety of gatherings from a group of researchers who meet to discuss scientific results to a group of sales people who are training.

Conference planning can be the responsibility of a corporate employee or a professional meeting planner.

Everything about the planning of conferences. From important steps in the planning process to conference types and their requirements.

5

Event Organization

Event organization can become a cumbersome process if not taken seriously. Thoroughly combing over as many details as possible is a great maneuver aimed to present an event worth remembering. Whether the event is of Business or Personal nature, details make a difference. The first line of business to consider in organizing an event is to decide upon the overall atmosphere to be projected by the event. How should the guests feel upon arrival and departure? Will all guests remain together during the event or will they be divided into smaller groups at some point during the experience? Should emotions of comfort, excitement, relaxation, romance, restfulness or pleasure be endured? Choosing the atmosphere is as vital as selecting the theme of a child's birthday party. This atmosphere/theme is the foundation in constructing the perfect event.

Organization of Events

Is the nature of the event casual, formal, romantic, or professional? Different Event Venues project different moods casting the tone of the event's nature. Most venues possess the ability to cast each of these tones to make the event successful. Many restaurants offer gathering rooms to project a formal, romantic or professional feel, while a portion of the main eating area settles guests into a more casual, laid-back retreat. The same is true for most venues. Yachts can be the perfect "wow factor" for intimate, casual bridal/baby showers as well as intriguing the professional crowds mixing business with pleasure in the sights and sounds integrated with elegance on this excursion. Next, location of the event, namely the event venue, should be selected. The event venue provides the background to the atmosphere draped upon guests. Venue needs to include consideration of several factors of location. How will guests arrive and will parking be an issue or inconvenience? How far will guests be willing to travel to reach their destination? Other considerations include event facilities. Does the event facility provide a catering service, technological equipment, DJ/ music or will it permit the use of such on its premises? How many guests will be attending the event and will the desired location accommodate this number of attendees? The location should comfortably allow guests to mingle and move without feeling crowded or lost in a vast openness of over-sized space. Finding this perfect zone of comfort is easily attainable with a little research or assistance of an event manager. Remember to consider the time frame of the event to offer guests quick access to hotels if an overnight stay is deemed necessary.

Event Planning

Event planning is a detailed immersion into planning and executing a memorable and exciting event for business promotion, recognition of achievement, or the introduction of new products and technology. Event planners pave the way to a streamlined unfolding of an event by the practical application of resources and methods to fulfill every conceivable need that might arise at such a gathering. Event planning sets the stage of the visual, culinary and experiential impact of the event, making a difference between money well invested and dollars poorly spent. Event planning is an art...and event planners are detail-oriented multi-taskers with an eye toward detail, a nose for expediency, and an ear for suggestions. The goal of the event planner is to please the event sponsors with delivery of an event that fulfills their expectations. More about the Planning of Events.

Promotion

Promotion is a necessity for any event as the means of informing interested people that an event will take place. Promotion requires a focused application of organization, branding and outreach, and is dependent upon defining an interested demography. Proper promotion also relies on correct information about the event and the event sponsors. Since promotion is the domain of the marketing expert, the event must provide a distinct benefit that makes people want to attend, that marketing efforts may promise, with reasonable surety, a large enough audience to make the event a success. Promotion can not be overlooked when planning an event that appeals to a diverse audience gathering together for a common interest. Attracting attention prior to the event is invaluable for bolstering ticket sales, increasing interest in a cause, or highlighting accomplishments. Promotion requires the use of advertising for stimulating the interest of the target demographic, by arranging appearances for event spokespersons on talk shows and radio programs, or by circulating information at related industry events or through other media.

Promotion also takes the Internet stage, providing web sites, or links to web sites relating to the event, industry or cause. Attention is paid to writing press releases, optimizing search engine content, and spreading the word through social media. Promotional tasks might also include writing blogs or conducting email programs to pave the way for subsequent information-gathering by prospective guests.

Not to be overlooked are the writing talents needed for developing direct-mail materials and invitations, as well as printing resources for the production of posters, fliers or brochures. In some instances, retaining event promotion personnel to distribute promotional materials at festivals or to man booths at other events offer keys to opening additional doors of interest in an upcoming event.

Good promotion imparts a sense of anticipation about an event. Often, to accomplish this, promotions revolve around a chosen theme that becomes the springboard for the entire event, affecting the choice of music, colour, décor, food and even the dress of event participants. Effective promotion brings with it the energy of enticement, is the harbinger of excitement, and offers a promise of things to come.

Advertising

Adverstising to promote your events. The event advertising budget is of utmost importance to the success of any event, for advertising reaches out to a broad audience. Advertising provides the means for attracting attendance to an event of greater numbers, a more diverse demographic, and a more interested audience than invitations alone.

Advertising takes form by way of newspaper advertisements, through full-page spreads or in-line column notices. The event advertising budget may be used to speak enticingly to television viewers during news spots, or during prime-time shows.

Websites offer an excellent, low-cost method of advertising through links placed on web pages that appeal to the target demographic most likely to be interested in the offerings of the event. Not to be overlooked is the vast audience served daily through radio programming, the event details presented by a popular radio host, or by way of an audio spot installed within regular programming.

Advertising is the realm of the marketing and promotion expert, who, through training and experience, knows the best methods to entice, attract and provide information to prospective event attendees. In addition, the advertising expert is well equipped to provide compelling copy, provide professional photography, actors, and voice-over talent for the constructing of audio and visual messages.

In addition, advertising professionals have within their bag of tools the means for extracting information regarding the most compelling aspects of the event itself, capable of targeting the emotions, needs and interests of their target audience with just the right mix of media. For determining the budget needed to conduct a successful advertising campaign, a well-versed advertising professional is invaluable for steering event monies toward those advertising mediums most likely to deliver a successful turnout.

To obtain the most bang for the advertising dollar, advertising is most successful when it revolves around a central theme targeting a sense of excitement, a possibility of romance, an opportunity for riches, or the mystery of the unknown. Certain planning details must necessarily be determined, however, prior to production of the advertising itself. The event date and time, venue, theme, programs, speakers, celebrities and ticket costs must all be finalized and in place, that advertising will correctly provide the information to spur event ticket sales.

Budgeting

Budgeting for an event is by far the most important aspect of a successful event. While budgets can be as varied as the occasions being planned for, a budget lays the groundwork for what can be included in the event, what details must be scaled back, and what ideas must be abandoned during the planning process.

Determining a budget is most easily accomplished when a specific amount of money is dedicated for the event in its entirety. Factors to be considered are deposits for event venues, speakers, caterers, photographers, bands, DJs, fireworks, audio-video and sound equipment, furnishings, rented lighting, limousines, floral displays, booth standards and panels, portable dance floors, stages, and printing services. If advertising and promotion are to be part of the event equation, funds will have to be allocated to newspaper, radio, and television advertising as well as contracting the services of writers, actors, voiceover talent, photographers, videographers, ticket master services and website marketing.

Event personnel and payment for such services must also be included. These cover security and information desk staff, food servers, bartenders, valets or parking attendants, set up and tear down workers, sanitation crews and drivers for transporting people and equipment to and from the event location. Other expenses to consider are gifts, signage, banners, posters, carpet runners, money to cover lodging and transportation of speakers and event personnel, special uniforms, cell phones, internet access to the event, special music CDs and the services of professional decorators, event and space planners. Even the most carefully crafted budget is prone to the need to cover last-minute surprises or overlooked necessities. Rule of thumb suggests an additional 10-15% above and beyond anticipated costs be allocated for unexpected expenses.

Event Security

Security at an event is comprised of individuals who are responsible for overseeing the safety and well-being of guests who attend an event. Security likewise monitors the stream of support personnel responsible for setting up to ply their respective services, providing safe access to guests attending the event, and steering away disruptive or unwelcome troublemakers. Security is an important consideration at events that center around visiting celebrities, political candidates and children, for these provide opportunity for argumentative, imbalanced or opportunistic individuals to play havoc with the overall good feelings cultivated by the event itself. Security is also a necessity for providing safe transport of monies gathered through ticket sales, or for providing vendor registers with necessary cash.

Security personnel further help deter the opportunities found among crowds for pickpockets, scam artists, and thieves. Monitoring the event floor, or stationed at points of ingress and egress to verify guest registries, the security force also observes the incoming and outgoing of equipment, breaks up arguments, and calls in emergency personnel if the need ever presents itself.

Security personnel can be obtained from company ranks or membership rosters. They can also be found among willing volunteers, a security company, or off-duty and retired police officers. The extent of security's responsibilities must be carefully defined so the event may progress with the least amount of disruption, the fewest unfortunate incidences with the greatest invisibility. While most guests will appreciate the presence of security at an event when entering a strange parking garage or finding themselves among people who've had a bit to drink, security serves its purposes best when it is not needed.

When planning an event, security needs to be adequate to provide observational coverage for the event floor as well as being adequate to handle crowd situations. Whether determining the number of security personnel in accordance to coverage of square feet, coverage by ratio of security personnel to guests, or manning specific stations such as ticket booths or parking garages, the basic requirements remain the same. Security should provide an assurance of safety for guests, event personnel and their equipment, as well as protection of displays, saleable products and event-goers' personal sense of security.

Invitations

Invitations are essential parts of many events. For small, personal or closed events, where only a specific number of people are invited to attend, invitations are a must. Invitations are typically chosen through a printing service, require postage for mailing, and require willing staff to stuff and address the envelopes. With today's casual attitudes and instantaneous Internet connectivity, such a formal request as an invitation automatically sets an event above the ordinary. A sense of exclusivity is commonly attached to the receipt of a written invitation, making it a powerful tool for gathering top-notch executives, powerful financiers, or noted academicians to industry events, political gatherings, new product releases or high-profile think-tank gatherings.

Invitations fall within the realm of the commercial printer. Selection of quality papers, distinctive fonts, properly sized envelopes and RSVP cards for return remittance compromise the classic invitation. Just as importantly, the tone of the invitation, the words used to express the invitation, and the times and location of the event must be obtained before the invitations are ordered, that printing and processing may be completed in a timely fashion.

Invitations are commonly distributed at least 3 weeks prior to an event, and if more time is necessary, determined by the size and scope of the event, they may be sent to recipients even earlier. Printing likewise takes time, and if it is part of the promotional process for the event, the invitations become one of the earliest details to attend to, once the venue and timeline of the event are established. For political, religious and business-related gatherings, the invitation may be included in a mailing with a newsletter or other information, such as brochures, or include prompts to encourage a remission of monies for reserving lodging, transportation, or banquet attendance. There may also be options presented for participating in special events related to, but not part of, the main event, such as the dedication of monuments, buildings, or the opening of new businesses.

Invitations express a profound intimacy as it relates to the event and the guests involved. Invitations not only convey a sense of special regard for the invited, but they also impart a sense of dignity and charm to the event. Invitations likewise suggest opulence befitting important, formal, and celebratory affairs.

Decoration

Decorations at an event are necessary for setting the mood, framing the emotion and underscoring the importance of the event. From crepe paper streamers to professionally-designed displays of colour and beauty, decorations generally work within a theme determined by event sponsors and coordinators, setting the stage for the bulk of the event proceedings. Decorating for large events can prove daunting, requiring equally large displays to be seen among a sea of people, vendors, event booths and accompanying equipment. Colors must be chosen and established for the event in keeping with the chosen theme, reflected in promotional materials, advertisements and floral arrangements, tying the whole together into a feast for the eyes, as well as imparting a visual sense of cohesiveness.

While decorating is often the most exciting part of event planning, it is one area where too many cooks can spoil the broth. The décor relies on collaboration among event coordinators to arrive at a common agreement of what the event theme is all about, then punctuates the idea with décor that is intrinsic to the theme.

Decorating can be simple, or as extensive as coordinated colors of tablecloths, napkins and the colors of clothing event personnel wear. Decorating with flowers is always a winner, and lends panache to banquet table centerpieces and anchors stage backdrops. Flags, banners and posters lend upward interest when hung from the ceiling, while floor-level display easels post information about event times, welcome messages, and directions to specific meeting rooms.

Not to be overlooked is the instant atmosphere suggested by clusters of balloons, centerpieces of fruit, or large urns flanking a main walkway. Ribbon streamers and bows also lend opulence to the affair, particularly when utilized as trimmings on tables, stages, or around entry doors. Not to be overlooked is the manpower needed to decorate a large hall for a special event, and the bucket lifts, ladders, tape, wire and tools to fashion an event to remember. A good source for experienced, and often free display artists can be found among the ranks of high-end department stores, whose extensive inventory of display items might be available for little more than an appreciative mention in the local newspaper.

Flowers

Flowers impart a sense of formality to an event, providing an attractive anchor to the event theme in the décor of reception areas, tabletops and stage backdrops. Flowers may also be incorporated into ladies' restrooms, flank entryways, or grace serving and buffet tables. In addition, serving personnel smartly accessorized with floral boutonnières incorporates them into the décor to impart a sense of richness and elegance that promotes an impressive and memorable event. Floral displays can be created in large, floor-standing urns, incorporated into long, sweeping swags, twine around stairway banisters, or curl lazily around supporting columns and posts. Available in silk, greenery can define paths and walkways, establish bowers and arches, or accent table fronts and booth backdrops.

Flowers cannot be overlooked for their special function as endowments of honour to special guests, as in a massive floral spray bestowed upon a visiting dignitary, contest winner, or political giant. Floral arrangements of marzipan, spun sugar, or carved fruits and vegetables delight the eye, as well as wetting the palate.

A champagne fountain is glamorous and beautiful, trimmed with flowers tucked among sparkling glass and delicate bubbles. Hors d'oeuvres arranged amid rose petals and delicate fern fronds are at once a culinary masterpiece as it is a feast for the eyes. Ice sculptures accented with flowers establishes a gleaming monument to the specialness of the event, just as giant flowers made of crinkled paper lend an air of festivity and fun.

Floral arrangements are best relegated to the services of a knowledgeable and experienced florist, well-versed in making suggestions for floral arrangements that maintain their good looks for the duration of the event. Choose a florist capable of meeting the needs of a large order; many smaller florists may not have the means for obtaining massive numbers of plants, or refrigerating large displays.

Check into the prices of silk flowers as well, and those businesses that provide plants to office buildings, malls and hospitals. Greenery may also be rented, both silk and real, which may be perfectly suited for an outstanding event.

Site Selection

Site selection for the purpose of an event can range from a small room in a borrowed or rented building, to an Outdoor Park, neighborhood, sports complex, or as in the Olympics, an entire city. Most importantly, the location of the event should be readily accessible, easy to find, and located in a safe area.

The site must be capable of fulfilling the requirements of space, electricity, bathrooms and other amenities to handle the event, and be of a proper construction, meeting zoning regulations and offering a contract to provide a seamless event with the least amount of hassles.

Selection of a site relates directly to the event function, and the degree of surety required for the event to proceed. Exposed sites, such as when events are held out-of-doors, may be subject to inclement weather, which is capable of shutting down an event or greatly diminishing the number of guests who attend. A site venue with inadequate parking may deter guests from attending as will the selection of a site in a crime-riddled or dangerous area.

The perception of the site itself is also key to a successful event. It may prove difficult to attract interest for a boat show in the middle of a dry parking lot, as it may prove wildly successful to sponsor a tractor pull at a local fairground. The site itself must lend it's own sense of anticipation and excitement to the event. Modern structures with grand scaling, parking garages, rich interior details, and carefully designed floor plans are suited for events, making such venues perfect for providing a site to host a memorable occasion. Hotels are always a suitable option, filling the lodging needs of out-of-town travelers, offering ready provision of catered food and beverages, and large rooms for classes, banquets, or vendor displays. In addition, they are usually located along major routes, may provide shuttle services to airports and train terminals, and can greatly reduce event staffing costs.

Event Equipment

Equipment to make your event a success. The need for special equipment to pull off a successful event may be as diverse as the event itself. From special lifts to hang decorations from a high ceiling, to hand trucks for transporting tables, chairs, and other supplies to areas within the event, careful consideration must be given to ascertain what equipment may be necessary. For those portions of the event to be captured on film, audio-video equipment can be as simple as a portable hand-held camcorder, or as high-tech as a full studio television camera, replete with audio grip and camera technician. Events featuring a beer garden will necessarily require the acquisition of beer kegs and taps, and bar areas might require soda canisters and dispensers. Events highlighted by dangerous performances usually require the presence of medical personnel and a ready ambulance, while fireworks should be backed up with a fire truck and crew. Children might be engaged at an event by pony rides or amusements, or adults equally tempted to ride high in a helicopter or balloon.

Other equipment to have on hand might be a ready battery of fire extinguishers, and walkie-talkies for event security or key personnel. Extension cords to run electricity to remote vendors and measures to contain cords and hoses to prevent falls are possibly in order. Remote video monitors to survey key areas of concern could prove helpful at security stations; lockboxes or safes could lend a sense of security to money stations. Flashlights could prove invaluable for personnel traveling through stretches of dark spaces when events are held at night out-of-doors, and are certainly needed for personnel, parking cars in open fields at night.

The reservation of portable toilets to accommodate very large crowds or the rental of office trailers for event administration might prove necessary. Power tools for the construction of stages and platforms, trailers for the construction of parade floats, golf carts for covering large event spaces, and even water coolers to prevent dehydration all fall within the realm of extra equipment needed to make an event a safe and memorable one.

Staffing

Staffing for an event is as diverse as the event itself. Adequate staffing depends on the number of guests anticipated to attend the event, and are employed to handle the multiple tasks that under-gird a successful event.

Staffing encompasses individuals such as servers, coat checkers, drivers, special needs assistants, valet parking attendants, customer information agents, and ticket-takers. Staffing may also attend to the details of directing the influx of guests, the positioning of booths and vendors, attending nurseries, assisting guest speakers, delivering supplies during the event, and containing litter.

Additional staff may be needed to set up tables, arrange chairs for seating, and on occasion, assist the decorating committee. Staff may also be required to oversee the direction of other staffers, or to handle the monies generated through ticket sales. Typically, many of these positions can be accomplished by event volunteers, filled by existing company employees, or may be included as services provided by the caterer, equipment rental service or event venue.

The roles of staff are reliant upon the event itself, and the variety of services needed to provide a pleasant experience for event guests. While event sponsors may envision a successful event, rarely do they comprehend the number of bodies required to handle all the details. Defining all facets of the event, from the arrival of guests to the after-party cleanup, will help to assuage those problems caused by the lack of adequate personnel. Many services contracted for the event, such as caterers, chair and table rentals, florists, ticketing agents, and the event venue or location itself commonly provides personnel to handle their respective services. These may be included within the scope of contracted services, or be offered at an additional cost. Savings can be realized with the designation of volunteers from company ranks, membership rosters, or interested individuals willing to perform these functions, provided direction is available to coordinate individuals to carry out assigned tasks. Often, it is to the benefit of event organizers to contract professionals offering such services, who likely provide adequate insurance and training to guarantee these functions are performed to event sponsors' expectations.

Ticketing

Ticketing is very important for commercial events that aim to make profits. For events sure to attract an interested audience, tickets are the means for producing revenue to offset event costs, raise funds, or turn a profit. Ticketing, while seeming a simple concept, may require printing, promotion, reservation, knowledge of event seating, working with caterers, providing information regarding event schedules, lodging and event transportation details. Ticketing is a specialty function often intertwined with and reliant upon advertising and promotion, requiring the knowledge, experience and resources of a ticket master. The ticket master's function is to attract attention to the event, handle the monetary details of ticket sales, and provide accurate reporting of ticket sales to event organizers.

Ticketing is important to any event where the number of persons attending determines the influx of revenue for the event. For events offering a banquet as the central focus of event activities, ticketing ascertains the number of guests anticipated to attend, as it also supplies needed money to offset the costs of food service and catering. Ticketing is likewise a marketing venue; and for the purpose of attracting interested parties to purchase tickets to an event, prospective guests must be made aware the event will take place. Ticket masters are geared toward the promotional advertising that garners attention for an event, and are perfectly positioned to suggest additional promotional aids to bolster lagging ticket sales.

The ticket master has, at his disposal, the means for distributing information regarding the reservation of hotel rooms, suggesting transportation routes to and from the event, and even providing ticket sales at the event. The ticket master also has the means to bolster ticket sales through related organizations, business publications, blogs, word of mouth, print or media advertising and other promotional events. The ticket master may also funnel ticket sales through a network of ticket masters throughout the nation, capable of stimulating interest from a far-reaching audience otherwise untapped by local ticketing resources.

Catering

Catering is one of the most important ingredients for the planning of some common events. Preparing the delicious delicacies that make an event special is the domain of the event caterer. Armed with specialty dishes, culinary delights and dietary alternatives, the many food options the caterer offers can entice, inspire and satisfy event guests, making it a central focus of event activities. Caterers typically offer a signature selection of hors d'oeuvres, salads and entrees, desserts and beverages.

Caterers can be individuals, small businesses, or chefs associated with a hotel or restaurant. Many hotel venues offer in-house catering services, or may suggest a proven and responsible catering service with whom they have enjoyed a professional relationship. Caterers typically provide the serving dishes for a buffet, such as chafing dishes, warming trays, serving utensils and beverages, such as tea and coffee. Artistic chefs may also offer hand-carved ice sculptures as the focal point of a special table, and some supply tableware with accompanying flatware to provide the greatest culinary impact.

A banquet serves the purpose of gathering event guests together for the purpose of presenting awards, recognizing achievement, celebrating accomplishments, or introducing new ideas. Banquets may be defined as those relaxed opportunities to introduce guests to like-minded professionals, long-lost friends, or new acquaintances. The banquet can be a simple affair served by a buffet of culinary dishes, or can be rendered in the more formal format of table service, replete with formally-attired waiters and waitresses.

The caterer offers dishes in accordance with the desires of the event sponsors, providing any number of menu options generally priced on a per-person basis. Caterers are also flexible, capable of producing variations of dishes or offering specialty menus to accommodate the needs of guests limited in their food choices due to diabetes, weight loss programs, or allergies. The caterer must have an idea of the number of guests expected to attend the banquet, and details must be defined as to the types of drinks to be served, the selections of hors d'oeuvres prior to the main meal, and the desserts that follow. In addition, the caterer may provide servers for the event, and needful equipment such as chafing dishes, plates, glasses, and tableware. Necessarily, these details must be carefully considered, that the event take place without experiencing the horror of a banquet marred by the lack of personnel, necessary tools to conduct food service, or worse, running out of food.

Determining the number of guests anticipated to attend a banquet is most easily ascertaining by on-line registry, return RSVP to delivered invitations, ticket sales, or sign-up sheets. Allotments should also be made for the occasional important guest whom fails to reserve a seat, as well as for unexpected guests, or last-minute invitations. For this reason, caterers often promise delivery of a reasonable excess to accommodate extra guests who might otherwise be turned away from joining in the festivities.

Event Photos

Photos taken during an event become an aid to sharing the event experience through house organs, the printed media, or on a website.

Event guests often desire the opportunity to obtain photographs of an event as keepsakes, or to display in their own organizational and business communications.

Photographs provide a record of past events for use in future event promotion, and become an archive of attending guests, speakers, or special moments. Photographers may be contracted to capture the event in its entirety, or retained to only cover a specific portion of it.

Photographers are responsible for providing their own equipment for shooting the event, replete with cameras, lenses, filters, necessary lighting and film. Pricing is generally in accordance to a specific number of shots, or by a package offering a diversity of finished photo sizes. Photographers may also offer photos developed by specialty darkroom techniques, such as newspaper-friendly half tones, collages of important guests or products, as well as colour-filtered or superimposed photographs. If the occasion calls for it, the photographer may be contracted for shooting portraits of attending guests, requiring backdrops or special lighting. The role of the photographer at special events has grown to also include the services of videographers, who by the wonders of technology, can pull from video footage a number of still shots to be converted for print.

The photographer may also be versed in photograph retouching, capable of air-brushing unwanted backgrounds from event shots for use in printed media, as well as correcting colour, red eyes, or the occasional unflattering photo capture. For large events, the services of a number of photographers may be necessary to cover the myriad goings-on at the event. The services of a reputable photographer can make or break the successful after-promotion of the event — because no one wants to see photographs that are blurry, poorly-lit or that amputate the heads from key speakers or honored attendees.

Floor Plan

When moving a lot of people through an event, knowledge of the venue floor space is crucial to proper planning. When a large number of guests require table accommodations for dining, attending classroom lectures, or perusing multiple vendors on display, floor space is taken up by furnishings, requiring adequate traffic zones to accommodate guests moving throughout the selections.

Location of electrical outlets, essential for lighting, computers, sound equipment and running vendor refrigerators will determine the location of display booths, ticket counters, and food carts. Stages require a lot of room, as do dance floors and areas determined for lecture seating. Product display booths may be joined together by means of backdrop curtain units used to define display spaces, and the widespread use of computers requires access to Internet capabilities.

Event guests themselves require space. The venue must comply with local codes, which establishes the number of bodies that can safely fill the venue, while making room for all the accompanying accoutrements that make the event a success. Live bands require space for the setup of instruments, the placing of speakers, and the positioning of related sound equipment, electrically driven. Furthermore, caterers will require food preparation areas, places to store needful plates, silverware and glassware, and areas for servers to congregate. Not to be overlooked are the facilities for after-meal plates to be washed, and garbage to be gathered for disposal.

Bar service areas necessitate storage for ice, space for guests to place their orders, and facilities to store liquors, mixes, glasses and garnishments. Display props also take up valuable floor footage, such as signage easels, urns and large floral displays. Placement of information booths and security stations, storage for gifts and give-aways, set-ups for concert back-stage areas and spaces to contain a queue of devoted fans for celebrity autographs are but a few of the many uses of floor space a floor plan helps to plan and define.

Speakers

Speakers are very important for some event types. The function of speakers at an event is to draw in guests who would like to take part in a live session with an expert on topics relating to the event itself. For the company event, the speaker may zero in on effective management, human relations, financial matters or future trends. For an educator event, topics may include the parent-teacher relationship, spurring creativity among students, or dealing with bullying. Speakers' bureaus provide a plethora of talent to make any event a memorable one by providing professional speakers versed in a wide variety of topics. Speakers for an event may likewise be obtained from club membership rosters, from among company ranks, or from among politicians, entertainers, sports figures or other newsworthy individuals.

A speaker must have the confidence to address a large group, share memorable experiences, offer sage advice, or instruct in established or new technologies. Speakers must also be capable of fulfilling the requirements of speaking for a specified amount of time, having suitable material and presentation skills to keep an audience engaged. The selection of a speaker or multiple speakers should be in alignment with the overall theme of the event, while meeting the expectations of the attending audience. The cost to engage a professional speaker relies typically on the fees they demand for their speaking performance. This might include lodging and airfare, if the speaker must arrive from a distance beyond comfortable driving range, or if time constraints are prohibitive.

Speakers performing at an event may provide instructional materials in conjunction with their field of expertise; including CDs, DVDs, books, software, and informational literature or signed photographs. If the speaker is a well-known entertainer or sports figure, the opportunity for guests to participate in special get-togethers, book signings, and autograph sessions are not uncommon. The appeal for guests to privately interact with celebrities through special parties, back-stage gatherings, or high-profile seating arrangements are the substance of promotional contests, often requiring payment of additional fees to the speaker for these extra demands.

Food

Food is a component of successful business and private events. The event theme plays an important role in helping to determine the menu to be presented at the event. While chicken cordon bleu may satisfy guests attending a semi-formal affair, the same dish presented amid tuxedo–clad gentlemen and women dripping with diamonds simply doesn't work.

Likewise, an event centered on a tropical theme seems amiss with chicken cordon bleu gracing guests' plates, where there should be lobster, prawns, fish, steamed mussels and fresh tropical fruits.

The cost of such meals plays an important role in the selection of food for the event. It is proven easier to offer a more selective, pricier meal when tickets are purchased by event guests prior to the event, that caterers may prepare the food in accordance with guests' selections. Events whose meals are an included part of the event are often less costly when choosing from the caterer's established menu offerings, than when the caterer must meet unfamiliar menu selections demanded by the event planning committee. Food has a natural place amid the bustle and excitement of events honoring achievements, celebrating anniversaries, or kick-starting a new business. Food also brings together event goers in a more relaxed atmosphere conducive to conversation, establishing broader social networks, or reuniting old friends. The offer of a meal is a necessity for events that center on industry training, where long hours of classroom lectures and immobility tend to make guests sleepy. Food refreshes the mind, cheers the soul, and makes a long afternoon easier to tackle, with a forward anticipation of evening socializing and camaraderie with newly developed friends.

At less-formal affairs, such as company picnics held in the open air, a barbeque is a natural choice. Likewise, the event which has as it's goal to present a number of industry-related products and services is very well served by the offering of a diversity of vended foods. The use of food vendors allows event guests to pay for their own meals in accordance with their appetites and their budgets. Vendors also offer the benefit of additional income for offsetting the costs of the event itself, typically requiring a deposit to reserve a space at the event well in advance, and contractually providing a portion of their profits to be paid to event sponsors.

DJs

DJs and the use of them for events has increased over time, not only for the ability to bring professional quality music to an event, but also to allow playing music which might not be suitable or available with a live band. DJs often provide their own sound equipment, and traditionally have an inventory of music at hand, as well as the ability to play music provided by event coordinators or guests.

The role of the DJ is to be a showman, an initiator, an entertainer, and an accomplished speaker. DJs bring with them a style of interaction with the audience that may range from a soothing crooner to an outrageous clown. Rarely does a DJ offer variations of personality that makes one DJ suitable for all audiences.

For events whose theme and guests revolve around a middle-age demography, the DJ must necessarily comprehend the music of the era, the popularity of the music, and provide materials from which to fulfill requests common to the age. Likewise, a young crowd may avoid the dance floor with the advent of pop-40's music, only making a stride toward the vacant space when music blares in rap, rock or techno-beats. DJs typically are paid in accordance for the time they are engaged, a price that should include accompanying audio speakers, music and the DJ's personal sound equipment to perform their services as contracted. The DJ requires space to set up his equipment and ready his musical inventory, which generally is little space at all, making the DJ a preference for smaller venues as well as smaller budgets.

Choose a DJ with a reputation for excellence, as the deposit required to book a DJ is typically non-refundable. Should the DJ fail to perform to expectations, the equipment fail, or the DJ suffer illness or injury which prevents them from fulfilling their contract, include the stipulations for payment in the contract. Inquire as to whether the DJ has in place the means for providing a backup to meet their obligations to event sponsors, in case they cannot perform as contracted.

Transportation

Transportation to and from an event is within each guests' responsibilities, but there are instances where providing transportation is a necessity. When individuals must arrive at a specific time for particular ceremonies, provided transportation reduces the possibilities of a late arrival, or worse, a no-show. Transportation also might be necessary to bring in a guest speaker to an event destination that lies beyond the speaker's comfortable driving range. Transportation is likewise a must for covering very large events by key event organizers or security personnel. The lowly golf cart has found popularity for this purpose beyond the rolling hills of the golf course, adapting easily to indoor spaces.

Transportation arrangements also prove necessary for the delivery of products for displays, and materials for the construction of special areas. Any event detail requiring the arrival of goods, materials or people to the event, that is necessary to the event, must be weighed and considered. Transportation of guests arriving at a transportation hub, such as an airport or train terminal, require transportation to their hotel rooms, or the event venue itself. Often, transportation is provided by hotel venues in which the guests will be staying as a service to hotel guests. If transportation is not a provided service, the assurances of public transportation, availability of taxis or proximity to rental car depots must be investigated.

Allotment of funds to cover transportation costs can be tricky to pin down. If rental vehicles are provided as a means of transporting key personnel to and from the event venue, the costs of fuel must also be included in the equation. Further, rental of items such as golf carts may require a fee for delivery of the carts, and trucks rented for the delivery of products and display materials must include the salaries of drivers retained to perform these functions. Transportation costs can easily blossom without a definitive and structured plan. Taking the time to make a considerate approach to transportation needs in event planning is an absolute must. This requires anticipation of every detail, forecasting needs for transportation in order to arrive at a calculable and attainable event budget.

Gifts

Gift-giving has grown in popularity as the means to promote an event, to sell tickets, to increase attendance, or to award attendees. It is not uncommon for gifts to be presented as the centerpiece of company holiday parties, and has become a popular way for businesses to promote products by supplying tax-deductible gift packages to celebrities or other spotlight personalities attending special events.

The giving of gifts can be made an integral part of the event itself. Gift-giving is a method for honoring accomplishments, serving as a thank-you, given as favors commemorating an event, or provided to promote new products and services. In preparation, gifts must be purchased or pledged, stored until the event, wrapped accordingly, labeled for distribution, and secured in a place to be drawn from during the event, safe from loss, damage or vandalism. Trophies, plaques, commemorative mugs, T-shirts, caps, printed totes and pens are among the most common gifts given to event attendees. Table centerpieces and floral arrangements might also be included in the list of gifts. For events that revolve around a particular company, jackets, tropical trips, tickets to amusement parks or gift certificates to popular stores might be in order. For companies introducing a new product line, samples might likewise be attractively packaged and distributed that guests may have a personal opportunity to try out the newly introduced products.

Certain events, particularly those relying on ticket sales, may offer extravagant vacations, boats, automobiles or even homes as an integral part of the promotional campaign used to entice individuals to purchase an event ticket. In this vein are also found the back-stage pass and invitations to celebrity band after-parties.

Tickets to an event may also be treated as gifts themselves; a popular promotional method employed by radio and television stations, local newspapers and related businesses to stir up excitement for an event. Opportunities to receive salon services and makeovers, special sessions with golf pros or even driving a race car are but a few of the exciting ways gifts can play a part in event promotion.

Furniture

The need for furniture is often the farthest thing from one's mind when planning for an event, yet plays an important part in assuring the event will proceed with the greatest comfort for event guests. Furniture necessary for an event will be dependent upon the event itself. Seating for dining, counters for bar services, tables for booths, backdrops for display spaces and desks for ticket agents are just a few of an event's furnishing needs.

It is necessary to determine what furnishings will be required for the event, what the selected event venue will supply, and what must be rented from outside sources. Also to be considered is the manpower needed to set up seating and banquet tables for hundreds of guests, who will provide serving carts, bar counters, display backdrops and booth tables. For a very large event, the need for necessary furnishings can be enormous; requiring careful pre-planning to assure the event is not marred by inadequate furnishings.

Many venues provide furniture for seating the established number of occupants their building may legally allow, or they may only include a limited number of seats or tables, and leave the remainder to be rented from an outside source. It is imperative to discuss options for seating, tables, and for meeting the needs of bar and table services prior to selecting the venue itself, for such things often play an important role in venue selection. Also to be ascertained is the manpower needed to deliver, set up and tear down the furniture for return to rental sources. Many furniture rental companies will avail event sponsors the people to deliver, set up and tear down their furnishings for an event, while others deal simply with furniture rental. Consideration should likewise be given to the costs for hired manpower, delivery trucks, and deposits that may be required when selecting a furniture rental company.

Special furniture, such as operator chairs for a salon show, plush chairs to accommodate special guests of honour, or stage furnishings for plays or skits may be borrowed for the event. These might be found from pieces already owned by members of the event committee, the furniture stock of a friendly business, or even found at a second-hand store. Simply ask for furnishings to meet the need and appearance desired and make sure to clarify the function for which they will be used.

Limousines

For those special individuals being honored at an event, there is nothing like a limousine to make them feel appreciated, appear important, and most of all, to arrive at the event on time. Professional limousine services can provide a plethora of limousine packages from one car to many, suitable for a few passengers or a large party. Limousines are typically leased, with driver included, on an hourly basis. A limousine is a specially altered luxury automobile suggesting wealth, importance, and above all, offering vast amounts of room. This makes the limousine a perfect vehicle for transporting several members of band, honored guests replete with spouses and friends, or popular celebrities invited to attend an event. The limousine shouts importance upon arrival, causing heads to turn and curious eyes to attempt a peek at the special passengers that ride behind the mask of dark, smoked glass. Limousines likewise offer extreme privacy, capable of hiding intimate moments and clothing changes from intruding or prying eyes.

Leasing a limousine is perfect for delivering key executives to an event, showcasing a winner of a promotional contest, or giving weight to a political candidate. A limousine should also be considered for transport of company founders, giving special treatment to investors, or collecting visiting dignitaries. Limousines can be offered with simple fare, such as plush, curved couches that face each other to provide a transportable "living room". They can also be stocked with the makings for cocktails or the cork popping of champagne toasts, complete with bar and working refrigerator. Stretch Limousines may be capable of holding the entirety of a football team, while yet other specialty limos have even been installed with working whirlpool tubs.

A limousine imparts a magical quality that only a limousine can deliver. Short of arriving in a private jet, a limousine instantly conveys a special message about it's passengers, providing a memorable touch for guests honored at a special event.

Sound

Sound equipment for an event is especially important when guest speakers will be delivering talks to event guests, announcements must be heard over the din of a large crowd, or the event is highlighted by a live band or DJ. While bands and DJs often bring with them the necessary equipment to ply their trade, very large rooms, outdoor events and events with a variety of activity occurring simultaneously within a number of separate areas often requires the introduction of additional audio speakers dispersed throughout event areas. Guest speakers will require the help of a sound system to be heard among a large audience, and with the advent of headphone microphones and wireless connections, such devices save countless dollars and time in setting-up. Still, the sound system cannot deliver audio information or music without the key elements of wiring, electricity, soundboards or CD players to provide the instruments of producing sound, or regulating their tone or volume.

The common complaints registered by guests at events are either the insufficiency of adequate sound volume, or the imposing excess of such. A professional sound technician or an enthusiastic audiophile found within company ranks or on membership rosters can prove an asset for regulating sound delivered to the comfort of most event guests. Sound is especially important for classroom and lecture portions of an event, with the assurance that feedback squeals and irritating static or sound shorts occur with diminished frequency, or not at all.

Bands and DJs also require adequate sound equipment to deliver soothing music, danceable beats and entertaining patter to keep audiences engaged, announce selections, or solicit requests. Not only do the rooms within which these entertainers perform need to be acoustically designed to dampen hollow echoing; additional speakers at strategic locations perform to diminish this effect. Monitors are necessary for guest speakers as well, giving performers the ability to hear their own delivery, thereby adjusting their vocalizations for clarity. Information desks and established security stations provide maximal performance when outfitted with microphones and connection into the sound system to announce lost items or persons, event schedules, or to command attention of event personnel to specific stations. The sound system is the voice of the event, offering encouragement, building excitement, or bringing attention to matters at hand, necessities for event coordination and visiting guests' enjoyment.

Fireworks

Fireworks can add precisely the right exclamation point to a fantastic evening. Fireworks have the ability to be potentially dangerous, particularly in the hands of amateurs, so individuals with extensive experience working with fireworks are a must for safely handling this unique addition to an event. Individuals or companies who provide professional fireworks displays offer a wide selection of effects, dependent upon having a large enough area to safely conduct the display. Insurance should be a primary concern, and the designation of responsibility in case of an accident should be carefully considered when choosing to include a fireworks display at an event held in a public venue. If fireworks are legal within an area, and insurance costs are not prohibitive, planning an event with fireworks can be a tedious process. The professional fireworks artisan proves to be invaluable for suggesting a display format to suit event coordinators, to fit within time restrictions, and to provide the safest possible experience for event guests. Contracts with a firework display service should also spell out the circumstances under which the display can be safely conducted, particularly those conditions that might precipitate a cancellation due to weather.

Fireworks would be considered a necessity for the celebration of a national holiday, such as the Fourth of July, but can also add just the right punctuation to a grand opening, a new product introduction, or a landmark anniversary. Fireworks lend themselves best to warm weather and outdoor venues, and by their nature, must be performed in the evening for optimal effect. Indoor fireworks displays are not without favor, however. Increasingly, the use of animated stands and displays of revolving sparklers, flaming pots and lasers set to music are within the realm of the fireworks artisan. It bears repeating the importance of checking the zoning rules and locals laws governing the use of fireworks for an event, and the assurance of insurance to meet the possibility of a potentially devastating accident.

Lighting

Lighting is an essential element for establishing the mood of an event, as well as providing illumination for displays and highlighting decorations. There also exists the need for lighting controls such as dimmers, to impart a mood for intimate evening affairs such as dances or speaker presentations.

Spotlights may be a necessary part of an event spectacular, bringing attention to a speaker, a product demonstration, or a stage performance. Guests should be able to move about with comfort, able to see the people and furniture in the spaces in which they are enjoying event participation.

Classic lighting for formal and informal banquets is found in the warming glow of candlelight, sprinkled across the gleaming tableware and muted shadows of a well-dressed banquet room. Practical lighting should optimally illuminate hallways and other traffic areas of guest ingress and egress. Parking areas need to be well-lit, as a deterrent to pedestrian accidents and opportunistic criminals. Lighting in kitchen areas should be brightly-lit, to facilitating delivery of attractive dishes and for the performance of meal preparations.

Bar counters work best when backlit and illuminated from a light source emanating from under the serving counter. Meeting rooms and lecture areas require a bright enough light to facilitate note taking and reading presentation materials. Twinkle lights are an invaluable aid for demarking the perimeter of stage edges amid the glare of spotlights in darkened rooms for fashion shows or other events where a misstep could result in a nasty fall. They also lend an air of starlight when draped as a canopy suspended amid the soaring spaces of a cavernous dance floor.

Can lights may be incorporated above booth displays, aimed at will to spotlight vendor offerings. As a means of attracting attention to specific areas of very large rooms, well-placed lights can essentially carve up the space into the appearance of multiple, smaller areas. Lighting serves to facilitate the attractive appearance of formally dressed women and tuxedo-clad men, who otherwise might appear garish beneath conspicuous fluorescent lighting. Lighting provides safety, encourages relaxation, flatters skin tones and draws attention to achievement. The proper selection and placement of lighting is perhaps the most important decorating element of all.

Bands

Bands provide entertainment to your event guests. Accommodating the needs of a band requires space for a stage, sound and lighting, as well as time for the band to set up and tear down equipment before and after the event. Bands generally perform specific music in accordance with their personal interests and talents, so choose a band that performs music suitable for the event occasion.

A band brings with them a sense of celebrity, and for a special event, a well-known band can provide quite a boost to promotion and advertising simply by recognition and the fan base their presence will attract. Cover bands, or those local musicians not necessarily known for cutting recording deals or enjoying wide celebrity, are also a popular choice when danceable music that stretches across a wide variety of ages and musical genres is desired. A celebrity band anticipates treatment in accordance with their celebrity, demanding thousands of dollars to perform. These typically bring with them stage hands to attend to the many details of setup and tear down, arriving in extravagant motor home busses accompanied by large trucks filled to the brim with lighting, special effects equipment, booms, microphones, speaker stacks and soundboards. Such a band requires vast amounts of electricity to power the specialized equipment that produces their signature sound, and may require additional spaces for dressing rooms, pre-concert gathering, and post-concert after-parties.

The cover band is an altogether different animal, with band members generally toting in the equipment for a gig themselves, setting up just prior to their performance, and personally involved in the break-down when their engagement concludes. The cover band also charges much less, making them a preferred alternative to a DJ for more formal events.

Expect to book a well-known band months in advance, for tight schedules and extensive travel are the bane of the celebrity band. A cover band, however, may be obtained on relatively short notice. Always have in place an alternative backup plan when engaging entertainers for an important event, in case the band cannot fulfill the contract set forth between event sponsors and musicians.

Internet Access

The myriad facets of an event often necessitate a requirement for Internet connectivity. Connection to the Internet is an increasingly popular method for providing the means to verify ticket sales and reservations. Vendors require Internet connections to share product information, order product through company sites, download paperwork, or for signing up interested consumers. Others use the Internet to provide special services, or for running presentation software. The introduction of wireless Internet service, or WiFi has made it a staple requirement for consumers who have incorporated computer technology into their daily lives. As a platform for doing business, a computer is an valuable tool containing much of the needed information for plying any number of trades. For the event planner, the assurances of internet connectivity goes hand-in-hand with providing the needful services necessary for conducting an event with efficiency. Accessible WiFi provides fingertip access to files, schedules, responsible parties, phone numbers, addresses and the plethora of information needed to carry out an event. A majority of hotels offer WiFi as a standard service to visiting guests, only requiring the presence of a properly outfitted laptop computer to pick up the

WiFi signal. As computer use becomes progressively relevant to the nature of business, so too, businesses such as fast food restaurants and coffee shops seek to attract customers who willingly tap into offered WiFi connections. When considering a venue to host an event sure to require Internet access by a large number of vendors, the major hotel venue presents an excellent choice. Event personnel can take advantage of any one of a number of free platforms to access the information they need by establishing no more than a link and a password to a shared website.

In more remote locations, Internet connections may be offered at an additional cost to contracted venue services. These might require arrangements be made in advance for accessing a WiFi connection, or to provide connection through more conventional wired Internet access methods.

Information Desk

Information desks are the communications hubs for conferences and other business events. At extremely large gatherings, particularly those events that encompass large spaces and a large variety of vendors or exhibits, the stationing of an information desk helps smooth the way through the confusion that can occur at an event. An information desk can also be the place to provide wheelchairs for the infirmed, strollers for small children, and a station for the Lost and Found. Locating the information desk is key to its successful use and application. Stationed near the main entry, where guests come in, is the most logical choice. Extremely large events may benefit from the placement of more than one information desk, particularly in those instances where there are multiple gates for entry to the event

The information desk is the communications hub for an event by way of knowing where specific displays can be found, giving event guests directions to restrooms, and acting as a place to lodge complaints. The information desk can also provide instruction to vendors for setting up, direct delivery crews to a particular location, or apprise event goers of scheduled meeting times.

The personnel manning the information desk should have the means for communicating with Security personnel, possess a roster of scheduled events, and be a source for providing maps of the event floor, if the event is spread over a wide area. Likewise, the information desk should be secure in it's own right, in the event items are delivered there that have been found on the event floor. The information desk will have it's share of lost persons to be found, found persons to be claimed, and cranky event guests with a complaint to air. Personnel chosen to man the information desk should be patient, helpful, and above all, knowledgeable of the event and what can be found where. Provision of two-way radios or cell phones and a list of numbers for key personnel are a necessity for conveying or obtaining information, and reducing guest stresses associated with maneuvering unfamiliar spaces.

Lodging

Lodging of guests for events that last for two or more days. When an event requires guests to travel some distance to another location, they may require lodging in hotels close to the event, with easy access to supporting eateries or public transportation.

Hotels are typically receptive to booking event groups by offering room discounts, particularly when such an event promises to fill a large number of vacant rooms. Larger hotels commonly offer adequate amenities to service the event itself, and may likewise offer excellent discounts on meeting spaces when attending guests reserve rooms in certain capacities. The provision of lodging for guest speakers is generally included in their speaking contract, or reimbursed as part of their fee. Special invited guests, or guests of honour are less likely to forego an event if lodging is already paid for them, or they at least have the assurance of a room already reserved in their name. Event sponsors may likewise require lodging during an event for convenient access to pre-event meetings, dinners with celebrities, engaging with speakers or entertaining special guests. Lodging may also be necessary for key event personnel, allowing them to be handily available for meeting the call of event set-up, dealing with momentary confusions and attending last-minute details of event direction.

Reserved lodging typically requires a minimal standard of rooms to realize discounts in room rates. Reserved lodging also requires record of a responsible individual or company credit card information specifically to honour subsequent invoicing of unfilled or unpaid rooms. By requiring response to invitations or the purchase of tickets for guests attending the event, this helps to offset the risks of reserving a large number of rooms, which may or may not be used. For financial protection, however, most hotels offer a 24-hour respite for canceling reservations, that event sponsors are not held responsible to paying for rooms that not used. This likewise opens rooms for the hotel to offer to non-event travelers at higher standard rates.

Accommodation

Every event will certainly have an individual or two that requires special accommodations. This can be in the form of specially-prepared foods for those with dietary restrictions to making room for wheelchairs and walkers. Accommodating guide dogs, providing seating for special assistants, assuring the service of milk-less, peanut-less, or MSG-less foods to those with allergies that can cause life-threatening health problems all fall within the realm of accommodations. If the selected venue is located in a multi-story building, access for the wheelchair bound, the infirmed, or the morbidly obese necessitates access to elevators to deliver guests to the event destination. Additionally, seating at banquet tables becomes quite crowded if inadequate space is not given to allow for wheelchairs to take a place at the table.

The occasional guest dealing with excessive weight might need the accommodation of a larger, stronger chair. A blind individual might require a space under the table during a meal to allow for a guide dog to curl up, away from the intruding feet of other guests. The Vegetarian will appreciate the offering of meatless dishes, and those involved in weight-loss programs or other menu restrictions will be more inclined to attend if food choices present favorable options. Additionally, restroom doors should be roomy enough to allow access by wheelchair, as well as providing at least one stall large enough to accommodate the wheelchair-bound and those with walkers. Those guests with visual or hearing impairments might be better served by seating placement closer to audio speakers or the event stage to enhance their experience. Accommodation of guest limitations is best served prior to the event, by means of a query written into invitations regarding special guest needs. Typically, the option of menu choices to meet the needs of the Vegan or those with food allergies will help facilitate preparations, which will ease the uncomfortable circumstances associated with such needs, and prepare the way for all guests to enjoy the event in it's entirety.

Parking

Parking to accommodate guests at an event is an essential part of event preparation. Not only does adequate parking serve to avoid making unhappy guests, it increases event attendance by guests who might otherwise stay away if they must walk a long distance. Inadequate parking can force guests into being exposed to adverse weather, or concerned over issues of safety, particularly when attending those events held during evening hours.

Consider the parking necessary to accommodate guests who will commute to the event as opposed to those that may be lodging in the vicinity. Venue selection will bear heavily on the amount of parking available to accommodate a large number of attendees, bearing in mind if the anticipated arrival of guests will occur all at one time, or as a constant ingress and egress of cars and people.

Event Venues

Event venues are locations where events are taking place. The definition of an event venue can be as endless as the stars in the sky; thus, when selecting the perfect venue for that important event, the sky is the limit. An event venue in simple terms is the location hosting an event. Some venues are more common than others, but there is a never-ending list when creativity comes into play.

Hotels

Hotels are a popular choice when it comes to event planning and the search for a perfect event location. An event venue providing accessibility to virtually every budget is the hotel. Hotels can easily be found on nearly every corner in larger cities and somewhere within or near other small towns. Finding a hotel is easy and makes the distance to be traveled by guests an issue of the past.

Hotels come in various shapes, sizes and number of stars awarded. Regardless of budget and taste there is a hotel to fit the bill. Up-scale, top-of-the-line, five-star hotels often feature on-site catering and meeting facilities ubiquitous with professionalism and formal elegance. Picturesque ballrooms and meeting rooms give guests the grandiose feeling leaving a good impression on the more affluent crowd. Mainstream hotels, perhaps with 3-4 stars, are none-the-less effective in achieving an overall ambience to event attendees. This caliber of hotels offers nearly the same facilities; however, on a much more affordable budget.

Events encompassing two or more days may find comfort in the choice of hotel with its on-site availability for lodging guests at their leisure. The convenience of a hotel for multi-day events is nearly unmatched providing guests with downtime crucial to refueling for the next day's agenda. For traveling guests, housing the event at a hotel makes planning and attending easier for them. Eliminating the amount of work on their part, ultimately allows them to have a better outlook with less stress going into the planned event.

Hotels lend themselves quite nicely to corporate affairs for the business crowd. Such professional events well suited for the hotel venue include award dinners, promotions of products, launching of new lines, partnership appreciation, client appreciation, staff appreciation, lectures, seminars and many other endeavors. This venue speaks volumes to the business crowd with its accessibility to technology and vast array of amenities. Easy to find with parking on location, hotels provide a great venue for the professionals of the business world. Amenities found within a hotel can make the affair flow smoothly with built-in necessities. Hotels feature staffs well prepared in handling business meetings and can be of assistance during any unforeseen issues should they arise. The facility is designed to meet the needs of all guests, including private events. Hotels are a familiar venue for good reason. They have in-demand technology capabilities, adequate space and ease of location while promoting productivity with networking, full functional computer labs.

Conference Centers

Conference centers are the perfect event venue to organize huge and professional conferences and seminars. When planning an event to include a medium to large number of attendees, a conference center provides a great choice. Events focusing on large groups and/or large groups that will break down into smaller units during the course of the program will find comfort in the facilities offered by a conference center. With on-site accessibility to technology capability, a conference center limits the amount of equipment necessary to transport by the event host. Some conference centers require an additional charge for the use of their equipment, while the access to the capability is included in the base fee. Some upgraded features may include use of a wireless microphone or an outside line entirely available for credit card transactions-very important in events where products can be purchased on-site.

Conference center facilities include various sized rooms with the option of renting one space or several spaces at a time. The rooms needed simply depend upon the number of expected guests or space needed for displays. With a variety of room options, there is the prospect of deeming one area for dining for maximum convenience of those in attendance. For events lasting more than one day/night, a conference center is a good choice due to its accessibility to hotels. Overnight accommodations are near or sometimes within a conference center and generally offer a discount to attendees or a group rate when combined with admission to the event. Many conference centers are an extension of a hotel providing everything on a guests' list when traveling and enjoying an important occasion.

Using a conference center is a great idea when planning graduation parties, receptions, farewell or welcome aboard parties, business transactions, monthly or quarterly company meetings as well as high school or family reunions. Conference centers may bring to mind destinations for conferencing with colleagues, which is a fundamental event occurring in conference centers worldwide.

With large well-equipped banquet rooms and medium-sized event rooms, conference centers add a personal touch with the option of small group discussions reassembling in the main gathering area to share and discuss ideas and/or conclusions. Keep conference centers in mind when planning professional events that require spatial and technological needs within a comfortable setting.

Meeting Rooms

Meeting rooms are the event venues of choice to host a business meeting. Probably the first venue that comes to mind is the meeting room. A convenient and tested venue, the meeting room is a great choice among business professionals and individuals alike. Even the term, meeting room, exudes a certain type of stern, important character often associated with corporations or other businesses.

Meeting rooms are great venues to interview future employees. The location and access are convenient for job seekers to attend. A waiting area and interviewing space can be separate to ensure privacy is maintained. Open forums can be conducted in meeting rooms. This can provide a platform for locals to make their voices heard in matters extending beyond their own city limits. Awards ceremonies that entail a quaint guest list and agenda are distinguished events often held in meeting rooms. Graduation and birthday parties often find themselves celebrating in this setting. With many meeting rooms being located within a hotel, an overnight stay is within arm's reach. What a wonderful way to kick-off a special birthday with an intimate party followed by a restful retreat? Kids and grown-ups alike will marvel in the ease and affordability of renting a meeting room for personal events. Businesses will savor the on-site technology demanded by nearly every function in the corporate world. Wireless Internet, networking, projectors, screens and sometimes in-house computer labs make meeting rooms a productive venue for business professionals everywhere.

The term meeting room can also be a generic term sometimes interchangeable with the term ballroom. The ballroom is one of the larger meeting rooms available. Those in attendance to events held in meeting rooms may harbor a sense of familiarity and security in the traditional setting this venue affords. With a staff on hand, meeting rooms take advantage of built-in bonuses and limit the need for outside assistance.

Restaurants

Restaurants are the best choice as venue for some events. With a numerous selection and cuisine to choose from, restaurants often find themselves a well-matched venue for many elite, exclusive and intimate events. Restaurants share something with their guests in their appreciation for great taste. Whether local fare or ethnic cuisine is your preference, there is most definitely a restaurant to whet your expectations and appetite.

Several restaurants feature meeting or gathering rooms for larger than usual party sizes. These rooms can be reserved in advance for planning the perfect event. Some restaurants even offer more than one room, allowing guests to be housed into separate dining quarters close by without trimming down the final number on the guest list.

Banquets honoring high achievement in business, social or personal life are quite common as restaurant events. Award dinners for employees show true appreciation in this casual or formal after-hours atmosphere. Restaurants are frequented by individuals due to their nature of routinely presenting a comfortable familiarity to even formal affairs. This familiarity often promotes a friendliness and inviting climate allowing guests to look forward to attending such an event.

Business ventures wishing to mingle and leave an at-home feeling with clients may find this setting a superior fit. Depending upon the menu, the seating capacity at restaurants can range from 60 for a seated luncheon to 250 in a reception style gala. Networking events are well received at restaurants with the leisurely laid-back position offered by this event venue. Many public and private parties function well by commencing within a large adjacent room that does not lose any of the amenities included in fine dining.

Determining the time of the event will aid in planning which dishes, drinks and/or desserts are to be featured. Guests do not expect or demand to be fed a four-course meal, but should not feel famished upon departure. Brunches make a very inviting option for guests and often afford convenience for everyone involved. Brunches and lunches alike lend themselves to a more casual attitude whereas dinners and cocktail parties have a touch of frill or formality not associated with the morning or noon crowd. Dinners may project a more serious outlook than the cocktail party allowing clients to ease into a more comfortable business

Convention Centers

Convention centers are the perfect venues to organize an host large events in a professional manner. Hosting a large event encompassing several vendors, businesses and/or groups demand the need for a spacious venue. A convention center is a great option delivering adequate space for large guest lists without sacrificing convenience. Most convention centers are within walking distance to hotels making overnight accommodations convenient for guests.

Convention centers are equipped with all the necessary tools typically needed when making formal presentations, including technology capability and catering. Within a convention center, there most often is ample floor space to comfortably contain several thousand individuals. This layout presents a great tool in accommodating audiences for large entertainment functions, as well as display space including plentiful walking room for attendees.

Events common to the convention center venue include corporate conferences, professional lectures, trade shows, concerts, recitals and conventions in general. Such events can be public or private in nature because convention centers are open to the general public, no membership required. Within the convention center, attendees can be contained within the main gathering area where more than a thousand guests can mingle and/or interact if desired.

Bringing branches or departments from large organizations together for an annual conference or meeting is a popular event for businesses and fits well within the parameters of the convention center. Trade shows highlighting specific industries fare quite well in this capacity with enough space to showcase tools, talents and/or products for guests. Within this setting, demonstrations are easy to perform giving guests a hands-on review of products. Other noteworthy events include seminars for districts or state-wide employees focusing on current hot topics or essential elements to aid in the production of employees and businesses. Convention centers have the capacity to house trade shows for remodeling, gardening, education, automobiles, crafts/hobbies, brand name accessories as well as job fairs. They provide a great avenue for those seeking employment. Job fairs comfortably fit into the scene of a convention center giving job hunters access to a wealth of opportunities inside one building. The convenience of identifying several potential employers under one roof is an enormous asset.

Outdoor

Outdoor event venues are important for both private and corporate events. When not even inclement weather can put a damper on event planning, the outdoor venue makes its voice heard. With a variety of options, choosing an outdoor venue has never been easier or more enjoyable.

Outdoor venues offer so many features unmatched in celebrating indoors. First, the sense of feeling carefree with room to spare is exquisite in comparison to jamming 200 people into a 100 person capacity room. Outdoor venues offer breathing room and then some.

Many options are available for outdoor venues including zoos, botanical gardens, parks, conservatories, camps, retreats and lawns. The location can be as simple or as sophisticated as desired. Several zoos even provide the use of LCD projectors, screens, sound, available AV technologists and wireless Internet connectivity. Perhaps a zoo is a great way to plan an informal day with colleagues followed by checking out the animals.

Some outdoor venues nudge people into possibly trying something new or something they never dreamed they would pursue. Horseback riding, rock climbing, canoeing, white water rafting and paint ball are just a few ideas for team-building events that might propel your business in the right direction.

Camps and retreats can offer scenic quarters for guests in mountain lodges, prairie ranches, and lake or ocean-side comforts. Cabins provide a fun-filled accommodation for family reunions or birthday parties. Close family and friends may reminisce on special memories while adding a few more to the collection.

When planning an outdoor event, it is vital to have a back-up plan, specifically a back-up location in mind. Some outdoor venues include a shelter away from the elements should inclement weather strike. Another important item for consideration in outdoor event planning is the use of technology and any extra equipment. Check to see if the site provides it or accommodates it. In most cases, outdoor venues will increase the amount of equipment brought to the site by the host/hostess of the event.

Theatres

Theatres are the perfect venues to host events that should express glamour and classiness. Setting yourself and your business apart from the crowd is easy to do when hosting an event at a theater. Decidedly a tasteful and classic landmark in most cities, theatres are beautiful backgrounds in creating memories of events lasting a lifetime.

Possibly overlooked as a venue option, a theater is a quintessential element is attracting a more affluent client or crowd where inclement weather has virtually zero interference. The elegance associated with a theater setting incorporates this attitude into the minds of everyone in attendance.

Perfect for ceremonies, lectures, presentations, awards and product launches theatres provide the technological needs and artistic imaging synonymous with modern entertainment. Guests will relish in the scenery and luxurious nature of the facilities. Even a trip to the restroom is a little more elegant than normal.

With a large and comfortable seating capacity, theatres appeal to the higher class of guests and larger numbered crowds as well. The tasteful decor of most theatres sends a message of class and style in a deep, meaningful way. There is no hint or subtlety in the formal elegance exuded by the theater venue. If making a statement of taste, high class and elegance is at the top of the list the theater is the ideal event venue. Some theatres have restaurants or cocktail lounges on-site adding a special touch by easing catering needs. Many theatres are created with a main stage area plus additional smaller stages. The multiple stages create an added element of entertainment resources for events. Theatres are great venues for fundraisers, corporate events, luncheons, social hours, recitals, performances, movie premiers and countless parties.

Theatres come in all shapes and sizes with the most common being found in larger cities; however, smaller cities and towns often have their own scaled down versions adding a personal touch which is commonplace in close-knit communities. With the capacity to project onto large screens, superb stage lighting and sound along with areas designated for catering, theatres should not be overlooked when planning that important event.

Stadiums

Stadiums are perfect venues to host events with a huge number of participants. A unique and unmatched creative ingenious idea for a venue location is a stadium. With obvious parking and seating capacities nearly unmatched, stadiums are great venues for tremendous events. Corporate or company picnics are very popular events held at stadiums. Corporate picnics often find themselves perplexed with the venue dilemma of finding a large enough facility along with a great atmosphere that is somewhat more impressive than a simple day at the park. Upon entering the stadium, guests can be greeted with scoreboard messages adding a personal and unique touch to this event that is destined to hit the ball out of the park with everyone in attendance. Being constructed in the heart of cities, stadiums tend to surround themselves with many attractions adding convenience for everyone. If an NFL stadium is selected for the important event, a locker room tour may be a great activity to liven up the crowd. Conducting business in a box seat or boardroom overlooking the field is a great way to kick of the day, which concludes with a little turf action.

Perhaps appearing informal, this setting is sure to please a diverse group captivating them with a big hearted and spirited day that has a more personal touch than frequently linked with business events.

Other noteworthy stadiums are former Olympic arenas. Perhaps re-living the games or role-playing your favourite dream into reality on this grand platform would show a corporation's ability to focus on human relations and not all dollars and cents. Conducting an important business transaction at a stadium may be an impressive way to mix business with pleasure in a higher scale version of the traditional golf outing.

Business can flex their corporate muscles while improving public relations when opting for a stadium event. A company softball game, flag football game, lacrosse match, soccer scrimmage or kick ball tournament are all great activities for bringing a little fun personal touch to the work place without losing respect. Employees and clients alike would savor the opportunity to conduct a celebration or transaction in such an opportunistic, popular venue as a stadium.

Yachts

Yachts are special event venues that are not fitting to any event. Growing in popularity, but often overlooked is the event venue of the yacht. Meeting the needs of a wide variety of event styles and purposes, the yacht speaks elegance and professionalism with a unique twist from more traditional event sites. Embarking on a yacht will leave guests with an experience they will not forget and cherish for years to come. If a dramatic impression or deep appreciation is the nature of the event, a yacht is a perfect choice. Yachts accommodate a large number of guests, while being pleasurable for smaller, more intimate groups as well. Some wonderful events for yachts include client appreciation/awards dinners, product launches/promotions, family or high school reunions, anniversaries, important business deals, bar/bat mitzvahs, graduations, bridal/baby showers, as well as engagement parties or weddings. Social and corporate activities alike, function well aboard the not-so-common event venue known as the yacht.

Most companies house several ships to meet the demands of a variety of seating/passenger capacities. A yacht can hold anywhere from 150-500 guests comfortably. Some consist of on-site catering and music/DJ or entertainment. However, outside vendors for such items are generally welcomed but must provide their own staff and supplies.

Weather is not typically a cause for concern when planning a yacht outing. In rare severe inclement weather conditions, the yacht will not sail and the event must be rescheduled; however, the ship sails rain or shine with covered areas making planning a little easier.

The backdrop of a beautiful skyline, day or night, exudes a special feeling upon every guest in attendance. Setting sail on a yacht can be the perfect way to say thank you, farewell or welcome to a special person or company. What better way to capture the attention of a new client or audience?

Onboard the yacht, businesses may delight in the diverse options offering brunch, lunch, dinner or cocktails to meet nearly every catering need. The added touch of a gentle breeze as you set sail skims the spirits of guests and is completed with a spectacular sunset or star-filled sky depending on the time frame selected for the event.

Rooftops

Rooftops are exciting venues to organize exclusive events. Breathtaking, magical, spectacular views are just a few of the mentions of appreciation heard when electing to entertain that special, important event on a rooftop. With panoramic views of cities, harbors, mountains or ballparks, rooftop venues are popping up on landmark facades all across the country. These spaces provide a unique private oasis for escaping the stresses of life below and rising up to the occasion.

Technology is no stranger to these areas either with outdoor plasma screens decorating the many hangouts located in the heart of many major cities. Fire pits, multiple bars, private cabanas and rooftop speakeasies are just a few eccentric accessories planted in these rooftop gardens of entertainment. There is no denying the unbeatable views afforded by this venue with groups attending corporate outings or private events seeking comfort in the warm hospitality of this laid-back setting. State-of-the-art DJs and entertainment are sometimes part of the package.

The unique identity of the rooftop venue is a great option for sports fans and enthusiasts with the capacity to seat many in stadium-style bleachers or more comfortably in over-sized extra wide stadium seats. Watching a game from this spot gives a memory like no other. The relaxed lounge feeling from a rooftop event exudes an allure to the business, social and family crowds. A business cocktail party held at sunset makes a strong statement, as any rooftop event would. The one-of-a-kind identity of the rooftop projects style without sacrificing space. Most venues are 3,000 square feet or larger and easily accommodate parties from 70 to 300 people.

An unmatched city perspective gained may incorporate itself into an unparalleled understanding or agreement of a business venture. Whatever the nature of the event, a rooftop venue is a chic atmosphere offering sprawling views and leaving guests with an empowering impression that can last a lifetime.

Ballrooms

Ballrooms are spectacular and often historic event venues. Considering a gala, dance or concert? Consider the ballroom. Dating back to prominent eras of history, the ballroom offers a look back into the past of luxury and pleasure at its prime. Ballrooms have the capacity to hold enormous numbers of guests with a dance floor area perfect for the obvious as well as displays and presentations. The warm character of many ballrooms are felt throughout the walls of the building in which it resides. Some ballrooms are within conference centers or hotels, while others are remodeled and repurposed old facades with genuine impeccable character. There is a vintage charm original to each ballroom of this nature.

High ceilings and elegance are only two traits awarded to ballrooms. Created with understated class, the ballroom is an enchanting arena combining an updated twist from historical times with contemporary technological amenities.

Wedding receptions fare well in this setting, but romantic endeavors are not the only option for this venue. Kick-off bashes, welcoming parties, appreciation dinners and dances as well as business social hours are in full swing across ballrooms nationwide.

On-site and valet parking are generally standard along with optional on-site or outside catering services. Ballrooms can be set-up to focus on entertainment, mingling, dancing, dining or a wide variety of combinations somewhere in between. Ballrooms within hotels make overnight stays more convenient for out-of-town guests. The facility is generally equipped with all necessary staff to take charge of any grand ballroom event. Dance or theatre groups may use the space for performances or competitions. There is adequate space for stage and audience seating available simultaneously. Auctions, fundraisers and concerts are great ideas for ballroom venue events. Seminars are fully function in the ballroom venue with the option of additional break out spaces if needed.

Gardens

Gardens are event venues that are often used for private events, but these event locations are also perfect to host certain business events. A romantic event, family affair or corporate activity can easily be configured on the grounds of a garden. Gardens are wonderful, whimsical backdrops to many spectacular events on small or large scales. Inclement weather is always a possibility with gardens, but most offer a haven from the rain with on-site indoor spaces as a great back-up plan. Getting in touch with nature has always been a tried and true measure for connecting and de-stressing-what better way to discuss an important product/decision, celebrate a special moment or honour those making a difference?

In the fairer months of the year, a cozy bridal or baby shower would be well spent at a garden. The fairy-tale atmosphere could make any girl feel like a princess or treasured storybook character, while the peaceful tranquility of flowers and plants may leave any expectant mother recharged and optimistic about delivery day. Businesses might enjoy a change-of-pace in the setting offered by a garden. Meeting rooms are sometimes available inside the main building of the garden, with outdoor spaces set-up for scheduled events. A product launch might be well received at a garden with guests leaving with 'product seeds' to plant out in the world. Birthday parties, luncheons and reunions are other great events well suited for the garden venue. Sprawling many acres, some gardens offer multiple spaces to facilitate larger functions as well. Within a city, it is sometimes reassuring to attend an event at a garden to remind oneself of life beyond the concrete jungle. Gardens take the cares of city life and momentarily set them aside to revisit the true beauty of this world.

Tea parties, buffets and picnic-style menus are featured dining cuisine at many gardens. These formats lend themselves quite nicely to the atmosphere encompassing the entire grounds at a garden.

Universities

Universities provide more than an academic setting for students and professors, it bestows large meeting facilities throughout its campus. Gymnasiums, libraries, centers for the arts, amphitheaters, college greens, lecture halls and classrooms or departments provide convenient settings for special events. Concerts can be held in the arts centers, college greens or gymnasiums to promote a singer, group or product as well as attract a specific crowd of clientele. Entertainment is easy to enjoy at a university since nearly every space available includes hook-ups and equipment needed for projecting, listening, viewing and/or participating in lively events.

Businesses and corporations may look to the university setting for appealing to a more youthful or academic crowd. Universities include ample parking providing space for various forms of transportation from cars to buses. The atmosphere of the university may bring back memories of college days and be a great place to reunite or reconnect with classmates and friends. It may be a popular avenue for highlighting special achievements or goals attained by individuals, teams and businesses. Many areas within a university provide workspace sufficient for lectures, small-group discussions and/or activities and many business related formats. Computer labs are also available enhancing productivity.

Special planning concerns include consideration of time of year for the event. Most universities or colleges are only available during the summer months; however, some have minimal vacancies throughout the entire calendar year.

Getting the most 'bang for your buck' is possible with the university. Small budgets with big guest lists can generally meet in the middle when choosing the university as the event venue. Multi-day or weeklong events are convenient with the use of on-site housing or dormitories. The state-of-the-art technology and design of buildings and residence halls adds a nice detail to this academic background. Camps or retreats find themselves housed quite nicely in the university setting with all the necessary amenities at your fingertips. Historical events may enjoy the progression put into action found within a university. Particular campuses may connect or emphasize aspects of a dedication, recognition or reception party.

Mansions

Mansions and villas are perfect venues to organize exclusive events in a breathtaking atmosphere. Looking for the magical setting for that spectacular grand event? Look no further than the venue of renting a mansion. Mansions can be rented in their entirety as well as by levels or rooms. The parlor and library rooms house a comfortable ambience with a secret getaway from the hustle and bustle of the dance floor in the ballroom. Perhaps the entire space of the first floor will fit the needs of the event which generally include the kitchen, backyard, garden area, ballroom, and other additional rooms all decorated with antiques to catch the flavor of the era of the mansion in its prime. The entire mansion can be rented opening its doors to guests as a luxury weekend home, per say. Some mansions contain a grand ballroom in their floor plans, which make incredible dance floors for wedding receptions, high school proms, college socials, business parties and family reunions. With dining adjacent in the next room, the convenience is similar to that of one's own home with an added touch of majestic elegance.

Noting the architecture of the particular mansion adds a nice delicate touch of charm to leave guests captivated. Other noteworthy areas within the mansion include, but are not limited to, a pavilion, tea garden, orangery, garden, greenhouse, second floor with balcony and patio. Such a historic building greets each guest with warmth and connectivity to years past. The timelessness of a mansion full of antiques and décor that is always in taste captivates the intimate setting desired for weddings and receptions, as well as intimate business retreats, meetings and celebrations.

Hosting an intimate tea party for new clients in the tearoom of a mansion signifies grace, style, class and elegance-all pleasing characteristics. Enjoying a brunch in the late morning hours or cocktail as the evening draws near an end are both breathtaking ways to make use of a mansion's greenhouse or orangery. A special gala for the utmost important clients headed up within the grand ballroom will make them feel as grand as the atmosphere experienced. A quiet, intimate book study group will feel at home in the neatly appointed mansion library overflowing with an abundance of books easily within reach.

Event Marketing

Event marketing is any action that you take to make your event known and desirable to your target audience. This includes the invitations (printed or electronic), promotions or advertisements and reminders. It also includes pre and post event surveys to better understand the interests of your attendees. Eventmanagement.com helps to make your events to a success. Event marketing, promotion and adverstising is a crucial ingredient for those. Learn everything about the Marketing of Events in the Internet and the marketing of Private Events.

Event Marketing in the Internet

Event marketing in the internet is a cheap and efficient way for the promotion of your events. Current trends in event marketing use web-based tools. Event websites can give attendees instant access to event details, travel accommodations and registration. Today's society expects immediate gratification which can be satisfied by a well-maintained event website. Most event management companies offer event marketing services including an event website, online registration and email reminders. The event website can provide testimonials from past attendees and publish a guest list of prominent people already registered for this event in order to encourage your target audience to attend. People are more likely to jump to action when they can see others have committed to the event. Another aspect of event marketing is well placed comments on social networking sites that can be linked to your website. Such posts can increase exposure to your target audience. Positive comments from others will lend credibility to your information and increase attendance to your event.

Professional event managers or event management software can help you market your event by customizing email communications to different target audiences, creating the event website, offering online registration and communication.

Event Marketing for Private Events

Event marketing for private events like birthdays, anniversaries, family reunions and weddings. Event marketing is not only for corporate events. Event marketing can benefit private events by keeping guests well informed and assisting with travel and hotel accommodations. A perfect example of a private event that can benefit greatly from marketing is the typical family reunion. In the past, reunions were promoted by word of mouth or paper invitations only with few details and poor RSVP rates. Imagine announcing the next family reunion with a website showing highlights from last year's event. The website can list the schedule of events and menu. Family members can respond online and even commit to tasks such as bringing the dessert. You can send email reminders to all attendees or just those participating in certain tasks. Proper event marketing such as this not only makes the event much more desirable to the attendees but much easier for you to manage.

Event Management Software

Event management software can be a lifesaver to anyone responsible for planning events whether it is a national conference, charity event or 50th wedding anniversary celebration. There are many different types of event management software that can be purchased or leased based on your needs. Some versions with basic management options such as online registration are even offered free online through event management websites. A full service system will allow you to manage every aspect of the event including the budget, registration, exhibits, appointments, housing, travel and email communications. These systems options can be grouped into a few main categories: Planning, Communications, Registration and Task or Program Management Most software companies allow you to purchase or lease only the tools you need for your event offering an affordable solution to planning any event large or small.

Event Planning Software

Event planning software and its planning modules are used in the conception phases in such tasks at facility management, travel and housing accommodations. Effective software will allow you to manage the event budget, create a theme and track vendors. Organization is vital to successful events and event management software allows you to keep every detail organized in one central tool.

Event Communication Software

Event communication software and its communication modules will manage invitations, online registration and event marketing.

These systems will allow you to create email templates that can be used across events or personalized to specific tasks. Having the ability to manage your email blasts by sorting attendees with different criteria will make your marketing efforts much more effective.

Event Registration Software

Event registration software is one of the most important software modules for professional event managers and planners of events that address a huge audience. The registration modules provide online registration and credit card authorization which is not only convenient for the attendees, but also an excellent resource for the event manager. Today's society demands instant gratification and is far more likely to act if they can register online and view that registration immediately instead of mailing in forms and waiting for a reply. The online registration can automate billing and ticketing of the event reducing staff needs and human error.

Task Management Software

Task or program management helps to coordinate the management of events. Gone is the day of clipboard sign up sheets. Task or program management modules allow you to schedule and execute each task of the event. Event software with appointment systems allows attendees to schedule themselves into the seminars or breakout sessions that meet their interest. It can also be used to match candidates with recruiters at job fairs. The appointment management option eliminates guesswork and allows you to plan according to the attendees' interest.

Air Show

An air show is an event at which aviators display their flying skills and the capabilities of their aircraft to spectators in aerobatics. Air shows without aerobatic displays, having only aircraft displayed parked on the ground, are called "static air shows".

Some air shows are held as a business venture or as a trade event where aircraft, avionics and other services are promoted to potential customers. Many air shows are held in support of local, national or military charities. Military air firms often organise air shows at military airfields as a public relations exercise to thank the local community, promote military careers and raise the profile of the military. Air show "seasons" vary around the world. Whereas the United States enjoys a long season that generally runs from March to November, other areas often have much shorter seasons. The

European season usually starts in late April or Early May and is usually over by mid October. The Middle East, Australia and New Zealand hold their events between January and March. However, for many acts the "off season" does not mean a period of inactivity, they use time for maintenance and practice.

The type of displays seen at an event are constrained by a number of factors, including the weather and visibility. Most aviation authorities now publish rules and guidance on minimum display heights and criteria for differing conditions. In addition to the weather, pilots and organizers must also consider local airspace restrictions. Most exhibitors will plan "full," "rolling" and "flat" display for varying weather and airspace conditions.

The types of shows vary greatly. Some are large scale military events with large flying displays and ground exhibitions while others held at small local airstrips can often feature just one or two hours of flying with just a few stalls on the ground. Air Displays can be held during day or night with the latter becoming increasingly popular. Shows don't always take place over airfields; some have been held over the grounds of stately homes or castles and over the sea at coastal resorts.

Attractions

Before the Second World War, air shows were associated with long distance air races, often lasting many days and covering thousands of miles. While the Reno Air Races keep this tradition alive, most air shows today primarily feature a series of aerial demos of short duration.

Most air shows will feature warbirds, aerobatics, and demonstrations of modern military aircraft, and many air shows offer a variety of other aeronautical attractions as well, such as wing-walking, radio-controlled aircraft, water/slurry drops from firefighting aircraft, simulated helicopter rescues and sky diving.

Specialist aerobatic aircraft have powerful piston engines, light weight and big control surfaces, making them capable of very high roll rates and accelerations. A skilled pilot will be able to climb vertically, perform very tight turns, tumble his aircraft end-over-end and perform manoeuvres during loops. Solo military jet demos, also known as tactical demo, feature one aircraft, usually a strike fighter or an advanced trainer. The demonstration focuses on the capabilities of modern aircraft used in combat operations. The display will usually demonstrate the aircraft's very short (and often very loud) takeoff rolls, fast speeds, slow approach speeds, as well as their ability to quickly make tight turns, to climb quickly, and their ability to be precisely controlled at a large range of speeds. Manoeuvres include aileron rolls, barrel rolls, hesitation rolls, Cuban-8s, tight turns, high-alpha flight, a high-speed pass, double Immelmans, and touch-and-gos. Tactical demos may include simulated bomb drops, sometimes with pyrotechnics on the ground for effect. Aircraft with special characteristics that give them unique capabilities will often display those in their demos; For example, Russian fighters with Thrust vectoring may be used to perform Pugachev's Cobra or the Kulbit, among other difficult manoeuvers that cannot be performed by other aircraft. Similarly, an F-22 pilot may hover his jet in the air with the nose pointed straight up, a Harrier or Osprey pilot may perform a vertical landing or vertical takeoff, and so on.

Safety

Air shows present some risk to spectators and aviators. Accidents occur, sometimes with a large loss of life, such as the 1988 disaster at Ramstein Air Base in Germany and the 2002 air show crash at Lviv, Ukraine. Because of these accidents, the various aviation authorities around the world have created set rules and guidance for those running and participating in air displays. Air displays are often monitored by aviation authorities to ensure safe procedures. Rules govern the distance from the crowds that aircraft must fly. These vary according to the rating of the pilot/crew, the type of aircraft and the way the aircraft is being flown. For instance, slower lighter aircraft are usually allowed closer and lower to the crowd than larger, faster types. Also, a fighter jet flying straight and level will be able to do so closer to the crowd and lower than if it were performing a roll or a loop.

Pilots can get authorisations for differing types of displays (i.e. limbo flying, basic aerobatics to unlimited aerobatics) and to differing minimum base heights above the ground. To gain such authorisations, the pilots will have to demonstrate to an examiner that they can perform to those limits without endangering themselves,.ground crew or spectators. Despite display rules and guidances, accidents have continued to happen. However, air show accidents are rare and where there is proper supervision air shows have impressive safety records. Each year, organisations such as The International Council of Air Shows and The European Airshow Council meet and discuss various subjects including air show safety where accidents are discussed and lessons learnt.

Weather

Air shows, and other big shows such as agricultural shows, on grassy land, are vulnerable to continued heavy rain waterlogging the ground, and making the cloudbase too low for flying, forcing cancellation, or the show ending early, costing much money for the show's organizers, as people and parking cars have difficulty moving about and turn the land into a morass, and the organizers may be tempted to put straw or cinders down to make movement easier, and the owner of the land cannot accept the resulting damage.

Exhibition

An exhibition, in the most general sense, is an organized presentation and display of a selection of items. In practice, exhibitions usually occur within museums, galleries and exhibition halls, and World's Fairs. Exhibitions include [whatever as in major art museums and small art galleries; interpretive exhibitions, as at natural history museums and history museums, for example; and commercial exhibitions, or trade fairs. The word "exhibition" is usually, but not always, the word used for a collection of items. Sometimes "exhibit" is synonymous with "exhibition", but "exhibit" generally refers to a single item being exhibited within an exhibition. Exhibitions may be permanent displays or temporary, but in common usage, "exhibitions" are considered temporary and usually scheduled to open and close on specific dates. While many exhibitions are shown in just one venue, some exhibitions are shown in multiple locations, such exhibitions are called travelling exhibitions.

Though exhibitions are common events, the concept of an exhibition is quite wide and encompasses many variables. Exhibitions range from an extraordinarily large event such as a World's Fair exposition to small one-artist solo shows or a display of just one item. Curators are sometimes involved as the people who select the items in an exhibition. Writers and editors are sometimes needed to write text, labels and accompanying printed material such as catalogs and books. Architects, exhibition designers, graphic designers and other designers may be needed to shape the exhibition space and give form to the editorial content.

Art Exhibitions

Art exhibitions include an array of artifacts from countless forms of human making: paintings, drawings, crafts, sculpture, video installations, sound installations, performances, interactive art, etc. Art exhibitions may focus on one artist, one group, one genre, one theme or one collection; or may be organized by curators, selected by juries, or show any artwork submitted. Fine arts exhibitions typically highlight works of art with generous space and lighting, supplying information through labels or audioguides designed to be unobtrusive to the art itself. Exhibitions may occur in series or periodically, as in the case with Biennales, triennials and quadrennials.

Interpretive Exhibitions

Interpretive exhibitions are exhibitions that require more context to explain the items being displayed. This is generally true of exhibitions devoted to scientific and historical themes, where text, dioramas, charts, maps and interactive displays may provide necessary explanation of background and concepts. Interpretive exhibitions generally require more text and more graphics than fine art exhibitions do. The topics of interpretive graphics cover a wide range including archaeology, anthropology, ethnology, history, science, technology and natural history. Examples of such exhibitions may be found at the Natural History Museum, museums of the Smithsonian Institution, the American Museum of Natural History and the Field Museum — to name a few of the largest museums of this kind.

Commercial Exhibitions

Commercial exhibitions, generally called trade fairs, trade shows or expos, are usually organized so that organizations in a specific interest or industry can showcase and demonstrate their latest products, service, study activities of rivals and examine recent trends and opportunities. Some trade fairs are open to the public, while others can only be attended by company representatives (members of the trade) and members of the press.

Art Exhibition

Art exhibitions are traditionally the space in which art objects (in the most general sense) meet an audience. The exhibit is universally understood to be for some temporary period unless, as is rarely true, it is stated to be a "permanent exhibition". In American English, they may be called "exhibit", "exposition" (the French word) or "show". In UK English, they are always called "exhibitions" or "shows", and an individual item in the show is an "exhibit". Such expositions may present pictures, drawings, video, sound, installation, performance, interactive art or sculptures by individual artists, groups of artists or collections of a specific form of art. The art works may be presented in museums, art halls, art clubs or private art galleries, or at some place the principal business of which is not the display or sale of art, such as a coffeehouse. An important distinction is noted between those exhibits where some or all of the works are for sale, normally in private art galleries, and those where they are not. Sometimes the event is organized on a specific occasion, like a birthday, anniversary or commemoration.

Types of Exhibitions

There are different kinds of art exhibitions, in particular there is a distinction between commercial and non-commercial exhibitions. Temporary museum exhibitions typically display items from the museum's own collection on a particular period, theme or topic, supplemented by loans from other collections, mostly those of other museums. They normally include no items for sale; they are distinguished from the museum's permanent displays, and most large museums set aside a space for temporary exhibitions. Exhibitions in commercial galleries are often entirely made up of items that are for sale, but may be supplemented by other items that are not. Typically, the visitor has to pay (extra on top of the basic museum entrance cost) to enter a museum exhibition, but not a commercial one in a gallery. Retrospectives look back over the work of a single artist; other common types are individual expositions or "solo shows", group expositions, or expositions on a specific theme or topic. The Biennale is a large exhibition held every two years, often intending to gather together the best of international art; there are now many of these. A travelling exhibition is another category of art exhibition.

Exhibitions of new or recent art can be juried, invitational, or open. A juried exhibition, such as the Royal Academy Summer Exhibition in London, the Chianciano Biennale at the Chianciano Museum of Art, or the Iowa Biennial, has an individual (or group) acting as judge of the submitted artworks, selecting which are to be shown. If prizes are to be awarded, the judge or panel of judges will usually select the prizewinners as well.

In an invitational exhibition, such as the Whitney Biennial, the organizer of the show asks certain artists to supply artworks and exhibits them. An open or "non-juried" exhibition, such as the Kyoto Triennial, allows anybody to enter artworks and shows them all. A type of exhibition that is usually non-juried is a mail art exhibition.

History

The art exhibition has played a crucial part in the market for new art since the 18th and 19th centuries. The Paris Salon, open to the public from 1737, rapidly became the key factor in determining the reputation, and so the price, of the French artists of the day. The Royal Academy in London, beginning in 1769, soon established a similar grip on the market, and in both countries artists put great efforts into making pictures that would be a success, often changing the direction of their style to meet popular or critical taste. The British Institution was added to the London scene in 1805, holding two annual exhibitions, one of new British art for sale, and one of loans from the collections of its aristocratic patrons. These exhibitions received lengthy and detailed reviews in the press, which were the main vehicle for the art criticism of the day. Critics as distinguished as Denis Diderot and John Ruskin held their readers attention by sharply divergent reviews of different works, praising some extravagantly and giving others the most savage put-downs they could think of. Many of the works were already sold, but success at these exhibitions was a crucial way for an artist to attract more commissions. Among important early one-off loan exhibitions of older paintings were the Art Treasures Exhibition, Manchester 1857, and the Exhibition of National Portraits in London, at what is now the Victoria and Albert Museum, held in three stages in 1866-68.

As the academic art promoted by the Paris Salon, always more rigid than London, was felt to be stifling French art, alternative exhibitions, now generally known as the Salon des Refusés ("Salon of the Refused") were held, most famously in 1863, when the government allowed them an annex to the main exhibition for a show that included Édouard Manet's *Luncheon on the Grass (Le déjeuner sur l'herbe)* and James McNeill Whistler's *Girl in White*. This began a period where exhibitions, often one-off shows, were crucial in exposing the public to new developments in art, and eventually Modern art. Important shows of this type were the Armory Show in New York City in 1913 and the London International Surrealist Exhibition in 1936.

Museums started holding large loan exhibitions of historic art in the late 19th century, as also did the Royal Academy, but the modern "blockbuster" museum exhibition, with long queues and a large illustrated catalogue, is generally agreed to have been introduced by the exhibitions of artifacts from the tomb of Tutankhamun held in several cities in the 1970s. Many exhibitions, especially in the days before good photographs were available, are important in stimulating research in art history; the exhibition held in Bruges in 1902 (poster illustrated below) had a crucial impact on the study of Early Netherlandish painting.

Preservation Issues

Although preservation issues are often disregarded in favor of other priorities during the exhibition process, they should certainly be considered so that possible damage to the collection is minimized or limited. As all objects in the library exhibition are unique and to some extent vulnerable, it is essential that they be displayed with care. Not all materials are able withstand the hardships of display, and therefore each piece needs to be assessed carefully to determine its ability to withstand the rigors of an exhibition. In particular, when exhibited items are archival artifacts or paper-based objects, preservation considerations need be emphasized because damage and change in such materials is cumulative and irreversible. Two trusted sources – the National Information Standard Organization's *Environmental Conditions for Exhibiting Library and Archival Materials,* and the British Library's *Guidance for Exhibiting Library and Archive Materials* – have established indispensable criteria to help curtail the deleterious effects of exhibitions on library and archival materials. These criteria may be divided into five main preservation categories: Environmental concerns of the exhibition space; Length of the exhibition; Individual cases; Display methods used on individual objects; and Security.

Environmental Concerns of the Exhibition Space

The main concerns of exhibition environments include light, relative humidity, and temperature.

Light

Light wavelength, intensity, and duration contribute collectively to the rate of material degradation in exhibitions. The intensity of visible light in the display space should be low enough to avoid object deterioration, but bright enough for viewing. A patron's tolerance of low level illumination can be aided by reducing ambient light levels to a level lower than that falling on the exhibit. Visible light levels should be maintained at between 50 lux and 100 lux depending on the light sensitivity of objects. An items level of toleration will depend on the inks or pigments being exposed and the duration of the exhibition time. A maximum exhibition length should initially be determined for each exhibited item based on its light sensitivity, anticipated light level, and its cumulative past and projected exhibition exposure.

Light levels need to be measured when the exhibition is prepared. UV light meters will check radiation levels in an exhibit space, and data event loggers help determine visible light levels over an extended period of time. Blue wool standards cards can also be utilized to predict the extent to which materials will be damaged during exhibits. UV radiation must be eliminated to the extent it is physically possible; it is recommended that light with a wavelength below 400 nm (ultraviolet radiation) be limited to no more than 75 microwatts per lumen at 10 to 100 lux.

Furthermore, exposure to natural light is undesirable because of its intensity and high UV content. When such exposure is unavoidable, preventative measures must be taken to control UV radiation, including the use of blinds, shades, curtains, UV filtering films, and UV-filtering panels in windows or cases. Artificial light sources are safer options for exhibition. Among these sources, incandescent lamps are most suitable because they emit little or no UV radiation. Fluorescent lamps, common in most institutions, may be used only when they produce a low UV output and when covered with plastic sleeves before exhibition. Though tungsten-halogen lamps are currently a favourite artificial lighting source, they still give off significant amounts of UV radiation; use these only with special UV filters and dimmers. Lights should be lowered or turned off completely when visitors are not in the exhibition space.

Relative Humidity (RH)

The exhibition space's relative humidity (RH) should be set to an value between 35% and 50%. The maximum acceptable variation should be 5% on either side of this range. Seasonal changes of 5% are also allowed. The control of relative humidity is especially critical for vellum and parchment materials, which are extremely sensitive to changes in relative humidity and may contract violently and unevenly if displayed in too dry an environment.

Temperature

For preservation purposes, cooler temperatures are always recommended. The temperature of the display space should not exceed 72 °F. A lower temperature of down to 50 °F can be considered safe for a majority of objects.

The maximum acceptable variation in this range is 5 °F, meaning that the temperature should not go above 77 °F and below 45 °F. As temperature and relative humidity are interdependent, temperature should be reasonably constant so that relative humidity can be maintained as well. Controlling the environment with 24-hour air conditioning and dehumidification is the most effective way of protecting an exhibition from serious fluctuations.

Length of the Exhibition

One factor that influences how well materials will fare in an exhibition is the length of the show. The longer an item is exposed to harmful environmental conditions, the more likely that it will experience deterioration. Many museums and libraries have permanent exhibitions, and installed exhibitions have the potential to be on the view without any changes for years. Damage from a long exhibition is usually caused by light.

The degree of deterioration is different for each respective object. For paper-based items, the suggested maximum length of time that they should be on display is three months per year, or 42 kilolux hours of light per year – whichever comes first. An exhibition log report, including records of the length of the exhibition time and the light level of the display, may prevent objects from being exhibited too frequently. Displayed items need to be inspected regularly for evidence of damage or change. It is recommended that high-quality facsimiles of especially delicate or fragile materials be displayed in lieu of originals for longer exhibitions.

6

Event Marketing

While marketing an event, there are a few key tactics and methods that can be employed to ensure that the event gains the maximum response and also that event is managed in the minimum cost possible. Event marketing has been a concept that has only recently been pioneered in India. But, though new, the concept has taken off very well with the Indian consumers who are evolving rapidly.

Some of the tactics and methods are listed below. Following them can ensure a cost effective implementation of the event marketing.

Event Marketing Hint 1: If the event is meant to market a certain product, then it is necessary to ensure that the purchase decision-maker attends the event. It is important to get the message across to the target audience and therefore enough research about the profile of the attendees is important to be able to communicate effectively to them about the product. It is important that least 50-60% of the people attending the event are targets of the product to be promoted.

Event Marketing Hint 2: It is also important to evaluate the value-added benefits that the venue or the trade show organizer makes available to your business. Make sure you find out if they allow access to the attendee mailing list so you can implement a pre-mailing process in order to promote your one-day trade show special, as well as the location of your booth.

Make sure you get participant contact information before the event as well as after. Other value-added benefits that can be expected from the show organizer include: being included in participant email distributions promoting the event, as well as an advertisement in the event show guide.

Event Marketing Hint 3: Before the event is undertaken, the cost effectiveness of promoting the product through the event should be questioned by asking yourself event qualifying questions around the "who" instead of the "how many"

Event Marketing Hint 4: The giveaways at the event should be relevant to the business being promoted through the event. And make sure you don't give something away for free just for the heck of it.

Event Marketing Hint 5: The location chosen for the event is perhaps the most important aspect. Make sure you don't purchase a cheap booth at a popular exhibition because there are strong chances that no one will be visiting you, since your booth will be tucked away hidden from all eyes. The most ideal locations in any exhibition areas are found at the entryway to the event and near the pathway to the food stations and restrooms.

Announcing Events

Why make sure that those you know do know about your event, and keep them informed with printed materials?

Announcing an event can range from very simple for a small party to an onerous task for a larger seminar event. Each has its method of informing attendees. The first thing that comes to mind for an event is the invitation.

I rarely get party invitations through the mail these days but I do get them by email. The chance of getting my response is actually higher through the use of print media. It seems like I am being treated as a special person when I get a mailed invitation. There are other ways, of course, that you can use print media to gain attention and attendees for your events.

If you are offering door prizes or free items to the first one hundred attendees, you are more likely to get a larger audience. In this case, you will want to not only have word-of-mouth advertising but also printed ads in the news media, or events listings in the news calendar page. If you want a large enough audience, you will need to choose a variety of ways to get people's attention. Do not just use email; combine it with print ads, and invitations.

Print media is not the cheapest way to inform others about an event, but it is longer lasting than electronic media, it takes more effort and thought to throw out an invitation received in the mail than it does to hit the delete key on your computer.

Plan for the Event or Flounder

Rather than being there to eat the food and drink the drinks, planning before attending an event will change your view.

Have you ever attended an event and seen all the people gravitating towards the food and the drinks? That is the first thing people seem to go for. Well, it is natural, especially if you are there alone and do not know anyone. It seems that food and drink are there for comfort. It is really difficult to talk to anyone with a mouthful, so if you can, stay away from the food, but certainly go and get a drink. You can still give your pitch with a drink in hand.

Take a look at your calendar before you head off to one of these events. You will need to know from memory when you are free for a follow-up appointment. This is part of the preparation you need to do before getting there. Then you can make a date and know there is no conflict with other items on your agenda. Nothing is worse than setting an appointment and finding out that you already have scheduled someone else in that time slot. It may seem like a good excuse for a follow up, but it usually does not bode well with a potential client.

You do not want to partake of any conversation that is whining about some guy that can never get anything straight. Just remember that you are at the event for one purpose and one purpose alone-it is not to eat and drink-it is to gain new business relationships and maybe cement some of the existing ones you have. The more visible you are and the more prepared you are, then the more likely someone will want to talk to you. You should also plan on how to get into private conversations without barging in and losing the flow of information.

Have you ever gone to an event and not worn the correct attire? Part of planning an event (seeing who will be attending) is to also research the nature of the event. Does the weather have an effect on who attends? Does the required dress have an effect on where it is held? Who will be leading the event and how are they regarded? What attitude does the event portray? It all comes down to knowing your audience and researching the event before you attend.

Super Lead Generation Event

One of the biggest boosts giving your company a barrage of new business is planning and hosting a Super Lead Generation Event. Unlike ads, squeeze pages or teleseminars—the targeted prospects get to see and meet you in person. If you're good, this is an immense credibility builder. And will lead to an incredible amount of new business.

If people know, like and trust you—it's much faster for them to become customers and a source of continued revenue. Probably for many years. And watching you in action can instantly establish that trust and position you as a leading expert in their eyes. Imagine your new leads buying your books, CDs or coaching program instead of buying from your competitors. Calculate the lifetime value each new lead is worth that will pay for your event many times over. And entertain the word-of-mouth advertising you get as they make referrals.

Here are the Top 10 Tips that will make this happen:

1) Booking the meeting room. If you were hosting a no-cost event, you'd want to save money on the room. Don't book a larger room than necessary. It's better to have a standing room only event than one where people see empty seats.

   You may decide to skip the refreshments. Coffee, tea, and pastries are added costs you may not want to incur. Besides this creates more distractions for your message.

2) Marketing the event. You've got to shout it from the rooftops. Mention your event on your website, e-zine, database, coaching calls, and even the local newspaper. Don't be conservative. Host a free teleseminar or advertise on local radio. Send a press release to online and offline media sources. Mention door prizes. Get noticed.

   Incorporate some type of capturing device to monitor the number of probable guests. This will aid in selecting the room size, number of seats and seating arrangement.

3) Guarding the registration. Collect business cards and contact details from all attendees. Ask if they would like to sign the guest book. These names become a valuable resource for you for future promotions. Beware of con artists who want access to your guest list or who are soliciting your leads for their deal.

4) Incorporating music. There's something about upbeat, up-tempo and driving music that electrifies the air with excitement. Music seems to draw us closer and tune our minds landing us on the same page. Best when used prior to the meeting, during breaks, and after your close. Coach or cue your sound guy on the volume levels.

5) Upbeat staff or volunteers. They are the speaker's extended eyes and ears. They should always wear smiles, offer firm handshakes and help with general questions. If the music's playing, they could show their involvement with light hand clapping. They can help guests find a seat and coordinate with hotel staff if there are unseen shortages. They should have the authority to invite hecklers to leave. And if you have a shy audience, they can help by leading them into exercises or Q & A sessions.
6) Connecting with your audience. Mixing humor, stories, case studies, mistakes and lessons learned make for a powerful and vibrant talk. It shows you are genuine and identifies you with your audience. When you empower them instead of instructing them—they'll be self-motivated to reach business breakthroughs sooner.
7) Acknowledging your scholars. This is an immense credibility builder as guests receive social proof of your system working for others. Ask for bullet style testimonials from your students. Keep this part upbeat and moving. Some have driven or flown in from other states to support you. Edify their hard work and dedication. 8) Keeping your program action oriented. Allow for audience mingling at specific intervals. Have them meet their surrounding neighbors. Encourage business card swaps.

   If you provide a workbook, have them fill it out. Keep them scribbling. Help them by saying, "On line seven jot down this answer..." And if a page in the workbook looks out-of-sync, acknowledge it, let the audience laugh, and continue on. They'll appreciate your sincere honesty.
9) Recording your event. Your recording becomes a powerful tool for your business. You can produce CDs or DVDs of your entire event to sell as a product, given away as a bonus, or passed around as a prospecting tool.

   It's important to have a professional recording so hiring a sound guy and/or camera person or crew can make you appear like an industry leader. Be sure to state your taping intentions in your marketing materials. People need to know prior to your event.
10) Being upfront with your motives. A sophisticated audience realizes you don't invest in any event without receiving

something in return. Let them know your intentions early on. Many will appreciate you candidness. It sends a message that you have nothing to hide.

Why is this Important?

Those who must leave early can make an early purchase or ask to receive more information. Those who arrive resistant to any offer can relax and enjoy your message. And the rest can decide by the end of the event. Your lead generation event can become a valuable source of future profits. And by following these tips: you can guarantee a great turnout, expand your territorial influence, and position yourself as an authority on your topic.

Trade Show Success

Trade shows can cost a lot-in time, energy and money. But there are ways to make sure your investments pay off. Start with these basics:

Are Trade Shows Right for You?

A trade show is the closest thing to a retail environment most B2B marketers will ever be in. If your products need to be seen, touched, demonstrated or otherwise experienced, trade shows can work for you. Be ready to make the most of the opportunity to meet and greet your prospects.

Are you Going to the Right Show(s)?

Each show attracts professionals who may or may not match your target audience. Before spending money on a booth, determine if it's your kind of show.

* Check with show management. They should be able to tell you who's come in the past.
* Scan the seminars and workshops to see if the topics will attract your kind of people.
* Look at who's exhibited in previous years (and who's coming back.) Talk to a few, if possible.
* Attend the show and walk the floor to get a sense of who comes, who exhibits and what draws crowds.

Will the Trade Press be There?

If yes, this may be a great time to schedule editor interviews. If there's a press room, you'll want to put your media kit in it. *Do you know what you're getting from your trade show investment?*

Build evaluation of results into your trade show programs so you know what you're getting. Leads or inquiries are a concrete measure. Lead quality is usually more important than quantity, so arm booth staff with qualifying questions. Once you know what you're getting from each show, you can focus on the most productive ones and eliminate others from your schedule. Trade show participation can be spendy. Make sure you know how to get the most out of your effort. Call in a marketing professional if you need one. It's a smart investment.

The Ins and Outs of Trade Show Exhibits

A trade show is an exhibition organised so that companies in a specific industry can showcase and demonstrate their new products and services. Some trade fairs are open to the public, while others can only be attended by company representatives (members of the trade) and members of the press. There are currently over 2500 trade shows held every year in USA alone. For people who are thinking of organizing or setting up a trade show exhibit, it is highly important that you know the factors that most affect the success of a trade show event. With a small a mount of attention, you can easily come up with a successful trade show exhibit.

Setting

Let's start with the place where the trade show exhibit will be held. The exhibit venue or the trade show space is highly reliant on the use of outstanding design for booths as well as other displays so that the organizers will be able to generate more traffic for the exhibit. For most trade show exhibit organizers, it is highly important that you are able to attract your desired customers in just under 10 seconds since the trade show exhibit viewers attention span can only last for so long.

Factors To Consider

- Location
- Theme
- Topic.

Budget Concerns

The trade show exhibit organizers must always keep in mind that some venues for a trade show may seem just too perfect for words- and this comes at a high cost. Money definitely does not grow on trees and even big multinational companies who hire trade show organizers to create a trade show exhibit for their company simply cannot afford atrocious rates, whether it be for the trade show exhibit's location, the design, or perks for visitors.

Examples of Trade Shows

- CeBIT
- ANUGA
- CEDIA Expo
- CES
- COMDEX
- E3
- Frankfurt Book Fair
- Global Gaming Expo
- HostingCon
- International Furniture Fair
- Macworld Conference & Expo
- Photokina
- Tokyo Game Show.

Displays

You can also opt to spend some extra money on the trade show exhibit displays. This is actually a good investment for you because the better your displays, the more people will be attracted to your show. When it comes to picking out a good trade show exhibit company, one should be able to effectively give a pre-show marketing for the trade show exhibit to increase traffic. According to the Center for Exhibition Industry Research, around 76% of the people who actually go would prefer to have some background information on what the theme of the trade show exhibit is and a selection of examples for the booths.

Engagement Marketing

Engagement marketing, sometimes called "experiential marketing," "event marketing", "live marketing" or "participation marketing," is a marketing strategy that directly engages consumers and invites and encourages consumers to participate in the evolution of a brand. Rather than looking at consumers as passive receivers of messages, engagement marketers believe that consumers should be actively involved in the production and co-creation of marketing programs, developing a relationship with the brand.

Multi Dimensional Communication

"Keith Ferrazzi suggests that we are moving out of the Information Age and into what he terms the Relationship Age. Emotion, empathy, and cooperation are critical to success, he says, at a time when technology and human interaction are intersecting in new ways. Trust and conversation are crucial in this new economy." Ultimately, engagement marketing attempts to connect more strongly consumers with brands by "engaging" them in a dialogue and two-way, cooperative interaction. Robert Gourley, the creative director of the participation marketing agency Mojave, sums up the idea this way; "People don't talk to brands, they talk to people."

This conversation between consumers and the products and services they consume is an attempt to take historical one dimensional communication to a new level. For decades, consumers would simply watch a commercial or look at a print ad that advertisers produced. That's one-way communication and doesn't qualify as engagement. Two dimensional (two-way) communication where consumers participate, share, and interact with a brand creates the engagement crucial to business and personal success. Two dimensional (2D) communication and engagement is where "both giver and receiver are listening to each other, interacting, learning and growing from the process." Three dimensional engagement, coined "3DE" in the book "The Relationship Age", has "not only length and width, but depth, where both giver and receiver connect to a higher power and are changed in the experience. Not just a conversation, but connection to a purpose that transforms all in the process."

The Brand Experience

The brand and the "brand experience" are directly taken to consumers through interactive channels of retail, digital and live events. Rather than wait for the consumer to find it, the brand takes itself directly to the consumer with campaigns that resonate on a personal level. This is closely related to the definition of transparent marketing. Transparent Marketing is a strategy used to personalize the content marketed to a customer by engaging them in Web 2.0 social media technologies such as blogs, live chat and product ratings. Through these web based technologies, companies are able to provide true transparency to their company and products, good or bad. In addition, they are able to build trusting and lasting relationships with their customers.

In an interview with Henry Jenkins DeFlorz Professor of Humanities and Founder and Director of the Comparative Media Studies Program at MIT, Alan Moore said...

Engagement Marketing is a very broad term, and purposefully so. At its heart, is the insight that human beings are highly social animals, and have an innate need to communicate and interact. Therefore, any engagement marketing initiative must allow for two-way flows of information and communication. We believe, people embrace what they create. And why is this important? Because in advanced economies the values of society and the individual change. At the heart of this is the key issue around identity and belonging. We have always had community. Pre-industrialization, we were tied to our communities by geography, tradition, the state and birthright. External forces shaped our identity. However, in a post-modern world we can have many selves, as we undertake a quest for self identity. This is described as Psychological Self-Determination the ability to exert control over the most important aspects of ones life, especially personal identity, which has become the source of meaning and purpose in a life no longer dictated by geography or tradition. The Community Generation, shun traditional organizations in favor of unmediated relationship to the things they care about. The Community Generation, seek and expect direct participation and influence. They possess the skills to lead, confer and discuss. These people are not watching television and have grown up in a world of search and two-way flows of communication. Going further Engagement Marketing is premised upon: transparency-interactivity-immediacy-facilitation-engagement-co-creation-collaboration-experience and trust these words define the migration form mass media to social media. The explosion of: Myspace, YouTube, Second Life and other MMORPG's, Citizen Journalism, Wicki's and Swicki's, TV formats like Pop Idol, or Jamies School Dinners, Blogs, social search, The Guinness Visitor Centre in Dublin or the Eden project in Cornwall UK, mobile games like Superstable or Twins, or, new business platforms like Spreadshirt.com all demonstrate a new socio-economic model, where engagement sits at the epicenter.

Alan Moore's Second interview with Henry Jenkins

Last Friday, I introduced my readers to Alan Moore — not the comic book creator but the brand guru — a cutting edge thinker about the ways that grassroots communities are reshaping the branding process. Moore, with Tomi T Ahonen, wrote a book called Communities

Dominate Brands. The book spells out their vision for where media is headed — towards what Moore described last time as a "connected society"— and what it means for the branding process. Here, Moore gets deeper into some of the issues which will be of particular interest to regular readers of this blog — the economic value of fans to advertisers and media producers, the issue of compensating for user-generated content, the case of Pop Idol as a global media franchise, and the concept of transmedia planning.

Early Examples of Successful Engagement Marketing Campaigns

PROMO magazine has credited Gary M. Reynolds, founder of GMR Marketing of New Berlin, Wisconsin, with being the pioneer in the practice of engagement marketing. It has cited Reynolds' formation of the Miller Band Network in 1979 as the seminal engagement marketing moment. In Japan, Tohato launched two new snacks brands, "Tyrant Habanero Burning Hell Hot" and "Satan Jorquia Bazooka Deadly Hot" in 2007 in an award-winning campaign which broke new ground in engagement marketing by combining multiplayer online gaming with advertising, on a mobile phone. Customers were encouraged to join nightly battles in a virtual game, on behalf of either snack brand, to determine the winner of the "World's Worst War". The games ran at 4 AM. The campaign was designed by Japanese ad agency Hakuhodo and won the Yellow Pencil award at the annual D&AD advertising awards ceremony where mobile ads were recognized for the first time in May 2008.

Another good example of engagement marketing is seen in the unique marketing strategy of Jones Soda. At the company website, regular customers are allowed to send in photos that will then be printed on bottles of the soda. These photos can be put on a small order of custom-made soda, or, if the photos are interesting enough, they can be put into production and used as labels for a whole production run. This strategy is effective at getting customers to co-create the product, and engaging customers with the brand.

Common Online Engagement marketing Tools

- Blogs: For engagement marketing purposes, companies can share content on their own blogs and participate as a commenter or content provider on relevant external blogs. Hosting a campaign that gives prizes to the readers of external blogs for their participation in some kind of contest is an example of an engagement marketing campaign aimed at external blogs.

- Social networking sites: Social networking sites (such as FaceBook, LinkedIn, and Twitter) are ideal for engagement marketing because they provide a way for people to interact with brands and create a two-way dialogue between customers and companies. Most companies maintain a presence on several of these sites.
- Webcasts: Differing from internal webcast meetings with a small, specific invitation list, engagement marketing online events are aimed at a much larger and public audience. They are typically available live or on-demand, which allows viewers to view content on their own schedule. Similar to conferences, audience members can ask the speakers questions and participate in polls during live webcasts.
- Email campaigns: One of the earliest online engagement marketing tools, email marketing requires target audiences to opt-in to directly receive a marketer's emails. Companies can also encourage individuals to share their messages virally, via the forwarding of emails to colleagues, friends and family.

Relationship Marketing

Relationship Marketing was first defined as a form of marketing developed from direct response marketing campaigns which emphasizes customer retention and satisfaction, rather than a dominant focus on sales transactions.

As a practice, Relationship Marketing differs from other forms of marketing in that it recognizes the long term value of customer relationships and extends communication beyond intrusive advertising and sales promotional messages.

With the growth of the internet and mobile platforms, Relationship Marketing has continued to evolve and move forward as technology opens more collaborative and social communication channels. This includes tools for managing relationships with customers that goes beyond simple demographic and customer service data. Relationship Marketing extends to include Inbound Marketing efforts, (a combination of search optimization and Strategic Content), PR, Social Media and Application Development. Relationship Marketing is a broadly recognized, widely-implemented strategy for managing and nurturing a company's interactions with clients and sales prospects. It also involves using technology to organize, synchronize business processes, (principally sales and marketing activities), and most importantly, automate those marketing and communication activities on concrete marketing sequences that could run in autopilot, (also known as marketing sequences). The overall goals are to find, attract and win new clients, nurture and retain those the company already has, entice former clients back into the fold, and reduce the costs of marketing and client service. [1] Once simply a label for a category of software tools, today, it generally denotes a company-wide business strategy embracing all client-facing departments and even beyond. When an implementation is effective, people, processes, and technology work in synergy to increase profitability, and reduce operational costs.

Development

Relationship Marketing refers to a long-term arrangement where both the buyer and seller have an interest in providing a more satisfying exchange. This approach attempts to transcend the simple purchase-exchange process with a customer to make more meaningful and richer contact by providing a more holistic, personalized purchase, and uses the experience to create stronger ties. According to Liam Alvey, relationship marketing can be applied when there are competitive product alternatives for customers to choose from; and when there is an ongoing and periodic desire for the product or service.

Fornell and Wernerfelt used the term "defensive marketing" to describe attempts to reduce customer turnover and increase customer loyalty. This customer-retention approach was contrasted with "offensive marketing" which involved obtaining new customers and increasing customers' purchase frequency. Defensive marketing focused on reducing or managing the dissatisfaction of your customers, while offensive marketing focused on "liberating" dissatisfied customers from your competition and generating new customers. There are two components to defensive marketing: increasing customer satisfaction and increasing switching barriers.

Modern consumer marketing originated in the 1960s and 1970s as companies found it more profitable to sell relatively low-value products to masses of customers. Over the decades, attempts have been made to broaden the scope of marketing, relationship marketing being one of these attempts. Arguably, customer value has been greatly enriched by these contributions. The practice of relationship marketing has been facilitated by several generations of customer relationship management software that allow tracking and analyzing of each customer's preferences, activities, tastes, likes, dislikes, and complaints. For example, an automobile manufacturer maintaining a database of when and how repeat customers buy their products, the options they choose, the way they finance the purchase etc., is in a powerful position to develop one-to-one marketing offers and product benefits. In web applications, the consumer shopping profile can be built as the person shops on the website. This information is then used to compute what can be his or her likely preferences in other categories. These predicted offerings can then be shown to the customer through cross-sell, email recommendation and other channels.

Relationship marketing has also migrated back into direct mail, allowing marketers to take advantage of the technological capabilities of digital, toner-based printing presses to produce unique, personalized pieces for each recipient. Marketers can personalize documents by any information contained in their databases, including name, address, demographics, purchase history, and dozens (or even hundreds) of other variables. The result is a printed piece that (ideally) reflects the individual needs and preferences of each recipient, increasing the relevance of the piece and increasing the response rate.

Scope

Relationship marketing has also been strongly influenced by reengineering. According to (process) reengineering theory, organizations should be structured according to complete tasks and processes rather than functions. That is, cross-functional teams should be responsible for a whole process, from beginning to end, rather than having the work go from one functional department to another. Traditional marketing is said to use the functional (or 'silo') department approach. The legacy of this can still be seen in the traditional four P's of the marketing mix. Pricing, product management, promotion, and placement. According to Gordon (1999), the marketing mix approach is too limited to provide a usable framework for assessing and developing customer relationships in many industries and should be replaced by the relationship marketing alternative model where the focus is on customers, relationships and interaction over time, rather than markets and products.

In contrast, relationship marketing is cross-functional marketing. It is organized around processes that involve all aspects of the organization. In fact, some commentators prefer to call relationship marketing "relationship management" in recognition of the fact that it involves much more than that which is normally included in marketing. Martin Christopher, Adrian Payne, and David Ballantyne at the Cranfield School of Management claim that relationship marketing has the potential to forge a new synthesis between quality management, customer service management, and marketing. They see marketing and customer service as inseparable.

Relationship marketing involves the application of the marketing philosophy to all parts of the organization. Every employee is said to be a "part-time marketer". The way Regis McKenna (1991) puts it: "Marketing is not a function, it is a way of doing business... marketing has to be all pervasive, part of everyone's job description, from the receptionist to the board of directors.

Approaches

Satisfaction

Relationship marketing relies upon the communication and acquisition of consumer requirements solely from existing customers in a mutually beneficial exchange usually involving permission for contact by the customer through an "opt-in" system. With particular relevance to customer satisfaction the relative price and quality of goods and services produced or sold through a company alongside customer service generally determine the amount of sales relative to that of competing companies. Although groups targeted through relationship marketing may be large, accuracy of communication and overall relevancy to the customer remains higher than that of direct marketing, but has less potential for generating new leads than direct marketing and is limited to Viral marketing for the acquisition of further customers.

Retention

A key principle of relationship marketing is the retention of customers through varying means and practices to ensure repeated trade from preexisting customers by satisfying requirements above those of competing companies through a mutually beneficial relationship This technique is now used as a means of counterbalancing new customers and opportunities with current and existing customers as a means of maximizing profit and counteracting the "leaky bucket theory of business" in which new customers gained in older direct marketing oriented businesses were at the expense of or coincided with the loss of older customers. This process of "churning" is less economically viable than retaining all or the majority of customers using both direct and relationship management as lead generation via new customers requires more investment.

Many companies in competing markets will redirect or allocate large amounts of resources or attention towards customer retention as in markets with increasing competition it may cost 5 times more to attract new customers than it would to retain current customers, as direct or "offensive" marketing requires much more extensive resources to cause defection from competitors. However, it is suggested that because of the extensive classic marketing theories center on means of attracting customers and creating transactions rather than maintaining them, the majority usage of direct marketing used in the past is now gradually being used more alongside relationship marketing as its importance becomes more recognizable.

It is claimed by Reichheld and Sasser that a 5% improvement in customer retention can cause an increase in profitability of between 25 and 85 percent (in terms of net present value) depending on the industry. However Carrol, P. and Reichheld, F. dispute these calculations, claiming they result from faulty cross-sectional analysis. Research by John Fleming and Jim Asplund indicates that engaged customers generate 1.7 times more revenue than normal customers, while having engaged employees and engaged customers returns a revenue gain of 3.4 times the norm. According to Buchanan and Gilles, the increased profitability associated with customer retention efforts occurs because of several factors that occur once a relationship has been established with a customer.

- The cost of acquisition occurs only at the beginning of a relationship, so the longer the relationship, the lower the amortized cost.
- Account maintenance costs decline as a percentage of total costs (or as a percentage of revenue).
- Long-term customers tend to be less inclined to switch, and also tend to be less price sensitive. This can result in stable unit sales volume and increases in dollar-sales volume.
- Long-term customers may initiate free word of mouth promotions and referrals.
- Long-term customers are more likely to purchase ancillary products and high margin supplemental products.
- Customers that stay with you tend to be satisfied with the relationship and are less likely to switch to competitors, making it difficult for competitors to enter the market or gain market share.

- Regular customers tend to be less expensive to service because they are familiar with the process, require less "education", and are consistent in their order placement.
- Increased customer retention and loyalty makes the employees' jobs easier and more satisfying. In turn, happy employees feed back into better customer satisfaction in a virtuous circle.

Relationship marketers speak of the "relationship ladder of customer loyalty". It groups types of customers according to their level of loyalty. The ladder's first rung consists of "prospects", that is, people that have not purchased yet but are likely to in the future. This is followed by the successive rungs of "customer", "client", "supporter", "advocate", and "partner". The relationship marketer's objective is to "help" customers get as high up the ladder as possible. This usually involves providing more personalized service and providing service quality that exceeds expectations at each step.

Customer retention efforts involve considerations such as the following:

1. Customer valuation-Gordon (1999) describes how to value customers and categorize them according to their financial and strategic value so that companies can decide where to invest for deeper relationships and which relationships need to be served differently or even terminated.
2. Customer retention measurement-Dawkins and Reichheld (1990) calculated a company's "customer retention rate". This is simply the percentage of customers at the beginning of the year that are still customers by the end of the year. In accordance with this statistic, an increase in retention rate from 80% to 90% is associated with a doubling of the average life of a customer relationship from 5 to 10 years. This ratio can be used to make comparisons between products, between market segments, and over time.
3. Determine reasons for defection-Look for the root causes, not mere symptoms. This involves probing for details when talking to former customers. Other techniques include the analysis of customers' complaints and competitive benchmarking.
4. Develop and implement a corrective plan-This could involve actions to improve employee practices, using benchmarking to determine best corrective practices, visible endorsement of top management, adjustments to the company's reward and

recognition systems, and the use of "recovery teams" to eliminate the causes of defections.

A technique to calculate the value to a firm of a sustained customer relationship has been developed. This calculation is typically called customer lifecycle value. Retention strategies also build barriers to customer switching. This can be done by product bundling (combining several products or services into one "package" and offering them at a single price), cross selling (selling related products to current customers), cross promotions (giving discounts or other promotional incentives to purchasers of related products), loyalty programs (giving incentives for frequent purchases), increasing switching costs (adding termination costs, such as mortgage termination fees), and integrating computer systems of multiple organizations (primarily in industrial marketing).

Many relationship marketers use a team-based approach. The rationale is that the more points of contact between the organization and customer, the stronger will be the bond, and the more secure the relationship.

Application

Relationship marketing and traditional (or transactional) marketing are not mutually exclusive and there is no need for a conflict between them. A relationship oriented marketer still has choices at the level of practice, according to the situation variables. Most firms blend the two approaches to match their portfolio of products and services. Virtually all products have a service component to them and this service component has been getting larger in recent decades.

Internal Marketing

Relationship marketing also stresses what it calls internal marketing. This refers to using a marketing orientation within the organization itself. It is claimed that many of the relationship marketing attributes like collaboration, loyalty and trust determine what "internal customers" say and do. According to this theory, every employee, team, or department in the company is simultaneously a supplier and a customer of services and products. An employee obtains a service at a point in the value chain and then provides a service to another employee further along the value chain. If internal marketing is effective, every employee will both provide and receive exceptional service from and to other employees. It also helps employees understand the significance of their roles and how their roles relate to others'.

If implemented well, it can also encourage every employee to see the process in terms of the customer's perception of value added, and the organization's strategic mission. Further it is claimed that an effective internal marketing program is a prerequisite for effective external marketing efforts. (George, W. 1990)

The Six Markets Model

Christopher, Payne and Ballantyne (1991) from Cranfield University goes further. They identify six markets which they claim are central to relationship marketing. They are: internal markets, supplier markets, recruitment markets, referral markets, influence markets, and customer markets. Referral marketing is developing and implementing a marketing plan to stimulate referrals. Although it may take months before you see the effect of referral marketing, this is often the most effective part of an overall marketing plan and the best use of resources. Marketing to suppliers is aimed at ensuring a long-term conflict-free relationship in which all parties understand each others' needs and exceed each others' expectations. Such a strategy can reduce costs and improve quality.

Influence markets involve a wide range of sub-markets including: government regulators, standards bodies, lobbyists, stockholders, bankers, venture capitalists, financial analysts, stockbrokers, consumer associations, environmental associations, and labor associations. These activities are typically carried out by the public relations department, but relationship marketers feel that marketing to all six markets is the responsibility of everyone in the organization. Each market may require its own explicit strategies and a separate marketing mix for each.

Live-in Marketing

Live-in Marketing is a term used to describe a variant of marketing and advertising in which the target consumer is allowed to sample or use a brands product in a relaxed atmosphere over a longer period of time. Much like product placement in film and television LIM was developed as a means to reach select target demographics in a non-evasive and much less garish manner than traditional advertising.

History

While LIM represents an entirely untapped avenue of marketing for both big and small brands alike it is not an all that novel an idea. With the rising popularity of experiential and event marketing in

North America and Europe, as well as the relatively high ROI in terms of advertising dollars spent on experiential marketing compared to traditional big media advertising, industry analysts see LIM as a natural progression.

Premise

LIM functions around the premise that marketing or advertising agencies go out on behalf of the brand in question and find its target demographic. From that point forward avenues such as sponsorship or direct product placement and sampling are explored. Unlike traditional event marketing, LIM suggests that end-users will sample the product or service in a comfortable and relaxed atmosphere. The idea behind this technique is that the end-user will have as positive as possible an interaction with the given brand thereby leading to word-of-mouth communication and potential future purchase. If the success of traditional event and experiential marketing is shared with LIM then it could indicate quite a lucrative and fairly low-cost means of product promotion. However, due to the fact that this means of advertising is still in its infancy more research is required to determine the true success of such campaigns. Because LIM is a fairly new concept many agencies are only now beginning to incorporate it into their advertising and marketing portfolios. The first such company to explicitly offer LIM services was Hostival Connect in late 2010. It is expected that more and more agencies will begin to sell LIM type campaigns.

Personalized Marketing

Personalized marketing (also called personalization, and sometimes called one-to-one marketing) is an extreme form of product differentiation. Whereas product differentiation tries to differentiate a product from competing ones, personalization tries to make a unique product offering for each customer.

Personalized marketing had been most practical in interactive media such as the internet. A web site can track a customer's interests and make suggestions for the future. Many sites help customers make choices by organizing information and prioritizing it based on the individual's liking. In some cases, the product itself can be customized using a configuration system. The business movement during Web 1.0 leveraged database technology for targeting products, ads, and services to specific users with particular profile attributes. The concept was supported by technologies such as BroadVision, ATG, and BEA. Amazon is a classic example of a company that performs "One to One Marketing" by offering users targeted offers and related products. Personalization is the term that later followed as a way of describing this evolution in Internet marketing. Drew Bartkiewicz and Bill Zujewski were two of the biggest industry advocates of the benefits and feasibility of One to One and later of personalization. Dr. Pehong Chen was the technologist who founded the software company, BroadVision, which enabled large companies to personalize their e-Business initiatives in the pursuit of One to One Marketing.

More recently, personalized marketing has become practical with bricks and mortar retailers. The market size, an order of magnitude greater than that of the Internet, demanded a different technological approach now available and in use. Many retailers attract customers to the physical store by offering discounted items which are automatically selected to appeal to the individual recipient. The interactivity occurs through the offer redemptions recorded by the point of sale systems, which can then update each model of the individual shopper. Personalization can be more accurate when based solely upon individual purchasing records because of the simplified and repetitive nature of some bricks and mortar retail purchasing, for example grocery superstores.

Don Peppers and Martha Rogers, in their ground breaking book on the subject, *The One to One Future* (Peppers, D. and Rogers, M. 1993) speak of managing customers rather than products, differentiating customers not just products, measuring share of customer not share of market, and developing economies of scope rather than economies of scale. They also describe personalized marketing as a four phase process: identifying potential customers; determining their needs and their lifetime value to the company; interact with customers so as to learn about them; and customize products, services, and communications to individual customers.

Some commentators (including Peppers and Rogers) use the term "one-to-one marketing" which has been misunderstood by some. Seldom is there just one individual on either side of the transaction. Buyer decision processes often involve several people, as do the marketer's efforts. However, the excellent metaphor refers to the objective of a single message source (store) "to" the single recipient (household), a technological analogy to a "mom and pop" store on a first name basis with 10 million customers. One-to-one marketing refers to marketing strategies applied directly to a specific consumer. Having the knowledge on the consumer preferences, there are suggested personalized products and promotions to each consumer. The one-to-one marketing is based in four main steps in order to fulfill its goals: Those stages are IDENTIFY; DIFFERENTIATE; INTERACT and CUSTOMIZE.

Identify: In this stage the major concern is to get to know the customers, to collect reliable data about their preferences and how their needs can be satisfy. Differentiate: To get to distinguish the customers in terms of their lifetime value, to know them by their priority in terms of their needs and segment them in more restrict groups. Interact: In this phase it is needed to know by which communication channel an in which way it is possible to optimize the contact with the client. It is needed to get the customer attention by engaging with him in ways that are known has being the ones that he enjoys the most. Customize: It is needed to personalize the product or service to the customer individually. The knowledge that a company has of a customers need to be taken into practice and the information about it has to be taken into account in order to be able to give the client exactly what he wants.

Examples of companies that have these techniques in order to persuade the clients:

- Market America;
- Dell Computers;
- Smart Cars;
- NikeID;
- Amazon.com;
- Sonae Distribuição (Modelo Continente SGPS).
- Printable Technologies.

Evangelism Marketing

Evangelism marketing is an advanced form of word of mouth marketing (WOMM) in which companies develop customers who believe so strongly in a particular product or service that they freely try to convince others to buy and use it. The customers become voluntary advocates, actively spreading the word on behalf of the company. Evangelism marketing is sometimes confused with affiliate marketing. However, while affiliate programs provide incentives in the form of money or products, evangelist customers spread their recommendations and recruit new customers out of pure belief, not for the receipt of goods or money. Rather, the goal of the customer evangelist is simply to provide benefit to other individuals.

As they act independently, evangelist customers often become key influencers. The fact that evangelists are not paid or associated with any company make their beliefs perceived by others as credible and trustworthy. Evangelism literally comes from the three words of 'bringing good news' and the marketing term justly draws from the religious sense, as consumers are literally driven by their beliefs in a product or service, which they preach in an attempt to convert others.

History

Many people believe Guy Kawasaki, the former chief evangelist of Apple Computer, to be the Father of evangelism marketing. In his books "The Art of the Start" and "How to Drive Your Competition Crazy" Kawasaki states that the driving force behind evangelism marketing is the fact that individuals simply want to make the world a better place. Evangelist customers spread their recommendations and recruit new customers out of pure belief, not for the receipt of goods or money.

Methodology

In their book, Creating Customer Evangelists: How Loyal Customers Become a Volunteer Sales Force, Ben McConnell and Jackie Huba outline six steps to creating customer evangelists:

1. Customer plus-delta (Continuously gather customer feedback)
2. Napsterize knowledge (Freely share your knowledge)
3. Build the buzz (Create intelligent word-of-mouth networks)
4. Create community (Encourage communities of customers to meet and share)
5. Make bite-size chunks (Devise specialized, smaller offerings to get customers to bite)
6. Create a cause (Focus on making the world, or your industry, better).

Kinds of Evangelism Marketing

- Evangelism marketing is applicable to any kind of product.
- Technology evangelism is the evangelism marketing of a tool.
- Platform evangelism is the evangelism marketing of the opportunity to create complementary goods for a multi-sided platform, which also involves non-marketing functions such as regulation of the platform's commercial ecosystem to maximize network effects.

Customer Communities

A strong avenue for evangelists is in the form of customer communities, which bring together groups of users of a product or service to share information and discuss common issues. Some companies assist with such events, for example General Motors' Saturn division in Tennessee organizes an annual summer picnic for thousands of customers. Another example is the Harley Owners Groups (HOGS), organized by Harley Davidson, which associate bikers locally and globally through quarterly and annual meetings held all over the world. Starbucks Corporation, the coffee company, started an online customer community in 2008 called My Starbucks Idea, designed to collect suggestions for products or services and feedback from customers. During the first year of the program, My Starbucks Idea generated 70,000 ideas through the site and approximately 50 changes based on customer suggestions were implemented.

Types of Events

The organisation of events is perhaps the primary activity of sport and recreation organisations. Workers in the sport and recreation industry, salaried and voluntary, are essentially organisers of people whether they be event directors, coaches, referees, instructors or facility supervisors. This organisation of people is manifest by what we see and call an "event". The term "event" in the sport and recreation industry usually refers to a situation where participants, facilities, equipment and other resources are co-ordinated to enable a form of sport or recreation or some allied activity to be undertaken.

The events conducted by Sport/Recreation organisations include:

- Competitive or non-competitive sport and recreation events
- Courses
- Promotional events
- Conferences
- Fundraising events.

Competitive events may range from the Olympic Games to a small local under 7's soccer match and anything in between. The scope of the events therefore depends upon the purpose of the event, the extent of participation, the facilities and equipment required, and the importance of the event in terms of community interest. The organisation of courses to assist participants learn more about playing, coaching and officiating are a fundamental part of the work carried out by recreation organisations. Such events must be carried out to ensure the continuance of the sport or recreation activity. Promotional events are not primarily organised for the benefit of the player or participant. They are organised to promote the sport or form of recreation activity to a target market with the underlying objective to increase participation. They may also have a second objective to promote the sponsor to the target market as well.

Conferences have many objectives. They may be organised gatherings of participants and/or members to carry out planning, to review progress, discuss important issues, circulate new information, select committee personnel, examine the position of the organisation and to impart new knowledge about the sport or recreation activity. Fundraising events include dinner functions, special entertainment functions, bingo or card nights, charity auctions and awards evenings.

Irrespective of the type of event, the skills required to manage an event are much the same and only the magnitude and complexity differs. Persons who are called upon to manage an event may acquire many titles but in this text for the sake of simplicity they will be called the Event Director.

Bidding for Events

The sport sector of the recreation industry abounds with events at local, regional, national and sometimes international level. It is important to consider that except for intra-club competitions, events are not "owned" by any one organisation. While the responsibility for organising a regional event may fall to one club, all clubs in the region have a stake in ensuring a successful outcome. Similarly all clubs in all regions of a nation have a vested interest in ensuring that a national championship is conducted successfully.

It is often the case that more than one club or association will desire to stage an event. Such a situation is healthy and generally leads to a striving by each bidding organisation to show that they can put on the best event. The decision as to which club will host what event is usually taken at meetings of the organisation that governs the event (the sport governing body). For example, the decision as to which club will host a regional championship will be taken by the regional association. The regional association comprises delegates and elected officials drawn from all the clubs in that region. In the case of a world championship, the decision as to which nation will host the event will be taken by the World Federation that is comprised of elected officials drawn from the member nations. It is a normal practice for any representative body, at any level, that has the responsibility to select which organisation will stage an event, to ask each and every rival organisation to supply a proposal detailing how they will organise and stage the event. This process of supplying a proposal is often referred to as the "bid process". The main purpose of the bid process is to:

- Demonstrate that the bidding organisation has the capability and resources to stage the event
- Provide additional reasons why the bidding organisation should be selected over other rival bidders. For example, these additional reasons may include:
    - Participants will have better facilities than other rival bidders
    - The event has greater financial backing than rival bids
    - Public support is more assured
    - Spectators will have better facilities
    - It's their turn.

When organisations are required to enter into a formal bid process in order to win the right to stage an event, there are two tasks. The first task is to develop a bid proposal and to submit the document to the selecting authority by the required date. In addition, it is often advantageous to attend a meeting of the selecting authority and make a formal presentation that draws out the main points or highlights of their proposal and to answer any questions that may arise. This is the second task.

Preparing the Event Proposal

The amount of detail required in the event proposal will depend on the scale and importance of the event. However event proposals generally share many common components The information that event proposals should convey includes but is not limited to the folliowing:

The Event Team

The proposal should provide information about the event management team in terms of the experience and qualifications of key team members. It is important for the reader of the proposal to feel that the event team have the capability to run the event and to be able to do what they say they will do.

If experience in staging events is limited then it is useful to mention any managerial, project management or co-ordination experience in any other field. Qualificatons of persons in the event management team may also prove useful to mention. The proposal should also describe any training that will be given to event volunteers.

Venue and Facilities

The reader of the proposal will want to know whether the venue is suitable for the event. The proposal should outline all facilities available at the venue, everything from toilets to car-parking. For indoor events, the type of surface, lighting, air-conditioning, seating, electronic equipment should be well described.

For outdoor events, the level of maintenance on turf, seating and shading for spectators, fencing, drainage and floodlighting is worthy of mention. The number of change rooms and their condition for teams/participants is always important.

There needs to be a detailed description of what would be attractive to event goers and how the venue will fully cater for the needs of the event, including performers, officials and spectators. Don't forget to include information about public transport to the venue, and car parking for those who arrive by car. If the venue has staged similar events in the past, you should make mention of this.

The Program

It is often the case that the host club or organisation has little or no say in setting the competition program when the date, or dates have been set by the sport governing body.

However, at the initial stage of bidding, the event proposal may suggest a competiton program in terms of the number of days, and the start and finish times each day. It is important for decision makers to know how many hours a day the venue is available. It is worthwhile to consider that the program shold also include cermonial events with visiting dignitaries who may make speeches or present awards, and also possibly entertainment events that may start or finish the program or fill any gaps.

The Budget

The club or organisation bidding for the event should draft a budget of probable income and expenditure. It is important that such a budget is realistic, and does not show a loss.

The club or organisation that wins the bid may be entitled to an amount of funding from the sport governing body to alleviate certain costs that will likely be incurred. However, there is also an expectancy that the host club or organisation will have an opportunity to make money through the canteen, bar, fundraising raffles and merchandising. These forms of income should be reflected in the budget in the event proposal.

The Purpose of an Event Proposal

The document may be viewed by many different potential stakeholders in the event. The table below provides examples of how an event proposal may be used by such stakeholders.

Stakeholder	*Need for the proposal*
A National Sports Organisation (NSO) Example: Athletics Australia Inc.	A NSO may receive requests from more than one organisation wishing to organise a National Championship. The NSO must therefore decide which organisation has the right to organise the event. Each state may be asked to submit a proposal to the NSO outlining how they will organise the event and how much it will cost. Based upon submitted proposals the NSO will make a choice of which organisation will host the event.
A sponsorExample: Telstra Corporation	Sponsors will view the proposal to gain an understanding of the scale and importance of the event, the potential exposure to their target markets to be gained and the relative strengths and weaknesses of forming a partnership with the event organisers. Sponsors will use this information to make decisions about whether to sponsor the event or not, and if so to put a value on the event as a form of promotion.
Government Example: A city council	The event proposal may be used as the basis of an application for funding to government agencies. They are often interested in supplying public funds to assist organisations to bid and stage major events. Governments are keen to attract events as they are viewed as a mechanism for attracting "sport tourists" who will provide increased revenues to local businesses, prestige to a city or region and have an impact on the development of a sport or recreation in there area of jurisdiction.

The Event Director

Managing an event is like managing a business, and like all businesses there needs to be someone who is the ultimate decision maker. In the case of an event, the final executive authority is usually referred to as the "Event Director". The role is complex and demanding even when events are small-scale. The primary role of the Event Director is to organise and mobilise considerable human resources such as participants, officials, administrators and helpers. They are a focal point for communication, internally and externally, and need to be contactable in and out of office hours, and over an extended period that may be many months. Managing people can be a burdensome responsibility and it is important that anyone undertaking the role of Event Director has the capability and personality to deal effectively with people in often-difficult circumstances. The ability to remain calm is perhaps a necessary prerequisite for an Event Director!

Structure of an Event management Team

The work involved in planning, organising and conducting a major event can be sufficiently great to require the employment of a team of people. It may require people to be involved on a full-time, part-time, contractor, casual and voluntary basis over a considerable period of time..

The organisation chart below indicates the magnitude and diversity of the team needed to run a major sporting event such as a National or State Championships. Smaller events will obviously require a much smaller team, and individuals in the team may be able to take on more than one role. The example organisation chart above has "departments" for Programme, Venue, Equipment, Promotions, Officials, Hospitality and Merchandising. The number of departments is arbitrary and depends on the size and complexity of the event and, importantly, on the ideas of the Organising Committee.

Furthermore, with small modifications, the same organisation structure could be applicable to running a different type of event such as a conference. An important aspect of the above model is that each department has a co-ordinator. As exceptionally important people in the event management team, they should be identified and recruited as early as possible. Co-ordinators should be a part of the organising committee and collectively they will share in decision making processes with the Event Director. The selection of co-ordinators is usually on the basis of knowledge or expertise and sometimes because only one person volunteers for the task. Whether co-ordinators have expertise or not, Event Directors need to appreciate that sport and recreation depends very considerably on the input of voluntary persons. Therefore systems should be put in place to recognise the contribution of volunteers and to provide non-monetary rewards. In consultation and close co-operation, the Event Director should develop and/provide a job description for each department head.

Financing the Event

The table below provides common sources of event revenue. Some differences exist between organisations that run events for profit motives and those that are not-for-profit oriented. Government grants are seldom achievable by for-profit enterprises. Small scale events run by not-for-profit organisations are likely to be funded by participant fees. Larger scale events, whether run by for-profit or not-for-profit enterprises will likely need substantial support through commercial sponsorship. In many cases, fees paid by people who spectate can be a worthwhile source of income.

Table: *Categories of Event Revenue*

Government Grants	Government grants to assist with the running of events are not easy to obtain. To be successful, applicant organisations need to demonstrate that the event has strategic regional importance. For example it may increase overseas tourists to the region.
Sponsorship	Despite the prevalence of event sponsorship in the sport and recreation marketplace is increasing, many organisations have great difficulty in achieving a significant amount of sponsorship. Competition between sport and recreation organisations for sponsorship is intense. Organisations need to be very professional in their approach to sponsorship and to be able to offer sponsoring companies outstanding value in promotional services. Event Directors need to exercise some realism and caution in relying to heavily on sponsorship.
Merchandising Sales	The term merchandising applies to the sale of a range of products that may be strongly identified with the event or the organisation hosting the event. A common example of merchandising is the production and sale of T-shirts, polo shirts, caps and other forms of clothing that are screen printed or embroidered with a design

Contd...

	or trademark of the event. Participants tend to purchase such articles for their commemorative value. Other typical forms of merchandise include glassware, pens, dish cloths, drink bottles and badges. Merchandising may be a form of income suitable for events that have larger numbers of either players or participants.
Participant Fees	The charging of fees to participate in the event is perhaps the most common form of event revenue. Sport and recreation events are a service provided and it is reasonable to suggest therefore that all basic costs of the event should be covered by participant fees. These "basics" include the hire of the venue, provision of appropriate equipment and the administration of the event.Sponsorship and government funding, if it can be achieved, allows the organisation of the event to go beyond the basics. The event budget should be set so that if sponsorship and/or government funding is not forthcoming the event does not have to be canceled.
Raffles	It is common to find that recreation organisations employ "on-the-day" fundraising strategies. The most common example is the raffle and a small amount of income can be achieved this way. Whereas it is difficult to achieve cash sponsorships, it is easier to obtain goods from sponsors which can be raffled.Event Directors should identify and research legislation in their own state/nation that pertains to raffles and other similar forms of fundraising. Raffles are often regulated by governments because of the potential for fraud and misrepresentation.
Spectator Fees	In some cases, events are sufficiently popular and entertaining to attract paying spectators. However it can be difficult to obtain money from spectators in circumstances where there no restriction of access(for example an outdoor event with no perimeter fence). If this is the case it may be better to make off-street parking for a fee.

7

Event Management of Corporate Events

Event management of business and corporate events is the essential activity of event managers and event agencies. While the objectives of corporate events can vary from Educational or Promotional to Ceremonial, the underlying goal of all corporate events is to create a positive image in the eyes of the target audience. One way to ensure a corporate event proceeds flawlessly is to hire a professional event management company. The role of the event management company is to take the stress off of you by managing the infinite number of decisions that go along with any corporate event.

Event Manager for Corporate Events

Event Managers manage the theme, location, marketing, entertainment and catering for the event. Online promotion and registration is another important benefit offered by most professional event managers. Online registration is not only a convenience for the attendees, but also a valuable tool that allows you to manage and track the event much easier.

Event management services can include virtually every detail of the event to your specifications and budget. A professional event management company can make your event less stressful and more successful.

Conference Management and Planning

Conference management and planning includes several key components:

Location

Conferences are held around the world in small and large cities. The venues range from Meeting Rooms in small hotels to large Convention Halls.

Cost

During the tough economic times, many companies are scaling back their conferences and some are even cancelling them altogether. The money crunch is sending many companies to smaller cities that offer cheaper rates. Some universities are hosting academic conferences on their own Campuses rather than hosting them at Conference Halls. Smaller colleges are taking advantage of the facilities at the larger universities in their area to save on cost.

Proximity to most of the Possible Attendees

A gathering of researchers from southern schools in the United States is not likely to be held in London. This just drives up the cost for the attendees and the planners.

The Accommodations Needed

Even if a school has an excellent conference hall, if there are not enough hotels in town for all of the attendees, it does no make sense to hold it there. While many attendees would be willing to drive from several miles to attend, many would not.

The Conference Room at the Venue

This may seem like a small detail to anyone who has never been involved in conference planning, but the conference room is very important. If you are going to make a presentation on a large screen, having the screen and a way to project those images available in the room is huge selling point in conference management. Many will pay extra just for the convenience of not having to lug their own Screen and Projector. The Acoustics and the Seating Arrangements also factor in to the room set up.

Types of Conferences

There are as many types of conferences as there are venues. While all of the conference types share some similarities, there are some differences: Here are some examples:

Academic Conferences

These can be held for two main reasons. University scientists hold them to announce research results. There is also a “call for papers” where newly published information is presented to a group. Many conference planning companies specialize in these types of gatherings for colleges and universities. These companies help in publishing the research or paper, as well. Many of these conferences are held on the campus of a large university.

Medical Conferences

Thanks to science, new advances in medicine are announced all the time. Medical conferences are a way for doctors and other medical professionals to keep up with these advances and to earn the needed continuing education credits to keep their license. Often professional organizations such as the American Medical Association host annual conferences to give doctors the opportunity to earn these credits.

Business Conferences

These can be several types. (1) Annual meetings. Many companies hold this type of meeting for shareholders to announce the company's accomplishments of the past year and to highlight the future. (2) If a company has many divisions around the world, often the management teams will get together to talk about the business' direction and to share best practices. This may be the only time they are in the same town. Often these conferences are held in the same town as the company's headquarters.

Training Conferences

Large organizations, such as United Way, will hold these types of conferences several times a year. This gives everyone the opportunity to learn new information and share best practices with their colleagues. Often training conferences will be presented by a marketing company and will be open to anyone from any company. These types of conferences require a classroom type of setting and easy access to restaurants if lunch and dinner is not included in the session.

Internet Conferences

These virtual gatherings have grown in popularity as travel costs have increased while company budgets have not. Even though they may seem as simple as just getting online, these conferences require planning—particularly if the participants are in different time zones.

Conference management may seem easy to an outsider: find a place, find a caterer and set up the room. But it is much more than that. Conference planning involves every little detail down to making sure there are enough water glasses on each table to making sure the sound system works. These tasks are usually distributed to several people and vendors but are usually over seen by a conference manager, who carries a huge responsibility. Any small mistake can put a damper on the entire event.

Event Management of Trade Shows

Event Management of Trade Shows: Trade shows are important for companies to present their products and to get in touch with its customers and business parties. If you have ever wondered about the success of trade shows, all you have to do is look at towns across America. Begin by looking at the community calendar in the local newspaper. You will like see an announcement for some type of "expo." These expos can focus on home improvement, senior care or the local businesses.

Pick up the phone book of even the smallest town. You will likely find some type of listing under "convention hall" or "room rental" that indicates a space large enough for a trade show. Finally, look at the annual events calendar for the local chamber of commerce. Most chambers host an annual business exhibition for the community. To the general public, these trade shows are an excellent way to find out more about local businesses, particularly if people are interested in a certain type of business. A boat show will draw people who love to be on the water and those who dream of owning the big Yacht. Home improvement expos are held in almost every town to showcase remodeling companies, contractors and even landscapers. For businesses, trade shows are a large part of many marketing budgets because:

They are a great way to meet many people quickly. Customers come to them! And if they stop by your booth, that usually means they are a great prospect. You can create a display that showcases the best of your business.

Cost of Trade Shows

The downside is the cost. Many trade shows require a huge booth fee that ranges from several hundred to several thousand dollars. This means that companies have to get the most out of these expos. Here are some tips for a successful trade show: Know what you want of the show financially and in terms of business leads. If you have a product you can sell, how many sales do you want to make. But if you offer a service such as insurance or marketing, determine how many leads you want to receive. This calculates your return on your investment and helps you decide if you want to attend the show next year. The host of the trade show and the venue will likely do some Marketing before the event. But why depend on them to market your business. Let people know that you will be at the expo. If you have regular Advertisements that run in various outlets, change these ads to mention the trade show.

Make sure you have a display that will attract visitors. Many companies give away novelty items and have a free candy jar at their table. This will attract the people who came to the exhibition for the freebies, but those people are unlikely to become customers. You don't have to have Music and Fancy Lights (but if you are a Disc Jockey they area good idea!). Have a display that gets across the key points about your business. Use videos that people can watch and allow them to watch before approaching them.

After a trade show or exhibition, you will get many leads. Those leads will only turn into customers if you follow up afterwards.

Most cities have many trade shows each year. If you attend each one, you will quickly eat up your Marketing Budget. Consider attending those that relate to your business. For example, many trade shows are geared towards women. If you know that women are the majority of your customers, sign up! You may not see as much traffic as you would at the large expo sponsored by the local chamber of commerce but may make more sales because you are hitting your target market.

Finally, work with the trade show organizers. Some private companies plan these shows but many organizations do the planning in house. If you are willing to help in the planning, donate door prizes or sponsor entertainment, you will likely get a prominent spot and free advertisement.

Event Management of Seminars

Event management of seminars and educational events. Who says learning ends outside the classroom? A popular source of academic, professional or technical instruction, seminars present information to diverse audiences. These tutorials may be private or public, series or single, commercial or informative, lecture-or dialogue-based. They are less formal than academic lectures, allowing audience members to interject opinions or discuss results.

In today's information-saturated marketplace, successful businesspersons are expected to learn new information quickly. 50-year-long careers are antiquated relics; mobile young professionals, equipped with powerful research skills and inter-career interests, swell the employment ranks. Seminars are a prime venue for dispersing important expertise in a condensed form. As such, event managers need to have a handle on how to plan a seminar.

Planning of Seminars

Like all successful enterprises, planning for a seminar should begin several months in advance by developing a theme. Is this seminar groundbreaking, philosophical, or technically-oriented? Who is the target audience? Select the niche market carefully.

When choosing a venue, do not select the nearest academic hall. Different seminar styles require different facility requirements. The higher the social caliber of the seminar, (e.g. the more VIP personalities) the more prestigious the venue must be. Additionally, the size of the location is dependent upon the estimated attendance figures.

Should the seminar be free? Incidentally, paid seminars typically attract more people than free seminars. Pundits believe that paid seminars present a visage of academic integrity, educational value, increases expectations, and elicit pre-paid customers to be there. An engaging keynote speaker is vital. After all, seminars are 60% information and 40% entertainment. A prosaic or ignorant speaker will kill and ruin a seminar. Seek respected, renowned speakers early on, and use their reputation as a marketing tool.

Solicit sponsors. Seminars are an effective method for corporations to "get their name out there." An automaker's seminar has already assembled a niche market, so local auto dealerships and repairs shops have a sure-fire guarantee of stellar brand positioning.

Develop an audience profile, then market, market, market! Use a descriptive title. Well-attended seminars are marketed 3-4 weeks in advance. Send e-mails (use BCC field to hide addressees), post flyers, write press releases, and use word-of-mouth. Eliminate direct mail – it normally doesn't work for seminars. Persuade audiences that they should want, or even need, to attend.

Secure audiovisual equipment and practice the presentation. Expect issues, so develop a contingency plan. Set up a basic registration desk, toss out a few refreshments, and enjoy the show. You worked for it.

Planning of Meetings

Planning of meetings :Often posted in cramped cubicles, a popular placard sardonically jokes: "Meetings: the practical alternative to work." But as far as event managers are concerned, a new definition is in order. Simply stated, a meeting is a gathering of individuals to achieve a common aim. In business meetings, leaders use oral communication, audiovisual productions, group discussions and other methods to accomplish corporate strategies. Idyllically, meetings spawn practical programs and marketable tactics. Realistically, meetings can be monotonous, time-sucking marathons of corporate hash. An event manager must dispel these negative notions and stimulate professionalism and creativity.

The two premises behind meetings are teamwork and passion. Both give vitality and energy to a corporation. Without meetings, corporate vision is lost, and employees labor for a paycheck rather than a shared dream.

Event Management of Meetings

Preparation should begin 6-18 months beforehand. Facilities, audiovisual rental equipment (which may include online conferencing equipment), caterers, tables and chairs, parking permits and accommodations need to be determined well ahead of time. Define the vision. Is it corporate growth? A product launch? After selecting a mission, deify it. Center all strategies on this central concept. Depending on client requests, an event manager may need to solicit businesses for sponsorships. If so, present sponsorship as proactive advertising to educated people in-the-know – an opportunity to be seized with vigor.

Choose a facility that is apposite to the vision. Producing a new line of burritos? Dine Mexican. Considering an IPO? Think of NASDAQ- and NYSE-reminiscent sites. While a complete menu is only obligatory for business dinners or all-day meetings, there should be an array of refreshments. Hire a caterer to provide light and simple culinary treats and do not ignore consider diet concerns (e.g. gluten-free, trans fat-free). Do not leave dishes on tables.

Depending on the duration of the meeting, transportation and accommodation may be vital concerns. At the minimum, select a venue with a nearby parking lot. If parking permits are required, then mail those to attendees as soon as possible. Attendees should be alerted of the meeting 2-3 months beforehand. Formal invitations should be sent by direct mail, while a polite e-mail or phone message will otherwise suffice. Send periodic reminders that prominently display dates, directions, agenda, and other important information. When attendees arrive, there should be a registration desk with name badges, itineraries and other information presented to them. Then, invite them to "invent, innovate, and design" – the new and improved definition of "business meeting."

Event Management of Team Building Events

Event Management of team building events that develop and motivate teams in companies and corporations. Team building events are perfect for companies and their divisions to motivate their employees and to develop real teams. In the United States, one of the most popular team building exercises is called the "Ropes" course. These exercises can range from taking a walk on a rope several feet in the air to just trusting that your teammates will catch you when you fall. Many corporations have used these exercises to motivate employees to work better as a team and the ropes course is just one example.

Even what seems to be the most isolation job requires team work. Accountants who may spend most of their time in an office crunching numbers will eventually need to present those numbers to managers and human resource officials to determine budgeting needs. Computer programmers will need to work with their colleagues to make sure that their systems are operating properly.

Team Building Events

Corporations have been using team building exercises for employee motivation for many years. What are some of the advantages?

These Exercises Build Trust

If you are scaling a wall and you are dependent on your team members to steady you, you learn quickly if they are trustworthy. In most team building exercises, you have to know that you can depend on others.

These Exercises Build Relationships

Most days employees sit in an office or work in a manufacturing plant and may have little time to get to know each other. During these team building exercises, they can chat about their lives. Most of these events begin with the participants telling more about themselves.

The Experience Builds morale

Most employees enjoy the day out of the office and enjoy the activities. They return to work excited about their participation and share stories from the event with others.

Team Building Increases Productivity

An energized, excited work force gets the job done. This is opposed to a work force that hates their job and has very little faith in the company or their colleagues. Planning a successful team building exercise requires planning and consideration of the employees' physical abilities and interests. Here are some guidelines: While the Ropes course is one of the most popular team building exercises, it is not for everyone. A group of computer programmers may not have the physical ability to do some of the stringent climbing exercises that are a part of the course. The course can be adapted, however. There are team building exercises that do not involve physical activity that will build trust and camaraderie.

Team building exercises like the Ropes course require an outdoor venue. Many towns have areas that are especially set up for companies and other organizations who want to host this popular course. However if your area does not have a place, you may have to consider hosting a retreat in another city. If you do, you have to consider travel expenses and how you will compensate your employees for their time. If you are doing some simple indoor activities, you can host the team building exercise at a nearby convention hall or even in your office.

In this economic downturn, you do have to consider cost. If several employees are away from their jobs during the exercise, productivity decreases. If you have to take the employees to another location, you have to consider costs for food and renting the venue. No matter how desperately you feel you may need a team building exercise, you may reconsider if you can't afford the costs. Set goals. If you hope to see productivity increase after the team building exercises, determine how much of an increase you want. You can choose if you let your employees know the goals. Especially if you invested money in sponsoring the team building exercises, you will want to see are turn on your investment. Employee motivation is a challenge in any business. That is why the Ropes course became so popular. Employees love the physical challenge and the fun of the event. They go back to work focused on their job and appreciative of the opportunity to spend a day with their colleagues.

Planning of Golf Events

Planning of Golf Events: Golf has evolved from an exclusive gentleman's game into an affordable public pastime. It is available to any man-jack who can purchase a cheap set of clubs and a few balls which he is guaranteed to lose in a few days. Because golf is such a popular trend, an educated event manager needs to understand how to manage golf tournaments and retreats. Tournament objectives should be established early on. Is the event a fundraiser or an exhibition? Sports, business, or personal related? Golfer caliber is important, as this will decide golfer handicap, course choice, and market approach. Probable celebrities and crowd size also affect course selection. Once the tournament type is decided, a course must be selected and carefully inspected. This entail its own set of conditions, including course rental, general insurance, Hole-In-One insurance (recommended), crowd regulations, etc.

Sponsors should be invited to subsidize the event. As much a cult sport as golf is, eager sponsors will seize advertising opportunities. Advertising works wonders – promotional gifts can be emblazoned with company imprimaturs, for example. Thank the golfing gods for their devoted following – not only will sponsors abound, but volunteers should come running as well. Use volunteers to clean and maintain the site, handle registration, set up concessions and portable bathrooms, etc. "The more the merrier" – with this mantra in mind, market, market, market! Golf magazines, shops and clubs can be used to distribute advertisements. If the purpose of the event is a fundraiser, this is the key factor in the event's success.

Although golf is not renowned for wild, unruly mobs, crowd management and security is a preeminent concern. A crowd control force and medical services, equipped with two-way radios, should be stationed around the course and at entrance/exits. While awarding green jackets may be slightly over-the-top, giving away scenic personal photographs is quite suitable. A professional photographer is a sure-fire ticket to freeze memorable moments on paper and present them to their respective winners – maybe surrounded by a walnut frame with a sponsor's logo engraved? Every golf tournament needs its own Orson Welles. A talented, knowledgeable emcee adds some spice and expertise to the day's events. Hire one. Last, but certainly not least, no golf tournament is complete with golf equipment. Rent clubs, bags, tees, balls, gloves, visors, and other assorted necessities. If possible, insure the equipment. And after all that work – find a five-iron and hit some hooks.

Event Management of Press Conferences

Event management of press conferences. Find out how to organize press conferences. Your idea of hell: pandemonium at the press conference; jostling reporters chomping after frightened keynote speakers and suit-clad business executives. Do yourself a favor by properly planning a press conference; and keep both the journalists and the executives in their places, grinning and glad.

Sometimes, a simple press release or email cannot suffice. When a company burns with the need to unleash a fiery new idea, it calls a press conference. Due to the hectic schedules of reporters, press conferences usually last for 30-45 minutes.

How to Plan a Press Conference

The first brick to building a successful press conference is determining its theme. Press conferences may promote products, apologize for incidents, launch marketing campaigns, or inform shareholders of finances. When to plan a press conference? Tuesday and Thursday late afternoons are prime time placement, while Mondays, Fridays and evenings are the worst choices. Check for competing events and conferences to avoid being one-upped.

The chosen venue should be easily accessible with an abundance of parking. No on-the-go journalist wants to arrive two minutes before the conference start and spend five minutes seeking a parking spot. Choose a location suitable to the mood of the event (e.g. secretive or informative). A dank and deserted basement may fit a "industry-domination-plan" type conference, but is less than apposite for a shareholders meeting. A triumphant press conference creates tidal waves; a pathetic one causes ripples and a few splashes. The differentiator: marketing. Target the primary audience (specific caliber and type of journalists) and distribute heaps of press releases, media advisories, emails, phone calls and worth-of-mouth tips.

Captivating speakers and presentations separate monotonous press conferences from dramatic ones. Choose 2-4 keynote speakers. They should be of high repute, with impeccable credentials and lots of charisma. Their presentations should not emulate one another – one can welcome and introduce, another present the main concept, and another relate the main concept to human interests. Powerful audiovisual materials will give journalists and photographers extra ammunition for their forthcoming articles. Opinions, disagreements and arguments may fly fast and hard in a heated press conference.

To avoid a Chernobyl-type explosion, with injurious media fallout, hire effective crowd control. Ushers should help seat journalists and arrange their equipment, and Q&A sessions require a neutral moderator to direction questioning. When journalists enter, they should receive a press conference packet. This should include an agenda, facts, statistics, graphs and charts. Then after 30 minutes, it's over. Such is the life of an event manager.

Event Management of Networking Events

Event management of networking events that may look like lavishly-funded business parties, but in reality, networking events are essential personal marketing galas. Thus, any event manager needs to know how to organize one whale of a party – er, one fantastic business networking event. Networking events are a key element to business success. They provide ample opportunity for brand positioning, contact establishment, future mergers, and personal marketing. There is strength in numbers. All companies have a vested interest in securing the support of a business friend (formally labeled as b2b [business to business] commerce). For aspiring businesspersons seeking some social capital, a networking conference is the prime spot to be.

How to Plan a Networking Event?

Due to the variety of size of attendees, a networking event needs to be planned at least 12 months in advance. In fact, the first invitation should be sent six months before the advent, which means the venue, accommodations, employment, entertainment and other essentials must be provided for by then. Networking events are best planned around weekends – because of weekday work schedules and hotel weekend discounts – and not in juxtaposition to similar occasions.

Note: the event manager should quickly determine maximum budget boundaries and operate strictly within that range.

The success of a business networking event, to a large degree, depends on the rate of attendance. Marketing is vital. Due to low return rates of direct mail, concentrate on social media marketing and that perennial favourite, e-mail. The requests should show the invitees why it is in their absolute best interest to attend.

When searching for a venue, select a location that is easily accessible, has nearby parking, and is near accommodations. The housing (required for traveling attendees) need not be four-or five-star resorts, but requires commodities like WiFi, free breakfast, etc.

Both the venue and housing selections should be selected with one theme in mind: comfort. How to pay for this gala? Sponsors. With the inbred marketing opportunities at business networking events, sponsors will jump at the opportunity to subsidize. In return for their financial assistance, allow them to set up shop at the event. Rental equipment is relatively straightforward: audiovisual equipment, lighting, sound, linens, tables and chairs. Entertainment and catering should subside into the backdrop, blending rather than interrupting. Likewise, catering should not emulate college buffets. When guests arrive, they are to be verbally welcomed and given a welcome kit. Hopefully, when they leave, they will be chock-full of another's business cards. Networking complete.

Incentive Travel

Event management of incentive travel events that motivate your employees and customers. Incentive travel is an event category that targets to motivate both key personnel and customers. Imagine sunning yourself on a beach in Jamaica or snow skiing in the Alps. Then imagine that your trip is completely free. Many companies use incentive travel as a marketing tool. These trips can range from a week in an exotic location to a weekend getaway in nearby resort. Most of the time all of the expenses are paid by the company including food, hotel, airfare (or in some cases a rental car).

How to Plan Incentive Travel Events

Learn how to plan incentive travel events: The incentives can be used in many ways:

Employee Motivation

What better way to spur a lagging sales team than by offering an all-expenses paid trip to Hawaii? If sales dramatically increase, the trip could be paid for by the proceeds.

Reward

Many companies don't tell their employees that they plan to reward them for good work. What a wonderful surprise when after a great month or even year, the employee is told her or she has won a trip. This surprise could stir enthusiasm in other to perform better and hopefully win a trip of their own.

Customer Loyalty

Customers come and go, but those that say are priceless. Many business owners choose to reward that loyalty with incentive travel.

Sometimes this is a surprise after a customer has placed a large order. Sometimes the trip is planned in conjunction with an event, such as the World Series or the debut of a Broadway show.

Customer Retention

Most businesses are competitive. If you don't want your customers taking their business elsewhere, incentive travel is a great way to let them know they are appreciated. So if you are a business owner who wants to motive employees and retain customers through an employee incentive program, how do you begin? Here are as few tips for planning perfect trips:

Research destinations. A tropical beach may seem like an obvious choice—unless you already live and work on the beach. Do you ever hear your employees or customers talking about where they would want to visit on a vacation? Do any of your employees or customers hobbies like golf or skiing? You may want to offer several destinations so that your employees or customers have a choice. Look for destinations that will highlight their interests and they will never forget.

Partner with a travel agency or other professional group to create a program. If you want to save on costs, consider trading service with the agency if that is possible. The program should include open-ended dates for travel, a choice of destinations and "extras." Those extras could include tickets to attractions or dinner at an exclusive restaurant in the area. If possible, visit the destinations yourself and stay at the hotel. Hotel brochures can be deceiving and that great room with a view may be a room with a view of the back alley. Even if you didn't know, your employees will blame you for their bad vacation.

Many business owners think that setting up a travel program is too much trouble and that the impact is minimal. They prefer to give cash or other gifts. But travel incentives have many advantages including: Employees and customers will know that you care enough to take time to plan the event from them. This takes more effort than throwing cash at them. Vacations create memories. Perhaps some of the beneficiaries have not had a vacation for several years. Or your incentive may have allowed them to visit a destination they had only dreamed of seeing. These memories are worth more to many people than money. Finally, travel incentives are great public relations and morale boosters. Employees and customers will tell others about the trip you provided. You will be seen as someone who cares enough to take the time to plan a wonderful trip!

Opening Ceremonies

Event Management of opening ceremonies that may be crucial when an event, a conference or a convention lasts for several days an when the event organizers want to gather, address and welcome the whole audience. No ceremony is as cherished at the opening ceremony of the Olympic Games. Athletes from around the world gather in preparation for competition of hundreds of sports. Celebrities perform, often singing songs written especially for the occasion. Preparation for the Opening Ceremony begins weeks before the event, with a traditional torch run around the world. The event is always one of the top rated shows as millions from around the world watch from the comfort of their homes.

How to Plan an Opening Ceremony

In small towns around the world, local sporting leagues imitate the Olympic ceremony. And when corporations have conventions or annual meetings, opening ceremonies are also held. While they may seem different, there are some key similarities between them.

All opening ceremonies usually involve some sort of entertainment. For a large corporation, that could include some subtle piano music that plays while presentations are made. For sports ceremonies, there could be marching bands and trained dancers. Celebrity singers may also perform. For sporting events, the athletes may march into the venue, much like the Olympic event. Even if the rest of the meeting is all business, the opening day may be fun.

In addition to entertainment, most opening ceremonies have a planned agenda. That agenda could include a guest speaker, the unveiling of a new product or product advertisement (if the convention is for a large corporation) or an announcement including some good news. Even opening ceremonies for the small sporting events have a planned agenda with a mix of entertainment and speakers. The agenda is upbeat and fun. Since it takes a lot of time to choose and book speakers, planning for opening ceremonies often begins a year before the actual event.

Deciding the venue is easy for some opening ceremonies, but some are more challenging. Sports ceremonies are usually held on the playing field which could be in an outdoor stadium if the game is baseball or on ice if the sport is hockey. Sometimes if there are enough participants, the event could be held at a large convention hall near where the games are played. If you are holding the opening ceremony for a convention or annual meeting, you will want to have it in the same place where the rest of the event is being held. Another possibility is to hold it at a fun venue nearby, which ironically can include a stadium or playing field. The possibilities are endless. You may need to do more as far as preparation and decoration for an opening ceremony for a conventions or annual meetings. Opening ceremonies are festive events and the tone of the rest of the meeting may be more solemn. If the conference is being held for a week, it is unlikely that music, food and drinks may not be on the agenda for the entire meeting. Depending on what time of day you host the first day event, it could double as a big party. The guest lists may vary for an opening ceremony. Like the Olympics, some people may only attend the opening ceremony, no matter what the event is. Large corporations or associations may welcome the media to this event to get coverage. During the opening ceremony for Little League Baseball, every team and their parents may be there, prompting a need for a bigger venue. The attendance should be considered when planning. Finally, opening ceremonies are held for the same reason that Olympic organizers hold them before each games—they inspire everyone who attends. Can you imagine anyone getting that excited about the Olympics without the fanfare that is held at the beginning? After being entertained, fed and encouraged, participants at even the dullest convention are ready to begin!

Event Management of Product Launches

Event management of product launches is essential components of the marketing mix of large companies. When Nintendo launches its latest game console or Pepsi announces a new type of soft drink, the companies hold product launches. These launches give the public and the media a chance to hear everything about the product before any negative reviews are given.

The task of putting together these product launch events could fall to a company employee who organizes meetings or an outside company. Product launch events have several purposes:

Why are Product Launch Events important?

To introduce the product to investors and other partners. Often new products are launched at the annual shareholder meetings. This gives the shareholders a chance to see and perhaps even test the product before it is introduced to the general public. However, if the product is huge the company may want to create a huge event and the shareholder may find out the same time as the media and the company's customers. To introduce the product to the old and new customers. Sometimes this is not a formal event. For example, a company announcing a new soft drink may set up a booth at a major sporting event or large fair. These events require just as much planning as setting up a major event at convention hall. Space has to be reserved, displays have to be set up and staff has to be hired.

To introduce the product to the media. Depending on the size of the company and the product, this could be in the form of a press conference. But many companies choose to have one big event and invite the media as well.

Planning a product launch where the media is invited is a bit of extra work. You must make sure there is room for photographers—both still photographers and videographers. And they must have an excellent view so that they can capture the action. You should make sure to prepare a "press kit" that will contain the information about the product and the company.

How to Plan a Product Launch?

Whoever has the task handling the market introdcution of a new product, has a huge responsiblity. Some of the things to consider are:

Venue

Most product launch events happen in big cities or in cities where the company is located. Sometimes these launches are held at big convention halls so that there is room for the shareholders and the media. However, some product launches are held in the board rooms of the corporate offices. The venue depends on how big the company is, how big the product is and how much money the company wants to invest in the market introduction.

Timing

When Nintendo and Sony launch a new video game console, the companies will usually release it in different places at different times. Sometimes a product will be a big hit in Europe or Asia before it is released in North America and vice versa. Usually the introduction of a new product, such as new toy or game console, coincides with the holiday season. New soft drinks may be launched during a big sporting event like the Super Bowl or the World Series. Millions of people watch these events and announcing the new product and airing commercials during these events will create a buzz.

Food

If the president of the company wants food at the event, the planner has a lot of decisions to make. Will it be finger foods or a full-course meal. What time of day with the new product launch event be held? What kind of food will be best for the attendees? How much food should be ordered? Will wait staff be needed?

The Small Details

These may not seem like a big deal, but they could make or break an event. Can you imagine Microsoft launching a new product and half the attendees having to stand because there are not enough chairs? Most product launches include an information packet that is given to the guests. These packages need to be ready to go and there need to be enough for everyone. The convention or meeting planner is responsible for making sure the small details are handled.

Product launches are some of the most exciting events for any meeting planner. Could you imagine putting together the product launch event for the Nintendo Wii? But these events are also the most stressful. The key, as it is for any event, is in proper planning.

Event Management of VIP Events

Event Management of VIP events which are an important marketing tool to increase and to maintain the loyality of key customers. Every company and organization has someone they consider a VIP. These people are often honored with VIP events. These people could be:

The company's top customer. In some cases, a top customer could represent up to 50 percent of a company's business. For a non profit organization, a VIP could be the top donor. Some companies value customers who refer other businesses to them. Non profit organizations may consider top volunteers as VIP.

How to Plan a VIP Event

These VIPs are recognized in several ways from invitation only events to special weekend out of town where they are shown the utmost hospitality at a resort or exotic destination. Here are some ideas for hosting a VIP event:

Awards ceremonies are popular black tie events to honour VIPs. Most non profit organizations hold annual banquets to honour top donors and volunteers. These events are often open to the news media so that pictures can appear in the local newspaper. The honorees often sit at a head table unless the award is surprise. Invitation only events are a way to let VIPs know how important they are to your company or organization. These events could include: 1. Box seats at a major sporting event where a gourmet meal is catered. This can include all sports from Indy Racing to baseball. The bigger the sporting event, the better. World Series or Super Bowl tickets are very impressive! 2. A day of golf at a country club. 3. Private parties. 4. Trips to private resorts. These events are exclusive and often created just to honour VIPs with hospitality.

Trade shows are a popular way for business people to network and meet potential new clients. Often a private invitation only party will be held in the evening. Invite your VIPs to this party. It is an excellent opportunity to network one-on-one with the people who do so much for your business or organization. Most companies and organizations host annual meetings. A private cocktail party before or after the public meeting is a great way to honour VIPs.

While there are many great VIP events, there are some pitfalls to avoid: If are in Chicago and your VIP is a Cubs fan, they probably won't appreciate box seats to a White Sox game. Find out if the honoree likes a team (and the sport) before choosing a VIP event that involves a sporting event.

Make sure your VIP can attend the event. It's like beginning a football game without the star quarterback. If you are hoping to honour the VIP in secret, let someone close to them such as a spouse in on the secret. They will find a way to get the VIP to the event! If your VIP doesn't drink, a cocktail party or other alcohol related events are not a good way to honour them. This could be disastrous if your VIP is a recovering alcoholic or doesn't drink for religious reasons. When planning trips, consider several options: 1. Some people don't like to fly. Find out if your VIP is one of them before offering to jet them off to an exclusive resort. 2. Some people don't have time for vacations. Consider a VIP weekend. You will save money with a shorter trip. 3. Make sure the trip is for two people. Most people like to take their spouses or companions on their trips.

Finally, some people who you consider VIPs don't want their good deeds revealed. This is particularly true in the non profit world where many large donors remain anonymous. The last thing you want to do is to alienate your customer or donor by giving them unwanted recognition.

Theme Parties

Event Management of Theme Parties that are popular for people of all ages. When someone invites you to a party, you always ask "What's the theme?" No one has 'plain Jane' events anymore where the guest are just expected to put on their Sunday best, eat appetizers and dance to boring music. Event planners caught on to the trend and now plan corporate and nonprofit parties with themes. Before getting into what it takes to have a successful theme party, let's examine some of the hottest trends:

Topics of Theme Parties

Casino Night

The increased popularity of poker has made Casino Night one of, if not the, most popular theme for all sorts of events. Charities use them as fundraisers. Participants purchase tokens that can be 'cashed in' for prizes.

Mardi Gras

These parties can be held any time of the year—not just at Mardi Gras time. What makes these parties so popular are the decorations — colorful beads and costumes set a festive mood.

Pick a Decade

Just a few years ago, the 50s were the most popular party them. Who could request poodle skirts, leather jackets and "Rocking Around the Clock?" But as the population has aged, the 50s have been surpassed by the 70s and 80s. Disco balls and bell bottoms are fun accessories. And the 80s brought colorful shorts and big hair—on both the men and the women!

Halloween

Pop superstar Michael Jackson can take much of the credit for bringing spooky back into style. More than 25 years after the release of "Thriller," many parties and events are based on that popular music video. Beyond the thrill the popularity of horror and slasher films give party goers a chance to be spooky. But costume parties don't have to be scary. Princesses, knights, cowboys and all sorts of strange animals have made their way to Halloween parties.

What goes into Creating a Successful theme Party?

Be careful which theme you choose : An organization that largely caters to seniors may not want to choose a Halloween theme. However partygoers may jump at the chance to try their hands at the casino tables. All generations will enjoy a trip back in time but all generations may not enjoy a Mardi Gras party. Consider the guest list when deciding which theme will be great for the perfect party. If possible, take a formal or informal survey of potential guests.

You must Decorate

What is a Halloween party without a few spider webs and spooky ghost hanging around? And can you honestly have a 70s party without a disco ball (or several) hanging from the ceiling? If you are on a budget, finding great decorations can be challenging. Don't limit yourself to the party store down the street. The Internet has a wealth of online stores that have great decorations at the price.

Don't take on the task of decorating all alone. Form a committee and make decorating the "party before the party."

Stay with the theme from the Beginning

Find invitations that are suited for what will happen the night of the party. Serve foods that coincide with the theme. This is easy if you are doing a Halloween theme because there are many ideas in magazines and books. If you are having trouble figuring out 'theme foods' keep it simple. Have a cake (or several depending on the crowd) that reflects the theme. You don't even have to make it—order it from a local bakery. Finally, be creative and create your own theme. If the members of your organization love a television show, create a theme party around that show. Have the guests come dressed as their favourite characters. Your themes are only limited by your imagination.

Trade Fairs

Event management of trade fairs where companies can exhibit their latest products and services. Definition, "fairs:" cotton candy, funnel cakes, hotdogs, and roller coasters. Actually, not all fairs possess such frivolity and festivity; trade and career fairs are decidedly less entertaining, albeit more useful. Headed by a knowledgeable event manager, a trade or career fair is a special opportunity through which buyers and sellers can meet.

Trade fairs are occasions in which corporations of a certain industry gather to display their latest products and innovations. Career fairs, a close cousin, occur when companies conglomerate to solicit potential employees. In today's competitive economy, both events are essential. Trade fairs are engaging, living advertisements, while career fairs are necessary to recruit college graduates and other superior employees from the rank-and-file lines of unemployment. When initiating the planning stages of a fair, first determine a theme. Is the trade show focused on florists or dentists? Will the career fair seek out engineers or marketers? Do not waste time marketing irrelevant prospects; select the target audience and focus accordingly. Before solidifying times and dates for a fair, be sure that no similar show is occurring nearby or has occurred recently. Additionally, check the success of past trade shows in the area. If they failed to elicit much interest, reconsider the location.

When an event manager selects a venue, he or she must anticipate expected crowd size and vendor participation. Locations should be easily accessible to the public with nearby parking lots. Add carpet, lighting, furniture, and perhaps some audiovisual equipment to enhance the atmosphere. Now, to solicit vendors. Aye, there's the rub. Vendors are the brick and mortar of a show. Prospects come for a vendor's goods; second-rate sellers will elicit second-tier buyers, which create a second-tier event.

After carefully listing a collection of targeted companies, send each company an e-mail, call their business executives and marketing branches and eagerly promote the event. Offer each company floor area and a space in the event directory, along with other incentives. After inviting vendors, market to prospective customers or employees. Avoid direct mail. Use worth-of-mouth, press releases, media coverage, newspaper advertisements, and industry-inside channels to disseminate invitations.

A few personnel logistics should be attended to during the actual event. A small crowd control force should patrol the area; a receptionist should welcome customers and offer pertinent information; and a set-up/tear-down crew (paid professionals) should take care of general equipment installation.

Definition, "fairs:" a place for a buyer and seller to meet. A place for an event manager to smile and say, "success."

Annual Shareholders Meetings

Annual shareholder meetings are import events for shareholders of listed and also unlisted companies. In the United States, every corporation is required to hold an annual stockholders meeting. Even corporations that are not based in the United States hold these annual meetings. There are several purposes for these meetings:

The focus of the shareholder meetings is the election of the Board of Directors. The board of directors makes many of the decisions of the corporation. The annual meeting is a chance for the shareholders to review the annual reports. This includes information about the fiscal well-being of the company. If there have been losses or gains, these will be included. Most companies allow shareholders to vote on certain key issues besides the Board of Directors. Some of the issues include investments and acquisitions of other companies.

The shareholders will get a look at new products or services that will be introduced in the upcoming year.

Planning of Shareholder Meetings

Many corporations have meeting planners on staff or allow their marketing department to plan these important gatherings. But often the planning is outsourced to a professional company. Some of the special considerations when planning an annual meeting include the corporate climate. Microsoft's annual meeting no doubt has a different "feel" than the annual meeting for a 'hip," youthful company that sells jeans. The corporate climate can affect every aspect of planning the meeting including:

An annual meeting for a conservative company may consist of sitting in a convention hall voting on corporate matters. Later a formal dinner with a guest speaker may take place. Some companies may create a 'rock-n-roll' atmosphere complete with a popular band. The attire may be casual. Even though it is not popular in this economic climate, many corporations have held their annual meetings in exotic locales like the Bahamas. The shareholders get to vacation and vote on important business. However, most corporations will hold these meetings in the city where the corporate offices are.

Some annual meetings are held over the course of a few days. Some are held on weekends or are limited to just one day. The length of the meeting can determine the accommodations, food options and other important details. If you are hired to plan the meeting, you need to find out who is responsible for compiling the annual report. Many corporations look for meeting planners who also have marketing departments that write annual reports. If you are not responsible for the reports, make sure you know who is. You will need to make sure there are plenty of copies available for shareholders and the media. What type of media coverage is expected? Is there a need to set up a special section for the press? Will there be special invites to the business media. If it is a large corporation, usually the press has an interest in the annual meeting and the naming of the board of directors. Smaller corporations usually send press release about the new board of directors and the highlights of the annual report.

Will bad news or good news be announced at the meeting? Will you, as the meeting planner, be privy to the news? If the company is going to announce that profits plummeted during the past year, you don't want to coordinate a fancy, black-tie party with all the expensive trimmings. Some of the shareholders may see this as a waste of money if you host an extravagant party when profits are down. On the flip side, if there is cause to celebrate, a grand party may be in order.

Finally, many corporations are choosing to hold virtual annual meetings to save money. These meetings include more planning than making sure everyone is online at the same time. You have to arrange for a secure connection for the meeting. You can find many free sites online that offer virtual conferencing for free. Votes can also be placed virtually. Most United States allows companies to host their annual meetings this way. Virtual annual meetings are very popular among small companies with limited budgets.

Event Management of Award Ceremonies

Event Management of Award Ceremonies that honour staff or acquire and customers. Award Ceremonies are an important type of events when you consider that we live in a society that loves to honour people for their achievements. Some of the most watched programs on television are award ceremonies including the Oscars, the Grammy's and the Olympics. Companies, organizations and other groups love to honour their own. These ceremonies are coordinated by in-hour meeting or marketing professionals or outside companies. The components of putting together an awards ceremony include:

Planning of Award Ceremonies

The coordination of the judging process. Particularly in a non-profit, this may be done by a committee. If you pick celebrities, particularly media celebrities to be judges, you will likely guarantee that your event will be on television or in the newspaper. Once you have the judges. Make sure they understand the rules and agree to keep their selections secret until the ceremony.

Once you have the judges, the next decision is how you will accept submissions. You can run an announcement in the local media if want to get submissions from throughout the community. If the awards are based on performance from within an organization, ask for submissions from within that organization.

The scope of the awards ceremony will determine where you will hold the event. If you are handing out awards to recognize community service, you may want to consider a large banquet room at a hotel. Small awards ceremonies that are just for the company could be held in the company board room or at a local restaurant. If you are planning a big community event, you will have unique challenges. If the ceremony is a formal dinner, you have to decide menus and make sure that the venue has everything needed for a successful ceremony.

Who will be the master of ceremonies? This is an important honour. If this is just a corporate event, the owner or other company executive may have this task. For large community events, having a celebrity as master of ceremonies will draw attention to your ceremony. This can be a local celebrity that everyone knows or if you have the budget, a well-known celebrity. Just make sure the person is comfortable with speaking in front of crowds.

You will likely want to have a guest speaker or speakers at your awards ceremony, particularly if these are community-oriented awards. Guest speakers can talk about the mission of your organization inspire others to be award winners next year. Again, you can choose a local celebrity, a well-known personality or someone from within your organization.

As guests are entering and even during the ceremony, you want them to be entertained. The type of entertainment will be determined by type of event. You don't want a rock band at an awards ceremony honoring those who have raised money for a conservative nonprofit. And the entertainment does not have to be extremely formal. Have someone playing the piano as guests arrive and possibly as they eat dinner.

The invitation to an awards ceremony needs to reflect the spirit and mood of the event. A community celebration should have a colorful logo from the sponsoring organization. Most formal initiations have a font that resembles elegant calligraphy. Make sure you include a way for guests to RSVP. You want to make sure the honorees are there. Thanks to advances in desktop publishing, these invitations don't have to be expensive. The invitations can be created online and printed from the office printer (if the printer makes quality copies).

Guest registration at the awards ceremony is especially important if you want to make sure the honorees are in attendance. You can set up a table outside the entrance to the meeting room and ask people to sign a sheet. If you are having a less formal event, you can even issue name tags to the guests at the registration table. If your awards ceremony is a community event, you will want to sell tables. You have a few ways to approach table sales. 1. You can run an announcement in the newspaper and local media announcing the even. Be sure to include information about how to purchase a table. 2. If this is an annual event, draft letters to past attendees reminding them of the event and asking them for their support again. 3. Have volunteers assist with table sales by asking their colleagues and friends.

Finally, remember you have to purchase the awards. These can be statuettes, like the Oscar, plaques or framed certificates. Make sure you order them in plenty of time for them to be ready for the awards ceremony and in enough time to correct any errors.

Event Management of Incentive Events

Event management of incentive events: Oftentimes, managers cocoon themselves in a business dream world. They believe in inherent employee competition and rely on the consumer rational evaluation. In reality, employees are frequently weary and worn down, and slog onwards for a bi-monthly pay check; and customers almost always buy based on emotion and brand loyalty. The solution: incentive events.

An incentive event is an interactive, engaging method of inspiring employee morale and consumer interest. Reminiscent of the religious Great Awakenings of American history, these stimulating revivals incite their audiences to evangelize new customers through telemarketing and the like. Successful incentive events are statistically linked to increased sales motivation, greater profit margins, customer loyalty, and new products and services. Properly used, they are an effective tool for renewing loyalty, provoking imagination, and stimulating success. A successful event manager captures and amplifies these attributes. Although the actual event should be relatively short (1-2 hours), 12-18 months are needed for proper planning. When starting preparation, answer two questions: What is the reason for the incentive event? And what should the theme be? Defining the reason for the activity (loss of morale, new product launch, or customer loyalty) directs the rest of the event; and a winsome theme engages attendees. Religiously abide by the three E's of event management:

entertainment, excitement, and enterprise. Focus on the first two. Bands, hypnotists, DJs, comedians, or other performing acts are critical tools in setting the mood. Motivational speakers should be carefully selected and reviewed. Create a lighthearted, excited atmosphere.

But not all presentation should be hype. To stimulate long-term motivation, a keynote business executive needs to appear and lay down the hard facts of success and present a plan of achievement. Prepare and test audiovisual equipment (e.g. soundboard, PowerPoint, mikes, etc.) to ensure a seamless speech. The speaker should also present employee recognition awards. Without these gilded wooden examples of success (order the plaques early with names engraved), employees may regard the event as propaganda more than a legitimate impetus. What's a party without food? Arrange for a full gastronomic smorgasbord of refreshing treats, snacks, delicacies and beverages. Most importantly, do not run out.

Ask for RSVPs and set up a registration desk at the event's entrance, where employees can quickly sign in and receive name tags. Using the RSVP and registration rosters, follow up the festival by emailing each employee and sincerely inquiring about their experience and any suggestions they may have. Fan the flames of motivation-without follow up, the event was nothing more than a subsidized business party masquerading as an incentive event.

Board Meetings

Riddle me this, dear reader: what type of board has nine heads and fights? Solution: a board meeting! Pitiable jokes aside, a board meeting can be a necessary evil or an enviable virtue. Properly planning a board meeting has drastic ramifications on its success and the ensuing effect on corporate growth. Event managers, proceed with caution. When members of a Board of Directors meet together to bat around corporate agenda, they create a board meeting. Board meetings focus on strategic goals and company vision more than detailed logistics and should be designed with big ideas in mind. Without these sessions, a company can soon become distracted, demoralized or lost within the corporate bureaucracy.

Due to the esteemed status of the attendees, a board meeting should be planned some time in advance (12-24 months). Develop a theme for the convention; it is not related to décor or festivity, but to what type of decisions will be made. The venue should reflect the prestigious nature of the occasion, set in an area evoking professionalism and imagination. Number of tables and chairs depends on the mood of the meeting and number of attendees. A U-shaped table is appropriate for assemblies with fewer than 40 people; a round table is suitable for smaller group; a square or rectangular table is apposite for other needs. Because many board members will be traveling, select a hotel, club or resort for the VIPs to reside. Hire a shuttle or cab service to transport the members from the venue to the accommodations.

Many board meetings are required to be held publicly. However, many such meetings attract little or no popular attention. If this meeting is expected to be swamped by the masses, prepare by using crowd control, abundant seating and a registration desk for agenda information and facility navigation. No board meeting is complete without dainty refreshments. While a Big Mac is far too plebian to be appropriate, fine wines, chilled deserts or salads are quite suitable for the debating bourgeoisie. All board meeting conversation must be recorded by a secretary. The secretary must be trained, competent and on-time. If the secretary is without his or her own recording materials, equipment should be provided.

Most importantly, follow up! Grandiose ideas are commonplace at board meetings, and can be easily snowed under by the return to daily routine. Do not allow board members to become bored and dismiss their dreams.

Executive Retreats

Event Management of executive retreats and the question "What is a successful executive retreat"? It is a paid-in-full escape from hectic work schedules, mundane daily routines and banal financial statements. Its mission is ingenuity and its charge is imagination. What is a successful event manager? A person who keeps the first list from filtering into the second.

Executive retreats are, in theory, getaways from prosaic business meetings and unendurable seminars. Retreats should stimulate free thinking and creativity. Unfortunately, due to the gargantuan size of some corporate budgets, many hard-earned dollars are wasted in expensive resorts and needless frivolities. A successful retreat should balance relaxation and entertainment with solution and enterprise.

Why hold an expensive executive retreat when a casual business meeting could serve just as well? Business meetings, pundits contend, may stifle imagination and direction due to locale stereotypes, venue choice, and the mish-mash of daily life. Setting aside an allotted time stimulates otherwise repressed innovation and boosts morale.

Planning of Executive Retreats

Business executives are busy people. Planning an executive retreat well in advance – 18 to 24 months – gives the event manager ample time to rent locations and fashion an agenda, and gives the participating executives time to mark their calendars. Anticipate how many people are coming (is executive attendance mandatory or voluntary?); the more attendees – or the more prestigious – the more planning time.

Before, executive retreats were renowned for frivolous locale. Now, budget-consciousness is all the rage, and many retreat managers opt for local venues to add down-home spice to the party. The venue should be clean, comfortable and fascinating. Also, it should have several meeting rooms for subcommittees can convene in. Get rid of posh protocol and red tape. Whatever setting is chosen, it should facilitate teamwork and communication. Regardless of whether the service personnel is employed by the venue or handpicked by the event manager, all must be spic-and-span clean, on-the-dot talent and spin-on-the-dime compliance.

Accommodation and transportation is of utmost importance. No executive wants his or her BMW ruined by a hailstorm or a rustic cabin bunk chock-full of fleas. Parking should be accessible (if permits are required, mail those early). Even business executives need their playtime, but not all events should border on frivolity. The proceedings should be a proper balance between festivities, brainstorming sessions and Puritan-ethic work assemblies. Once the executive retreat has concluded, an event manager needs to condense plans and concepts into emails, messages or memos, and distribute the information to participants. With all that work, why let the ideas go to waste?

Business Dinners

"Be our guest!" Thus, Lumiere, Beauty and the Beast's iconic speaking candle, introduces his gigantic smorgasbord with gusto and fanfare. While mimicking Lumiere's gargantuan feast is unnecessary, taking a leaf from his hospitality book guarantees an event manager one amazing business dinner. Business dinners are a long-standing corporate tradition, used to conclude fiscal years, celebrate new milestones, introduce new management, or a host of other prestigious events. They integrate entertainment with professionalism and allow different corporate levels and branches to mix and mingle. A successful business dinner commemorates company achievements, recognizes successful employees, and entertains the guests. Planning starts approximately 12-28 months before the event. Before anything else, ask the question, what should be the atmosphere? A business dinner may be formal or relaxed. A hint of caution: any company who is barely bobbing their head above the fiscal water should refrain from formal, expensive dinners. These may be construed as wasteful spending. A posh, roomy venue is an appropriate choice for a business dinner. There should be plenty of space for guests to walk by tables. The location should be booked sometime in advance. Also, a contingency date should be selected.

How to contact attendees? Formal dinners require elegant letters, while less posh parties need little more than a well-written office memo or even e-mail. Regardless of method, the first invitation should be sent 2-3 months before the advent, with the last reminder one week beforehand. All solicitations should prominently include dates, times, basic agenda, and a well-placed marketing ploy to attract the wavering. As for food choices, Lumiere may be on to something. Formal dinners require four-and five-star courses, while casual festivities need three-star (think Applebees) fare. This choice, however, leads to another quandary: self-serve buffet or maitre d' service? Buffets promote community and congeniality but sacrifice sophistication; maitre d' service reeks of elegance and French hospitality but leaves the palate wanting. Simply decide which set of attributes is most important.

When selecting entertainment, local burgeoning bands, DJs, rank-and-file comedians, puppeteers, etc. should be foregone. The event manager should carefully choose professional, engaging keynote speakers (motivational or informative) and classy musicians to set the mood. When attendees enter, they should sign a master RVSP roster (yes, RSVP's are essential) and be lead by ushers (solicited volunteers or paid staff) to their assigned seats – give VIPs subliminal preferential treatment. Nobody is looking. Snatch a martini. You've earned it-and thank Lumiere.

Event Management of Private Events

Event management of private events like birthdays, weddings, birthday and wedding anniversaries or other family events. Private events are celebrations with family members and friends. Moments of a lifetime refer to those special events that often happen only once in a lifetime. These private events such as weddings, golden anniversaries and special birthdays are marked with special celebrations. Celebrations that you want to remember fondly because of the beautiful ambiance created by lighting, decorations, music and food rather than the DJ that alienated the audience or the caterer that ran out of food. Learn more about personal events.

Event Management of Weddings

Event Management of Weddings: Weddings are among the most important events in a woman's lifetime, and every bride wants "the perfect wedding". There are many different variations from the traditional church wedding to the theme wedding to the outdoor wedding, and each wedding presents its own set of challenges. There are many details to coordinate, and a small glitch can turn into a major emotional crisis. So it is important for someone to monitor the details to keep things running as smoothly as possible.

Wedding Planning

The couple usually chooses the church and the reception location. Even so, it's advisable to double check the facilities' use policy. For example, some church fellowship halls may prohibit alcohol or dancing at the reception. The couple will also probably choose their own clothing, but it helps to at least be aware of the style and colour in order to coordinate the other aspects of the wedding. Colour scheme and theme if any will help in the planning process. Flowers, both for bouquets and Decorations, will need to be chosen and ordered. Music for the wedding itself may provided by an organist or vocalist, or may be a recording, in which case someone will be needed to operate the Sound System. A Photographer may provide both video and still photographs. Again, check policies; some churches restrict photography within the sanctuary. Following the wedding is usually the reception. Refreshments may consist of punch and Wedding Cake, or may encompass a Full Meal. Simple refreshments allow more options in seating; while sit-down dinners require Table Settings. Music may either be live or recorded. A DJ will probably have his own Sound Equipment, as will most Musicians. It's a good idea to review specifics with the DJ—"oldies" for a baby boomer may mean 50s or 60s music, while a younger DJ may consider 80s music to be "oldies". Decorations may be suggested by colour or theme.

A professional wedding planner can help to coordinate all the details to make sure that the wedding runs smoothly. Making sure that expectations are clear and reasonable will go a long way in preventing disappointments and making this special day the memory of a lifetime.

Event Management of Birthday Parties

Event management of birthday parties, events and celebrations. Learn how to organize birthday events by yourself or what professional event managers can do to assure a successful party. Details about all planning steps and potential mistakes. Birthday events recognize the milestones in a person's life. These festivities can be casual or formal. They may be intimate, with just a few close friends and family; or they can be grand events. There are two basic types of birthday parties: children's and adults', and each present its own set of challenges.

Birthday Parties for Children

Children parties are often Themed, which aids in putting together a coordinated look. For example a circus themed party may include colorful décor, brightly colored tableware, circus themed games, foods and party favors, and entertainment by a local clown. While a cowboy theme birthday party may feature cowboy hats, barbecue, and pony rides. Children's parties also often include party favors such as balloons or small toys.

Birthday Parties for Adults

While adult parties may or may not have a theme such as luau or fiesta, the Planning Process is similar, and just as important.

The date is usually on or near the birthday. Location may depend on the type of party and number of guests expected. Party décor may include Flowers, Streamers, posters, Decorative Lighting, or theme items. Tableware is usually chosen in coordinating colors which reinforce the theme or tone of the party. Food can consist or refreshments or a meal, again depending upon the type of party, party theme and budget. The location of the party may limit available options for Food and Refreshments: many church and community venues prohibit alcoholic beverages; some commercial venues require that food be catered by them. Entertainment can consist of games, activities, or performances. By knowing in advance what games will be played, preparations can be made for both game supplies and prizes. Activities such as pony rides or a sing-along can provide a fun way for guests to participate. Performances can entertain either adults or children: independent performers are available for anything from a magic show to a tasteful musical performance. There are many details to coordinate to host an unforgettable birthday party. By using a professional event planner the host/hostess can devote more attention to the guest of honour, help attend to the guests, and enjoy the festivities.

Event Management of Wedding Anniversaries

Wedding anniversary events celebrate important milestones in a couple's life together, and provide an opportunity for friends and relatives to join in celebrating that milestone. While most anniversary events occur at milestone intervals such as 10 years, 25 years, or 50 years, any anniversary can be a celebration. For many couples, the anniversary celebration includes a renewal of vows. This may be quite similar to an actual Wedding, with all the same detailed facets to coordinate Flowers, Décor, Music, and Photography, as well as details of the reception. Almost all wedding anniversary events include a reception. They are commonly held in an "open house" format where guests come and go during the specified time frame usually a weekend mid-afternoon. A small event may be located at the couple's home; if many guests are expected, another Venue may be chosen, such as a church fellowship hall, community center, or commercial venue, such as a Hotel.

Once again, Refreshments and Food are a central aspect of the festivities. Food may be provided by the family, friends, an outside caterer, or the catering staff of the venue.

Birthday Parties for Children

The menu usually consists of light refreshments, such as cake and punch, but may also include nuts, mints, coffee, and even light sandwiches or deli trays of finger foods. Décor can include flowers, paper streamers, and table decorations. Traditions for 25th anniversaries often feature a silver colour theme, while 50th anniversaries are gold.

Photo displays or slideshows add an interesting dimension to the celebration. Slide shows can be easily created with uploaded photographs and then enhanced with the addition of favourite music and slide transition effects. The slideshow can either be projected onto a screen or displayed on a large screen TV, and can be set so that the show progresses automatically once started.

Guests may be Invited privately, by formal invitation or phone call, or publicly, as with a notice published in the local newspaper. With both public invitations and especially church locations, there may be party crashers looking for free food.

A professional event planner can coordinate all the many details and help in overcoming any obstacles to making the anniversary celebration another successful milestone in a couple's life together.

Event Management for Family Events

Family events are fun and enjoyable to participate in. But they offer a number of challenges in the planning. The host of the event will usually select the date, and have some ideas about preferred locations. The host's home isn't usually a good choice due to parking constraints, so another location may be preferable. Before Choosing a Location, determine the scope of the event and estimate who will be attending. If there will be a large number of children, choosing a location with an adjacent playground may eliminate the need for planning ways to entertain the children. On the other hand, disabled family members may require facilities to be accessible. Facilities costs and amenities may widely vary, and some public facilities may require reservations up to a year in advance.

Food, Invitations and more

Food may be provided by the host, Outside Caterer, or the caterer affiliated with the facility where the event is to be held. The menu can consist of simple refreshments or a meal. There may not be a lot of Decorations; there may, instead, be souvenirs such as t-shirts, memory books, or cups printed with family Photographs. The family may want to have games or entertainment. Games can range from quiet table games to family sports competitions that can include everything from three-legged races to softball games. And entertainment may be impromptu skits or a sing along with a talented family member providing the music. Invitations are usually prepared and sent by the host. Double check about a week before the event to make sure it's been done.

Many family events are held Outdoors. Be prepared with a contingency plan for bad weather. Will you choose an alternate "rain date"? Or erect canopies to give shelter to guests? In extreme heat, some foods may spoil, and cold drinks will require extra ice. Family events can be a memorable, fun occasion. But sometimes the details don't come together, and they turn into a nightmare. The host doesn't have time to visit with guests, because he's busy scrambling to attend to the latest crisis. A professional event planner can attend to the details, leaving you to enjoy the party.

Event Management of Personal Events

Event management of personal events like birthdays, weddings and other events with family and friends. Many people may not realize that large corporations aren't the only ones that benefit from a professional event management company and that an event planner can be an affordable way to make those precious moments in life, or private events, even more memorable.

Whether you are hosting an 80th birthday party in your back yard or a wedding at an exotic location, an event manager can eliminate the stress and ensure the event is flawless. The event manager can help you choose a venue, plan a menu, visualize a theme, create an event website and carryout the endless details.

Planning private events such as a wedding can become overwhelming as you deal with multiple vendors. Interviewing caterers, entertainers and venues is time consuming and stressful. Hiring a professional event manager will ensure that you have one contact who is tracking all of the details for you.

Event management companies have a database of approved vendors, or will interview vendors you request, to ensure that your expectations are met. An event manager may even save you money, as the management companies are often able to negotiate prices with their vendors. Using an event planner can ensue that your theme carries throughout the event in the decorations, invitations, websites, food, entertainment and photography, providing a lasting image of the wonderful event for you and all of your guests.

8

Online Event Marketing Strategies

Placing a sales message in front of a qualified prospect is always a marketing goal. One way to accomplish this is through event marketing, in which a company is associated with a special event. This can work well when the company's products closely tie in with the event. The key to this strategy is finding or creating an event that opens prospects' minds to the marketing message.

Traditionally marketers have thought of event marketing as sponsoring a sporting event, industry conference, or even a social cause or project. Here is how these efforts can be translated online:

- Advertise on a site associated with a major event. Take a look at what sort of advertising you could do that would tie in with an upcoming sporting event. For example, the Kentucky Derby web site offers several advertising opportunities for companies.
- Sponsor an organization's online event. Sponsoring an event that is closely related to your product or company has the advantage of being seen as helping make an event or activity possible. This could be a community-service project that includes an informational web site.
- Donate to a nonprofit's auction. Fund-raising activities help many nonprofit organizations, and donations from businesses provide many of the products sold through auctions. An example is the online auction of the American Heart Association.
- Tie into a product. Dole, the fruit and vegetable company, has a product tie-in promotion with the Zany Brainy chain of toy stores and e-commerce web site. This association helps consumers see Dole as being interested in helping kids grow mentally and physically.

- Create a content site. Many times, it is possible to create a content site that educates and informs customers about your product category and leads the audience back to your web site. Dole's 5 A Day web site provides educational materials and lesson plans for teachers, information for parents, and activities for kids.

Most of the time, being closely associated with an event or activity is beneficial. But there are cases when it's not helpful and when it's even harmful. Say a nonprofit organization decided to discontinue an important event; negative feelings about this can spread to encompass a sponsoring company. It sometimes seems that the best way to avoid these problems is for a company to run the sponsored event or project itself with no outside control. However, if the public discovered that an organization thought to be completely independent were actually run by the sponsoring company, the publicity problems could be significant. Even ads running on the sites and materials associated with events or community projects can present problems. A content site covering an event might have material so timely and compelling that the audience doesn't even consider clicking on the sponsor's banner ads or links. For example, the recent presidential election resulted in a tremendous increase in traffic at news sites and other sites that focused on the political environment. On election night, however, the attention of the audience was so focused on the actual event that click-through rates possibly were below average.

Often, being associated with an event or a worthwhile cause can help a company reach an appropriate audience with a targeted message. It's important to choose these marketing opportunities carefully so that they highlight the company and present appropriate venues in which to deliver the company's marketing message.

Exhibit Marketing Mistakes: Ten Tips on How to Avoid Them!

The key to great exhibiting is marketing. But marketing is a very inexact science that leaves room for a multitude of errors to occur. The following are 10 of the most common marketing mistakes that exhibitors often make. Learn to avoid them and you will increase your chances for a successful tradeshow.

Have A Proper Exhibit Marketing Plan

Having both a strategic exhibit marketing and tactical plan of action is a critical starting point. In order to make tradeshows a powerful dimension your company's overall marketing operation, there must be total alignment between the strategic marketing and your exhibit marketing plan. Tradeshows should not be a stand-alone venture. Know and understand exactly what you wish to achieve-increasing market share with existing users; introducing new products/services into existing markets or into new markets; or introducing new products/services into new markets. This is the nucleus on which to build.

Have A Well-Defined Promotional Plan

A significant part of your marketing includes promotion pre-show, at-show and post-show. Most exhibitors fail to have a plan that encompasses all three areas. Budget is naturally going to play a major role in deciding what and how much promotional activity is possible. Developing a meaningful theme or message that ties into your strategic marketing plan will then help to guide promotional decisions. Know whom you want to target and then consider having different promotional programs aimed at the different groups you are interested in attracting. Include direct mail, broadcast faxes, advertising, PR, sponsorship, and the Internet as possible ways to reach your target audience.

Use Direct Mail Effectively

Direct mail is still one of the most popular promotional vehicles exhibitors use. From postcards to multi-piece mailings, attendees are deluged with invitations to visit booths. Many of the mailings come from show management's lists and as a result, everyone gets everything. To target the people you want visit your booth, use your own list of customers and prospects—it's the best one available. Design a piece that is totally benefit-oriented and makes an impact. Mail three pieces at regular intervals prior to the show, starting about four weeks out, to help ensure your invitation is seen. Wherever possible, use first-class mail. There's nothing worse than a mailing that arrives after the show is over.

Give Visitors an Incentive to Visit Your Booth

Whatever promotional vehicles you use, make sure that you give visitors a reason to come and visit you. With a hall overflowing with fascinating products/services, combined with time constraints, people need an incentive to come and visit your booth. First and foremost their primary interest is in "what's new!" They are eager to learn about the latest technologies, new applications, or anything that will help save them time and/or money. Even if you don't have a new product/service to introduce, think about a new angle to promote your offerings.

Have Giveaways that Work

Tied into giving visitors an incentive to visit your booth is the opportunity to offer a premium item that will entice them. Your giveaway items should be designed to increase your memorability, communicate, motivate, promote or increase recognition of your company. Developing a dynamite giveaway takes thought and creativity. Consider what your target audience wants, what will help them do their job better, what they can't get elsewhere, what is product/service related and educational. Think about having different gifts for different types of visitors. Use your website to make an offer for visitors to collect important information, such as an executive report, when they visit your booth. Giveaways should be used as a reward or token of appreciation for visitors participating in a demonstration, presentation or contest, or as a thank-you for qualifying information about specific needs etc.

Use Press Relations Effectively

Public relations is one of the most cost-effective and successful methods for generating large volumes of direct inquiries and sales. Before the show ask show management for a comprehensive media list, and find out which publications are planning a special show edition. Send out newsworthy press releases focusing on what's new about your product/service, or highlighting a new application or market venture. Compile press kits for the press office that include information about industry trends, statistics, new technology or production information. Also include good product photos and key company contacts. Have staff members at the booth who are specifically assigned to interact with the media

Differentiate Your Products/Services

Too many exhibitors are happy to use the "me too" marketing approach. Examine their marketing plans and there's an underlying sameness about them. With shows that attract hundreds of exhibitors, there are very few that seem to ";stand out from the crowd." Since memorability is an integral part of a visitors show experience, you should be looking at what makes you different and why a prospect should buy from you. This is of particular concern with generic products in your industry. Every aspect of your exhibit marketing plan, including your promotions, your booth and your people should be aimed at making an impact and creating

Use The Booth as an Effective Marketing Tool

On the show floor your exhibit makes a strong statement about who your company is, what you do and how you do it. The purpose of your exhibit is to attract visitors so that you can achieve your marketing objectives. In addition to it being an open, welcoming and friendly space, there needs to be a focal point and a strong key message that communicates a significant benefit to your prospect. Opt for large graphics rather than reams of copy. Pictures paint a thousand words while very few exhibitors will take the time to read. Your presentations or demonstrations are a critical part of your exhibit marketing. Create an experience that allows visitors use as many of their senses as possible. This will help to enhance memorability.

Realize that Your People are Your Marketing Team

Your people are your ambassadors. They represent everything your company stands for, so choose them well. Brief them beforehand and make sure that they know: why you are exhibiting; what you are exhibiting and what you expect from them. Exhibit staff training is essential for a unified and professional image. Make sure that they sell instead of tell; don't try to do too much; understand visitor needs; don't spend too much time; and know how to close the interaction with a commitment to follow-up.Avoid overcrowding the booth with company representatives. Have strict rules regarding employees visiting the show and insist staffers not scheduled for booth duty stay away until their assigned time. Assign specific tasks for company executives working the show.

Follow-up Promptly

The key to your tradeshow success is wrapped up in the lead-management process. The best time to plan for follow-up is before the show. Show leads often take second place to other management activities that occur after being out of the office for several days. The longer leads are left unattended, the colder and more mediocre they become. It is to your advantage to develop an organized, systematic approach to follow-up. Establish a lead handling system, set time lines for follow-up, use a computerized database for tracking, make sales representatives accountable for leads given to them, and then measure your results.

How to Prepare for a Fundraising Event

Well, that time of the year is upon us once again. People from all walks of life start to band together in pursuit of one common goal, to get their favourite candidate elected come November. Yes, election season is just about to arrive, meaning that we can now start flooding our candidates with enough wads of money to ensure that their campaign will stay afloat all the way up to the day we vote in these midterm elections. One of the most important aspects of any respectable campaign is the need to raise enough money to pay for advertisements, mudslinging jabs at an opponent, and all of the supplies and wages that are ultimately necessary to keep any campaign running at full steam. A lack of funding can easily mean that a candidate who should have otherwise easily swept the votes at the poles could end up simply treading water in a feeble attempt to save his political life.

No campaign can run without the need for fundraising. The act of raising funds for your favourite candidate is totally necessary even if the that candidate has an amazing track record, supports all kinds of initiatives that the average person is rooting for, and has enough charisma to be able to put a smile on even the most aggressive opponents. Unfortunately, most of the highly qualified candidates who should have won find themselves coming in last place in a two man race simply because not enough time was devoted to fundraising efforts. Without the money which acts as the lifeblood for any successful political campaign, a candidate will never be able to take any office in this country. No how, no way.

So, if you are highly supportive of a candidate and you want to help him or her win this coming election, what can you do to help? Without a doubt, a fundraising event is the best way to go about helping your favourite candidate. Since money is involved, you will have no problem getting the potential political winner to come to your fundraising event, so you already have the keynote speaker all lined up. All you really have to do is figure out what type of fundraising event you want to host and how much you should charge your attendees. While there are many different choices for a great fundraising event, many people simply choose to host a fundraising dinner because they are an excellent way for attendees to meet the politician and socialize amongst themselves. A successful fundraising dinner should have a wide selection of meals and a price tag per person that is not astronomically high considering the location and the event. Even though people will show up no matter how much the dinner at your fundraising event costs, it may be a better idea to have a lower priced meal and encourage that all of those in attendance contribute a bit of extra money on the side.

How to Organize a Shining Event

An event is any activity that requires you to make arrangements before the program can actually take place. It may be anything from an introductory meeting to a conference. No matter how small or easy an event may seem some forethought is required. A successful event is the result of a major investment of time and sound planning. Since many dynamics and factors are involved working with assumptions has to be avoided. The following are the ingredients of a successful event:

Have Good Event Pre-planning Processes

Have a clear vision for the event. There is need to create a vision for what the event will look like. In pre-planning (planning that is done before the event commences) one should:

a. Declare the event's purpose. In other words be clear about why you are having the event. The event purpose will help you from drifting off.
b. Identify the key driver of the event and stick to it. [It can be to wed to people, or get people save, etc.]

Have a clear picture of the People, Resources and Activities in the event

a. Decide who will be involved and assign specific responsibilities to each volunteer in the committee. All key areas of responsibility have to be monitored and supervised regularly. There might be a need to have subcommittees for different areas
b. Determine the amount of available funds and the amount you are willing to spend. Consider and contact potential co-sponsors for your event and decide each co-sponsor's responsibilities
c. Know who your intended audience is and determine a realistic expectation of event attendance in terms of numbers and the type of people
d. Identify potential locations where the event could be held. Apply for and be sure to receive a written confirmation that the event spaces you want are available for you to use
e. Begin developing an effective advertising campaign

Have means of measuring and monitoring event progress

a. Develop a realistic timeline for beginning and completing the various components of the planning process

b. The 7 questions: What, why, how much, who, how, when, where must be asked at all times in the planning process to ensure that all areas are covered and justified for.

c. The three key factors of an excellent event: Time factor, Quality factor and Cost factor have to be closely monitored and controlled effectively throughout the event planning process.

Conclusion

In conclusion, a good event is a result of proper pre-planning and it is easy to run and control. Proper monitoring and evaluation of an event will distinguish a successful from an unsuccessful event. An event with properly monitored processes will always shine out. Finally, investing quality time in pre-planning, avoiding making assumption and dealing with all key issues will guarantee that you will have a successful, shining event.

Reduce Event Management Cost with Online Registration Software

In today's events industry, with the rising price of materials and services, it can be a real challenge to grow your event and maintain the quality experience that your loyal attendees have come to expect. If inflated costs are contributing to a slow-down in growth for your event, event management software may be just the thing you need to streamline administration and do more with the human resources and budget you already have. Here are some ways that online registration software can help streamline event management:

Reduced Printing Costs

It used to be that all event registration, marketing and communication were done on paper. The event would print advertisements and post them all over town, the attendee would fill out a paper registration form, the event staff would mail a paper confirmation back to the attendee, and after the event was all over, the event organiser would send out a flyer to his attendees with an announcement about following year's event. Taking your event online with event management software will easily cut your printing costs and paper consumption in half. Pre-event marketing can be done with email advertising campaigns that have been proven to be more effective than post. Your event participant can register online and submit their data and payment through a customised online entry form. Registering online means that the attendee will receive an automatic confirmation email eliminating the need for your staff to print one and mail it off. After the event, a good event management software will allow you to send an electronic survey form and notification about the date for next years event.

Reduced Staff Hours

As mentioned above, one of the great advantages to offering event registration online is that your participants will receive an automatic confirmation email immediately following the submission of their data and payment. This not only eliminates the event staff's need to print and mail a confirmation but also puts the registrant's mind at ease. If your participants are currently registering on paper forms, your staff probably spends a good portion of their day answering phones and email from registrants who are concerned that you have not received their payment. If you are hosting registration online, the automatic confirmation email should reduce registrant inquiries considerably.

Event management software will also dramatically cut the number of hours your staff spends manually entering participant data into a spreadsheet or event database. Offering online entry for your event means that all data collected on the online registration form will be automatically sent to a secure database. If you currently collect paper forms you know how many late nights are spent transferring data from the hard copy over to the database. Those last days leading up to the event will be much less hectic with a system that automatically sorts and houses your data. You only need to log in to the event administration area of your software and check your numbers.

Reduced Over-Purchase of Merchandise and Food

One of the most challenging things any event organiser encounters in those last weeks leading up to the event is accurately predicting the number of event shirts he should order from his vendor or the number of hamburgers he should buy as opposed to hotdogs. Collecting event participant data by way of paper form means that there is lag time between when the form is received by mail and when that data is available in your database. In those last few weeks before the event, the speed at which you are able to get your participant data updated in the database is crucial. With online event management software, this is a non-issue because attendee data is automatically added to your database and available for viewing with real-time online reports. Adding shirt size and food preference questions to your custom online entry form will allow you to get quick accurate reports and email them on to your vendor or caterer at a moments notice. This will eliminate the need to guess how many orders to place which oftentimes ends up being more than you actually need and a waste of money.

In conclusion, growing your event without an increase in staff, payroll, and hours in the office is possible! Cost efficiency without a cut to the services you offer the attendee is the smart way to grow your event. A good event management system will help you streamline the logistics involved in planning your event and enable you to get more done with the money and staff you already have.

Marketing Optics can Cloak Reality

When I was young my parents told me to study hard, I would sit at my desk with a pile of books on one side, an open workbook book in front of me. When my parents would peak into my room they would say "It's nice to see you so busy." That's optics. Making decisions based on optics alone can catch up with you sooner or later resulting in bad grades, foiled campaigns and lost opportunities.

One of the concerns that many marketers face in these troubled times is a reduction in marketing budgets. The knee jerk reaction is to chop the number of shows and events. Other marketers are reluctant to reduce their face-to-face marketing exposure, continue their program, albeit with a reduced budget, for fear of creating a negative impression on potential buyers.

During the past few years there has been much talk about the value of face-to-face marketing. Industry experts, including myself, have detailed the process that will help exhibitors calculate a return on investment and return on objectives. Yet, surprisingly few have adopted this basic business tenant and integrated the practice into their exhibit plans. Some opt out when they learn that their efforts have not been as good as they would have imagined, other stay because they are led by the mistaken idea that the calculation of results are only for those who sell products. If more marketers would take the time to calculate their results, they would have the crucial answer on their return of their exhibiting investment. But the issue of optics involves one more criteria. You also have to look at the cost of not exhibiting. This may seem a more difficult number to calculate, but there is enough industry data around to help. For example the CEIR recently (Spring 2009) found that the cost of obtaining a high value lead at an exhibit was about half the cost of obtaining a similar lead without a trade show. The cost of an initial visit with a high quality contact was about a fifth of the cost when compared to non-show activity.

Statistics like these and the many more that are available point to a clear value for maintaining an exhibit program. However, what about those non-monetary values such as reinforcing a brand or gaining market share. Similar studies provide evidence that there are definite values in these non-monetary goals. In a CEIR's recent census, a survey of exhibitors found the following:

Exhibitions increase corporate and/or brand recognition 67% Agree or strongly agree.

Exhibitions assist in gaining/retaining market share 67% agree or strongly agree.

Source: CEIR, The cost effectiveness of exhibition participation, spring 2009.

With these numbers in mind the issue of optics comes into play. When you withdraw your support for your face-to-face program you run the risk of losing the direct advantage you sought by choosing to be there in the first place but of equal importance is that you also create a negative impression in your customer and industry's eyes that can be irreparable. Even if you can't justify your show participation by new contacts or orders written it is important to let the rest of the world know that you are not hurting. Stay visible even if you participate in a show with less space. However, don't shortchange your overall look and feel of your display just to be there. Stay visible in a smaller space but maintain the optics of success. At the end of the day your investment is sure to reap rewards.

Planning Your Fundraising Campaign-How Nonprofits Raise More Funds Online in a Global Recession

Fundraising for your nonprofit or charitable organization should be a positive happy experience, right?

It's about helping a great cause-sending kids to a national competition, improving a community, finding medical cures, saving animals, and more. These are important issues in our lives, to the tune of over $1 trillion dollars a year in donations!

But times have become more and more challenging for fundraisers.

Here Are Two Challenges Fundraisers Now Face When Planning Fundraising Events & Activities to Raise More Funds:

1. We deal with uncertain revenue streams, escalating overhead, and generating new interest from patrons and donors. Now as we're experiencing one of the worst recessions in decades, you may not be sure how to plan your fundraising. What can you expect from donors? Will they be there for you? Even if they want to give, do they want what you're offering?
2. Another big challenge is the way we've approached the job in the past. Usually the process is shared by parents, kids, and small business professionals. We "fan out" with our products and ask for the sale or set up sites for donations. Then, since most of us don't like to actually "sell stuff," we put it off. Ultimately, many people on the team end up buying "the stuff," only to give it away or store it in the garage-again.

So How Can Nonprofit and Charitable Organizations Raise More Funds Now

One innovative alternative has evolved and is getting lots of attention. The concept is based on the rise and undeniable appeal of global e-commerce. According to independent business researchers at Forrester Research, online retail sales reached $175 billion in 2007 and are projected to grow to $335 billion by 2012 in the United States. E-commerce has consistently grown by double digits each year for many reasons like convenience, variety and savings. And, most importantly, online shoppers seem to be less sensitive to adverse economic conditions than the average U.S. consumer.

How Can Nonprofit Organizations Raise Money Online

Your organization can send donors to a professionally designed and managed website that displays your charity's identity. People could shop for merchandise and services they want and need and you could be in a commissionable position without having to do anything! No recruits to find. No doorbells to ring. No inventory to manage. Just checks to cash. With the growth of e-commerce, successful businesses are emerging that distribute merchandise to online customers. This opens the door for others like you to earn commissions by bringing consumers to the online stores and malls.

Here Are 4 Benefits of Raising Money for Nonprofits Online Using Auction Sites:

1. It's a win-win fund raising option for you and your donors
2. You will start an excited buzz among patrons of your organization which means one customer can bring in many more
3. It's a possible source for tremendous revenue for your nonprofit organization
4. It's an inexpensive system with hands-off maintenance.

Thousands of online shoppers are already searching for their own personal bargains every day. It makes sense that the world of fund raising should be a part of the fun-and the profits. For example, one very enterprising fund raiser, a radio station in Germany, sold over $10,000,000 in e-commerce credits to 100,000 customers in 18 months on their privately branded site. The radio station was paid 30% of the sales, or over $3,000,000! By creating a business-to-business partnership with an e-commerce company, you can experience the above results. And, with an insignificant capital investment and essentially no financial risk, you can participate in the parent company's success and dynamic global presence. Good luck exploring new possibilities for your next fundraising campaign!

10 Reasons Meetings and Events are Important in Tough Times

When the powers that be come swinging the axe towards your event or meeting, here are ten points to make so they think twice. The arguments below are very similar to those offered by advertising professionals over the years when advertising is looked at as an unnecessary expense by the cost cutters. These arguments take a different twist, however, since they were developed with input from meeting planners. Stand firm and you just might be able to convince the powers that be that it is still necessary to hold your meeting or event!

1. Companies that do hold meetings set themselves apart from the masses that are slashing and cutting back. They will have an edge when the economy picks up again.
2. Holding off-site meetings and conventions sends the message that 'we' as a company are solid.
3. We can have the meeting, but we will keep it low key. It's not politically correct to do something extravagant right now.

4. ROI (return on investment) is always tricky to measure, but for meetings and conventions, we can prove they boost the bottom line: solidified relationships are more important now than ever.
5. Sharing information with all who need it at the same time is critical to the success of our new project or new product launch.
6. Meetings create enthusiasm that is contagious.
7. Hearing an outside voice makes the message more memorable. Enlisting the support of an industry expert will give our content more impact.
8. Using a trained facilitor assures that all points of view are aired and considered.
9. Many members of our organization rarely see each other-productivity will rise from being able to solve common problems that are never broached in e-mail exchanges.
10. For motivation, there is nothing better than face time.

How to Run Stress-Free Events

Hi there,

Some time ago I attended three major events, two were well-run, the third was a shambles. All three had a number of speakers and more than 200 hundred people present.

The Disorganised Event

This is what happened at one of those events:

On arrival, there were two people at the front desk who completely ignored me, so I walked straight in and organised my own stand. (This was a combination expo/seminar event).

There were no name tags for stallholders or attendees.

Refreshments were non-existant. Even water was unavailable.

Instead of briefly wrapping up at the end of each presentation, the Master of Ceremonies wasted at least another 10-15 minutes rambling on. A sponsor who wasn't scheduled to speak was 'squeezed' into the programme for a SHORT 10 minute promotion. He prattled on for 40 minutes boring everyone. No one, including the organiser or the MC stopped him.

At one point, the audience had been sitting for two hours with no break.

The last speaker who was scheduled to speak at 3.30 p.m. presented at 5.00 p.m... that's how poorly organised the event was. By this time many people had left (including me).

The sad part about the lack of organisation is that some of the presenters were great and so were many of the people who attended. The event management by the organiser would have tainted their reputation and reflected extremely badly on the company they represented.

Unfortunately, many of the attendees will remember more of the negative aspects, rather than the positive ones.

The Ingredients of Successful Events

With the end of another year in site, many of you will be in the process of planning events for your clients and your people in the new year, so I've put together a special event management tip sheet to help you save time, money and stress when preparing for your next event. Click here to receive "How To Run Stress-Free Events".

Speaking of running events in 2006, I'm presenting a terrific seminar to kickstart the new year together with Shelley-Taylor Smith, 7 time World Champion Marathon Swimmer and Motivation Expert. This one of a kind event will be held in both Melbourne and Sydney. If you seriously want to "Skyrocket to Success in 2006" then click here to book today as numbers will be limited and we've already had bookings pouring in.

The Final Word

Organising and attending events where you'll meet new people and expand your mind is crucial to stay ahead in both your personal and business life. The world is constantly changing and you need to change with it. Fresh input gives you a different perspective. It's very easy to stay in your comfort zone. However when you expand your mind, you learn more and can earn more. When you apply what you learn, you'll enrich your own life and can help others to do the same.

How to Get the Most Out of a Networking Event

Networking events take place all over the country. From small towns to big cities, networking is a part of any business model on the planet. Perhaps the biggest part of networking is convincing yourself to be social and not just a wallflower. The next time you attend a networking function consider the following tips to help you become more successful and bring in more business

What to do before a Networking Event

Before you attend the event write down what your strengths, attributes and special skills are. This way you will know exactly why someone should be interested in what you have to offer. Keep these strengths in your head in order to boost your confidence and remind yourself of why people should be talking with you and listening to what you have to say. Another great idea is to picture the room in your mind and picture yourself shaking hands and talking with people. By visualizing everything you will be doing it can really help even they most shy individual. Visualization is a powerful tool used by many successful people whether it is in business, sports or entertainment.

What to do when you Arrive at a Networking Event

When you finally show up make sure you have a confident posture, a controlled walk, a smile on your face and a firm handshake to those you meet. And never forget to make lots of eye contact. Then be sure to use the immediate environment to start a conversation such as the venue or the host. This will help you to find a common bond and to keep the conversation going. Always start with small talk before you get down to business.

What to do during a Networking Session

When you need to get down to business have some questions prepared to ask people in order to find out what their needs are and if your services will help people. You don't have to be pushy, rather soft sell yourself and build interest. This will make people more receptive to be helped by you.

Talking is only half of the event. When it comes your turn remember to repeat the individuals name back to them, actively listen to what they have to say and keep a mental database of as many details you can about the person to whom you are talking. If possible always get a business card and don't be afraid to ask for it. The best time to ask is usually after they have talked about what they do and then you can offer yours in return.

What to do after a Networking Event

Then when you return home be sure to write out information on the back of the card or a sheet of paper that can be stapled to the card. This way you can maintain and build and rapport for a future meeting, email or phone call.

Everyone likes a person who remembers them. Within twenty-four hours be sure to email everyone you met and say you enjoyed meeting them. It's also good to mention a detail you remember and suggest that they keep in touch with you.

By incorporating these simple tips and strategies into your next networking event not only will you enjoy yourself more but also bring in more customers to your business.

How to Plan a Successful Corporate Event?

A successful corporate event is very important for your company. When it leaves a memorable experience for your guests, it can help to increase your company goodwill and branding. Therefore, it is very common to see corporations investing their money to hold annual events to help boost up their branding awareness.

So, suppose you have been chosen to organize your company's corporate event. What are some of the things that you need to do in order to plan out a successful corporate event?

The first thing that you will want to consider in the planning process is the food. Food is an integral part of any event. Often, the potential success of any event is determined by the quality of the food. You should hire a professional catering service company to help you handle this process. With the help of a catering service company, you can channel your energy and focus on other important details when planning a corporate event.

Before you set out to hire a catering service, there are a few important things that you need to take note of. You need to know exactly what the mood of your corporate event is. Is there a theme? Is your event elegant or casual? These are important information that you need to let your caterer know so that the theme of your event can be reflected in your cuisine.

You should also find out whether your caterer provides you with amenities such as tables, chairs, decorations, and linens. A quality catering service should provide all of these amenities so as to make your event as successful as possible. Another thing to note is the number of people who are attending your event. It is very common for people to not turn up on the actual day itself even though they have already registered for your event. Therefore, ask your co-worker to do an attendance check so that you will not over-order the amount of food needed.

Some points to consider when planning out your corporate event are:

1. What is your event's intention? Is it a thank you party for clients and vendors? Or are you planning to reveal a new service or product to your potential clients?
2. Set the time of your event. Often, 3 hours is appropriate for a corporate event. Then, prepare your guest list and send out invitation to them.
3. If you intend to serve alcoholic drink, you should hire a bartender. 4. Think about your menu options and discuss with your caterer. Are you preparing a buffet style or a sit down dinner for your guests? Also, consider your guests that may have special dietary needs.

With early planning, you will be able to organize a successful event for your guests to enjoy.

Short Changing Your Trade Show ROI by NOT Planning

It seems to be a fact of life-we are poor planners.

And it is surprising, especially when we talk about planning for various marketing activities which have high price tags. Trade shows have proven to be an effective tool for marketing. Still, there are far too many exhibitors who rush into the activity, throw money at it, and then leave wondering where their money went?

What was all that fuss and expense for?

Why is this happening?

Is it because companies don't know how to plan for the best way to spend marketing dollars? Are they too caught up in negotiating the ups and downs of other marketing activities?

Is it the culture of the organization to always be rushing about and entering into all and sundry activities?

"Exhibitors know how to plan,but they are so overloaded with their many projects; they just do not take the time to plan. It is sad to see, but it is what it is." Bob Dallmeyer, RD International. One thing is for sure. Poor planning can be costly in time, human effort and most importantly dollars. Cynthia Stine, President of Promote Success PR, say that some of her clients are use to "casting a net at a trade show and coming home with some fish. But if they were to do planning the catch could be twice, maybe triple the amount!" Dedicated time and proper planning must to be devoted to trade show activities for maximum success. Cynthia urges companies to spend at least two months planning before a show and several weeks after a show to get the maximum benefit from it.The planning process is part of the marketing function and is comprised of multiple tasks and responsibilities leading up to the event. This include planning your booth space, graphics, booth personnel, communications, media exposure, white papers, lead criteria sheets, and on and on. You've got to rehearse.

This kind of investment of time, human recourse, and material means that last minute planning for trade shows has to stop!

So how does one go about that within their organization? Take the first step and start holding meetings about the upcoming trade show effort. Make sure these meetings are power packed with information and then action items, so that the entire team is well versed in what will take place at the show.

* Step 1-go over the last trade show facts and figures to assess what was great about it, as well as where there were areas that could use improvement?
* Step 2-outline what will take place at this show and how it can be different from the last experience. What are the major reasons for this show? Do you have all parties involved in the planning process?
* Step 3-assign team members various tasks concerning the show activity. One might be responsible for the booth design, graphics, etc. while another for the communications strategy involving customers and prospects. For each aspect of the show tasks, a person should be assigned to that task and held accountable.
* Step 4-map out all the tasks and personnel responsible, so that the entire team can see where they fit into the whole. Apply peer pressure for the team to fulfill their roles.

It is vital that the sales team be involved in the planning process. Upfront team member involvement means a greater likelihood that appropriate action will be taken when post-show leads are turned over after the show. They should have input on what information is captured on the lead forms-then they know they have the correct information to act on all the leads captured at the show.

There is a saying I use to remind myself: ONE hour of planning saves THREE hours of execution. I don't know about you, but I can use all those saved hours for more productive endeavors.

9

The Event Budget

The event budget is a projection (forecast) of the income and expenditure that the event will incur based on plans made and information gathered. The preparation of a budget is an essential part of event management. It is fundamentally important that Event Directors are able to predict with reasonable accuracy whether the event will result in a profit, a loss or will break-even. This is achieved by identifying and costing all probable expenditures and by totalling all expected revenues (income). By comparing expenditures and revenues, it then becomes possible to forecast the financial outcome of the event. The construction of an event budget allows the Event Director to exercise financial control. Many organisations have run into severe financial difficulty and even bankruptcy as a result of staging events. The budget therefore enables the Event Director to make sound financial decisions about the choice of venue, and expenditure on promotion and equipment. The process of budgeting also enables the Event Director to calculate how much revenue is needed to stage the event in accordance with all plans.

The preparation of an event budget is one of the earliest tasks to be undertaken in the event management process. However, it should be expected that there will be numerous adjustments and refinements to the budget throughout the whole project life-cycle. It is not possible to know every cost from the start, nor is it possible to know whether efforts to secure sponsorship and government funding will be successful. Event budgets by the event management team as better information comes to hand. Although the budget takes time to develop, there are some rules that should be observed throughout:

- Budget to avoid making a loss
- Be realistic about event incomes
- Have a financial contingency plan i.e what happens if the sponsorship is not forthcoming?

Once constructed, the budget assists the Event Team to determine whether a proposed course of action fits within planned financial strategies, or not. If the answer is in the affirmative, i.e. the item is said to be "within budget".

If the answer is in the negative, then there is an understanding that continuing to pursue that strategy has a higher degree of risk, and the event profit will be reduced. This does not mean, however, that any departure from the set budget is inadvisable. It may be that the "unbudgeted" cost item has obvious financial benefits.

Typical Event Expenditure

For information on typical forms of event income click here.

Events costs will depend on the scale and type of event. Not all the categories stated in the table below will apply to every event.

Travel and Accommodation	Costs associated with officials needed to run the event may have to be borne by the event organisers. Event participants are generally responsible for their own travel and accommodation costs. In minor or local events travel and accommodation costs are unlikely.
Trophies, Awards	The cost of medals, trophies and other awards requires detailed knowledge about the number of competitors, the categories of divisions of the competition and the format of the competition.
Salaries	Applies only events are organised by professional staff.
Postage and telephone	Events usually require considerable communications with participants and the event management team.
Stationery and Photocopying	Special event stationery may be printed but otherwise there is always a lot of photocopying and usage of organisation letterheads to write correspondence.

Contd...

Medical Fees	Events require persons with at least First Aid training to be in attendance. Larger events may also warrant the employment of a doctor and physiotherapists.
Venue Hire	A critically important aspect of the budget. Information about the probable cost of the venue needs to be obtained as early as possible. Beware that there some hidden costs such as security and supervision costs, and heating and lighting costs.
Insurance	Additional insurance can be taken out to cover risks of injury and/or financial losses associated with events.
Printing	Event programmes, posters, fliers and other promotional documents may need to be printed-especially where quality and colour is required.
Promotion	Expenditure on promotion may be considerable where a significant proportion of the event revenue is likely to be earned through spectators. Promotion covers items such as advertising, give-aways, costs associated with promotional events and sponsors' signage.
Equipment Hire	Includes equipment directly used by participants in the event and also any equipment used by the event management staff including sound systems, computers, mobile phones, two way radios, etc.
Transport	Includes costs of transporting equipment and hire of buses.

Selling the Event

For several reasons, promotion is a key factor in the success of a special event. The main purpose that promotion serves is to attract participants, spectators or both to the event. A football match without a crowd is always disappointing and so is a local tennis tournament with only half the expected number of players. It is essential therefore that the efforts of many people over many months to organise a special event produce a result i.e. a good attendance. Promotion is also important to the sponsor, if one exists. The objective of the sponsor is to achieve as much exposure of their name, logo and other properties as possible. Sponsors therefore have a keen interest in pre-event promotion such as publicity in the media and advertising and in the promotion they can achieve on the day through erecting signage and product displays in view of all participants.

Promotion is also important to the organisation for reasons other than attracting a crowd on the day. A well promoted event increases public awareness of the organisation. This is a chief reason why special events are important. Achieving an attendance target is not only good for the atmosphere of the tournament but also it is often a critical component that determines the event's financial success. Event organisers require income earned from spectator attendance or participants fees to pay for costs of the event. Any shortfall in expected revenues can have a disastrous effect on organisations that stage special events. There are numerous cases of sport and recreation organisations that have suffered major financial loss and even bankruptcy as a result of staging one event.

The means of promotion should be considered from the outset i.e. in the feasibility analysis. Organisers need to consider promotional strategies in order to estimate the total costs of the event. They must select strategies that are most reliable and cost effective in terms of achieving the target participation or patronage. Promotion is a key result area in event management and as such is deserving of adequate human and financial resources. Appointing a manager or co-ordinator for promotion is a sensible strategy. Methods of promotion are often classified into three categories:

1) Publicity
2) Advertising
3) Promotional events.

Organisers are often disappointed when the result of their promotional efforts is less than desired. One key concept to consider is that decisions to "purchase" a good or a service are usually the result of repeated exposure to promotional messages.

Choosing to participate or spectate in an event is a form of deciding to purchase. Potential purchasers need repeated exposure to information and promotional messages about the event. With each exposure, the potential customer's attitudes and intentions to purchase may change. The following diagram serves to illustrate how this works in theory.

Therefore it is vital that event managers plan multiple promotional strategies and employ these strategies in an orchestrated campaign.

Managing Event Staff

The success of the event will be very largely determined by how well event staff carry out their allocated tasks before and during the event. Although the event plan may stipulate and provide details of every task that needs to be completed, it is still necessary for the Event Director to ensure that every task is completed by the required date and time. It is the nature of event management that one small task, if not completed, can have a major effect on the success of the event. Supposing that someone forgets to pick up the trophies the day before the event and now the trophy shop is shut for the weekend. Perhaps, no-one checks the electronic scoreboard before the start of the event and it fails to work.

Although the Event Director has ultimate responsibility for all matters concerning the event they cannot and should not try to be in all places at the same time. Instead they must devise systems that result in:

1. The development of a management structure (i.e. area co-ordinators) so that responsibility can be shared among many
2. The provision of job descriptions for all event staff
3. The creation and use of systems that provide feedback to the event director when tasks are completed
4. Implementation of systems that enable staff to self-check the completion of tasks
5. The organisation meetings between event management team and director.

Online Learning for Sports Management

- Boards & Committees
- People Management
- Budgeting
- Financial Management
- Event Management
- Service Delivery
- Funding & Sponsorship
- Legal Issues

- Planning
- Policy Development
- Risk Management.

Study Menu

- Types of Events
- Bidding for Events
- The Event Director
- The Event Team
- Financing the Event
- The Event Budget
- Selling the Event
- Managing Staff
- The Project Schedule
- The Event Programme
- Event Safety
- Student Activities
- Site Map.

The Timeframe for Event Management Tasks

The table below includes the majority of tasks that must be carried out in order to successfully stage an event. Some differences may arise where venues are owned and operated by the event organisers and where the scale of the event is very small e.g. an intra-club event (in which case timeframes may be smaller) or very large e.g. The Olympic Games (in which case timeframes will be greater).

The Event Programme

The "Programme" is the schedule of activities from the start of the event to its conclusion. For a sport event, the programme governs which competitors participate at what time. For a conference, the programme stipulates the times of lectures and workshops, what topics are offered and who is presenting. If the event is the annual awards dinner, the programme sets out what time people should arrive, what time each course will be served and the times that each award ceremony will take place. The programme is therefore perhaps the central organising component of the event. Keeping to times as advertised on the programme is a key performance measure from the standpoint of the participant's satisfaction. An event that fails to run on time will inevitably cause complaints from participants and frustration on the part of all persons. People can be very adversely affected if the event runs overtime and obviously commencing before the advertised time is definitely NOT something to ever contemplate.

In setting the programme, event organisers need to estimate as accurately as possible the time that each and every activity in the programme will take. Furthermore, it is necessary to include in this calculations a time interval between each activity. This time interval is very important. There is usually always a need to move people and equipment, allow for introductions and thank-you's, make announcements and allow time for refreshments to be served and toilet breaks. Preparing the official programme will inevitably require someone to make many computations with calculator or spreadsheet. The draft programme produced is likely to changed and amendment many times before it is ready for publication.

The important factors to consider in preparing the official programme are:

1. Consultation with all parties directly involved in the programme
2. Calculating the time of each and every activity
3. Ensuring that the programme has time for "ceremonial" activities e.g. opening and/or closing ceremonies, speeches, the presentation of awards, entertainment
4. Ensuring that the venue is available for the FULL duration of the event
5. Choosing the date(s) so that the event does not clash with other major events
6. Allowing for a little "slack" time between activities
7. The order of activities
8. How the printed programme will be published.

Ceremonies

Ceremonial aspects of events should not be underestimated in importance. They include opening and closing speeches, musical fanfares, playing of national anthems, presentation of awards and flowers, visits from dignitaries, flag raising, and special displays. While not a necessary component, there is an increasing trend to add ceremonial activities to the event programme. They add greatly to the emotion, symbolism and entertainment value of the event. The inclusion of ceremonial activities is more common where events are of national importance, are televised and have major sponsors. Nevertheless adding a little ceremony to the event programme, which often costs very little, should be considered for smaller events.

A failure to include ceremonial activities is an opportunity lost for the organisation hosting the event.

Some points to consider in adding ceremony to the event programme are:

- Dignitaries that fail to show or arrive late-make contingency plans
- Capturing and positioning the crowd to witness the ceremony-they tend not to be effective if the people are dispersed too widely
- Ceremonies that are not well organised may backfire badly-include rehearsals
- Consider carefully the best time for ceremonies in the event programme-try to avoid dignitaries arriving at bad times or when there a few to witness i.e crowd at its smallest.

Event Safety

Below are a number of scenarios that indicate the range of risks associated with crowds at sporting events. Although some of these scenarios may seem to have a low probability, they do actually occur. As an event manager you are expected to have some kind of plan to deal with these problems if and when they occur.

- a spectator in one of the stands has a heart attack and requires urgent medical attention?
- someone in one of the stands sets off a smoke canister and there are surges of people pushing in all directions trying to get away?
- one of the parachutists (as seen in the picture above) lands badly and is suspected to have spinal injuries?
- the number of people in one of the stands exceeds the design limit?
- there is an earthquake during the event?
- there is an electrical storm during the event?
- and of course there are many more possibilities!

It is extremely important for event organisers to have an emergency plan in place.

The objectives of such a plan would be to reduce the possible consequences of an emergency through the provision of training to event staff in:

- early recognition of emergency situation
- actions to be taken to bring medical services (e.g. ambulance) to those in need
- crowd communication, direction and control
- accelerating the resumption of normal operations.

An emergency plan specifies the organisation's policies and procedures for handling sudden and unexpected situations which require immediate attention.

Elements of an Emergency Plan

1. An Emergency Plan should include the following elements with the appropriate documentation:
    - Assessment of the size and nature of the events foreseen and the probability of their occurrence. It is highly recommended that a vulnerability analysis be instigated.
2. Formulation of a plan in consultation with outside authorities such as emergency services, fire department, police
3. Procedures;
    - raising the alarm
    - invoking the emergency plan
    - communication both within and outside the site
    - evacuation of non-essential personnel to pre-determined safe assembly points by pre determined exits
4. Appointment of key personnel and their duties and responsibilities
    - site incident controller
    - site main controller
5. Emergency control centre (if required)
6. Action on site, for example alerting staff and students, ordering evacuation, confirming evacuation is complete
7. Action off site, alerting external agencies, alerting population, requesting external aid, advising the media

8. Where and how injured persons are to be treated. Are suitable first aid facilities on site?
   - The plan should define the way in which personnel at the incident site can initiate action. The plan should also contain the full sequence of key personnel to be called but consideration needs to be given to absences due to sickness and holidays, and any other changes in manning.
   - Emergency planning should consider the need to make arrangements for an authoritative release of information to the media. A person whould be appointed to receive enquiries from the public.
   - Appropriate training needs to be given to all personnel who are part of the emergency plan.
   - Once the Emergency Plan has been finalised and appropriate training has been conducted then the plan should be tested in one of three ways:
     * full scale exercise to test command, co ordination and communication setups
     * tabletop exercises can be used to test some aspects of the emergency plan, and has the advantage of not interrupting normal operations
     * specific aspects of the plan can be tested, for example communication and evacuation.
   - The Emergency Plan must be regularly updated. This will take into account changes in personnel, telephone numbers and storage areas. This requirement should be written into the plan, and should be responsibility of a particular individual.

Promote Events Through Social Media – Part One

Social media is continually changing how we plan and promote events, especially how we engage with attendees. Event planners can use social channels to improve their events while also increasing attendance. When we started to write this, we realized we have a lot to say on this topic. From promoting an event beforehand using social media to using social channels at the event to engage your attendees, and leveraging social media afterwards, is content worthy of three blog posts. Here are a handful of helpful tips. If you have others, please let us know in the comments section.

Using Social Media as a Pre-Event Marketing Tool

First, you have to set yourself and/or your event up on the social channels you would like to leverage. Sounds easy, but do you know which channels your audience uses most? Are they more active on Twitter, Facebook, or LinkedIn? Perhaps all three? A quick search of Twitter lists, popular industry hashtags, relevant industry LinkedIn Groups, and even Facebook Groups, can help you find people already discussing your company or industry. This can help narrow the channels of focus.. This can also help create your own lists of people to begin engaging with. Perhaps invite them to be a Fan of your Facebook Page, join your LinkedIn Group or follow them on Twitter (and engage with them so they will follow you back). Once your accounts are established and you're comfortable using them, you will need to make sure people know about your new online presence. Notify employees so they can add the links of the social media accounts to their email signatures and follow them. Also make sure to add URLS to your email newsletter, customer emails, promotional materials for your event, website, event homepage, and your blog.

Leverage Social Media Channels to Increase Attendance

One of the benefits to social media is that you can easily identify people with similar interests to that of your industry or event. As mentioned, a search of Twitter lists, popular industry hashtags, LinkedIn Groups, and even Facebook Groups can help you find people who are already discussing your company or industry. You can leverage this research and these individuals to increase your attendance through targeted messages that encouraging engagement with your social channels.

Provide Event Giveaways

Make it worth someone's while to follow your event through social networking. Provide valuable content regarding the event and the industry being represented. Offer followers early-bird registration offers, discounts (the 100th follower gets in free), contests, and sneak peeks of products or services being announced at the event.

Create an Event Page

A professional, interactive, and detailed event page is key. However, customizing an event page to look like an organizations website or adhering to branding standards can often be costly and time consuming. Through RegOnline, the new Theme Designer makes creating a professional and great looking event website easier for everyone. You can match the appearance of your event to your existing website, even using the site's CSS code to match the look and feel exactly. You can also build a custom theme that will look clean, professional and trustworthy. Or, simply choose from our library of custom-designed forms to put the skills of our professional designers to work for your organization. Regardless of how you build your page there are key elements you need to make ensure you include. The obvious: important dates, event location, contact information, how to register, etc. But is also important that the event page has information/ links to all your social channels.

Add Your Event to Facebook

RegOnline recently added a Promote page to help you publish your event to Facebook and a handful of event directories. Unlike simply posting a link to your event in a Facebook status update, the Add Your Event to Facebook feature creates a Facebook Event tied to your Facebook account that other users can register for. If you have ever received a "Sandra D invited you to the event "Sandra D's Birthday Party..." message from Facebook, you are familiar with the concept of Facebook Events. They are a fantastic tool that you can use to increase awareness of your event among your friends, colleges, and all other Facebook users.

Note: *You do need to remember, however, that just because someone signs up for your Facebook Event, they are not automatically signed up for your event in RegOnline.*

Create an Event Blog

Your event page will house all the details for the event but your blog can go into much greater detail. For instance, you can have your speakers post their bios or even short posts regarding what to expect from their sessions.. Your blog posts also provide more content to share on your other social channels – tweeting about the post with a link back, posting the URL to your Facebook page, and sharing it with relevant LinkedIn groups.

Crowd Sourcing for Events

Solicit feedback from your followers to help plan the event. Ask people what *THEY* want through surveys and polls. You can also ask for recommendations for caterers, photographers, and musicians, or any other vendors you might be looking to hire for your event.

Brand Events with Designated Hashtags

Hashtags are typically a word preceded by a # sign and can be used to unify tweets from multiple people on the same subject. (For example, #SXSW is the hashtag for the popular South by Southwest event.) It is important to promote this hashtag at the event and beforehand so people will be aware and use it. You can add this hashtag to your event page, marketing materials, blog content and other social and marketing channels. When creating your hashtag, keep in mind that you want something unique, since using a generic tag for your event (like #event) will just ensure that it gets lost in a sea of tweets.

Event Chain Methodology

Event chain methodology is an uncertainty modeling and schedule network analysis technique that is focused on identifying and managing events and event chains that affect project schedules. Event chain methodology is the next advance beyond critical path method and critical chain project management.. Event chain methodology helps to mitigate effect motivational and cognitive biases in estimating and scheduling.. In many cases, project managers intentionally or unintentionally create project schedules that are impossible to implement. The methodology also simplifies the process of defining risks and uncertainties in project schedules, particularly by improving the ability to provide reality checks and to visualize multiple events. Event chain methodology is used to perform more accurate quantitative analysis while taking into account such factors as relationships between different events and actual moments of the events.

Event Chain Methodology Principles

Moment of Risk and State of Activity

An activity (task) in most real life processes is not a continuous uniform procedure. Tasks are affected by external events, which transform an activity from one state to another. One of the important properties of an event is the moment when an event occurs during the course of an activity. This moment, when an event occurs, in most cases is probabilistic and can be defined using statistical distribution.

Event Chains

Events can cause other events, which will create event chains. These event chains can significantly affect the course of the project.

For example, requirement changes can cause an activity to be delayed. To accelerate the activity, the project manager allocates a resource from another activity, which then leads to a missed deadline. Eventually, this can lead to the failure of the project.

Monte Carlo Simulations

Once events and event chains are defined, quantitative analysis using Monte Carlo simulation can be performed to quantify the cumulative effect of the events. Probabilities and effects of risks are used as input data for Monte Carlo simulation of the project schedule. In most real life projects, it is necessary to supplement the information regarding the uncertainties expressed as an event, with distributions related to duration, start time, cost, and other parameters.

Critical Event Chains

The single events or the event chains that have the most potential to affect the projects are the "critical events" or "critical chains of events." By identifying critical events or critical chains of events, we can mitigate their negative effects. These critical chains of events can be identified by analyzing the correlations between the main project parameters, such as project duration or cost, and the event chains.

Performance Tracking with Event Chains

Monitoring the activity's progress ensures that updated information is used to perform the analysis. During the course of the project, the probability and time of the events can be recalculated based on actual data. The main issue with performance tracking is forecasting an activity's duration and cost if an activity is partially completed and certain events are assigned to the activity. The simple heuristic approach to this problem is to analyze the moment of risk, which is defined as one of the event parameters. Advanced analysis can be performed using a Bayesian approach.

Bibliography

Brunt, Paul: *Market Research in Travel and Tourism*, Oxford, Butterworth Heinemann, 1997.

Cukier, J. : *Tourism Employment in Bali: Trends and Implications*, London: Thompson, 1996.

Donald E. : *Public Personnel Management: Contexts and Strategies*, Upper Saddle River, NJ: Prentice Hall, 1998.

Douglas C: *Practical Tourism Forecasting*, Oxford, Butterworth Heinemann, 1996.

Eberts, Marjorie: *Careers in Travel, Tourism, and Hospitality*, Lincolnwood, VGM Career Horizons, 1997.

Hoffman, Edward: *Project Management Success Stories: Lessons of Project Leaders*, New York, John Wiley & Son, 2000.

Ireland, Lewis: *Quality Management for Projects and Programs*, Upper Darby, PMI, 1991.

Larkham, P J: *Building a New Heritage: Tourism, Culture & Identity in the New Europe*, London, Routledge,1994.

Lewis, Robert C.: *Cases in Hospitality Marketing and Management*, New York, John Wiley, 1997.

Lucas, Rosemary E.: *Managing Employee Relations in the Hotel and Catering Industry*, London, Cassell, 1995.

Madhukar Manoj : *Hospitality Industries in Next Millennium*, Rajat, Delhi, 2001.

McNicol, B.J. : *Views of Residents, Developers and Government Planners About Tourists and Tourism Resort Developments in Canmore, Alberta*, The University of Galgary, Alberta, 1996.

Moscardo, G. : *Tourism Community Analysis*, London and New York: Routledge, 1999.

Nijkamp, Peter: *Sustainable Tourism Development*, Aldershot, Avebury, 1995.

Norman G.: *Hotel, Restaurant, and Travel Law: A Preventive Approach*, Albany, Delmar Publishers, 1993.

Peter J.: *College & University Foodservice Management Standards*, Westport, AVI Pub. Company, 1985.

Prentice, R: *Conceptualising The Experiences of Heritage Tourists*, 1997.

Ratti Manish : *Hospitality Management : Theories and Practices*, Rajat Pub, Delhi, 2007.

Richards, G. : *Culture, Crafts and Tourism: A Vital Relationship*, Tilburg: Atlas, 1999.

Robert C.: *Cases in Hospitality Marketing and Management*, New York, John Wiley, 1997.

Rosenzweig, J. E.: *Organisation and Management*, New York, McGraw Hill International, 1963.

Sabharwal Rajiv : *Tourism and Hospitality Management in Liberalised Era*, Pacific, Delhi, 2011.

Sharma Sunil : *Planning and Development of Tourism and Hospitality*, Rajat Pub, Delhi, 2007.

Slinn, Judy A: *Tourism: Management of Facilities*, London, Pitman: M & E, 1993.

Smith, G. : *International Tourism and Hospitality Careers through Education and Training*, CHRIE Annual Conference, Washington DC, 1996.

Stallworthy, E.: *Waste Management Towards a Sustainable Society*, Auburn House, New York, 1990.

Swarbrooke, J.: *Marketing Tourism, Hospitality and Leisure in Europe*, London, International Thomson Business Press, 1996.

Thomas, F.: *Introduction to Management in the Hospitality Industry*, New York, Wiley, 1995.

Timothy, R.: *Cases in Hospitality Management: A Critical Incident Approach*, New York, Wiley, 1995.

Vallette, J.: *The International Trade in Wastes: A Greenpeace Inventory*, Washington, Greenpeace, 1989.

Index

A

Announcing Events, 227.
Annual Shareholders, 278.
Art Exhibition, 220, 221, 222.

B

Business, 1, 5, 8, 10, 11, 21, 24, 25, 26, 27, 30, 31, 32, 33, 34, 35, 36, 38, 42, 44, 45, 47, 49, 50, 52, 55, 56, 57, 60, 61, 62, 63, 65, 66, 68, 69, 73, 76, 78, 81, 82, 99, 101, 109, 110, 115, 117, 120, 121, 125, 126, 128, 130, 139, 140, 141, 142, 143, 144, 145, 146, 147, 148, 149, 151, 152, 153, 155, 161, 162, 163, 164, 165, 173, 174, 179, 181, 184, 186, 188, 191, 192, 197, 198, 202, 203, 204, 205, 206, 207, 208, 209, 210, 211, 212, 213, 216, 221, 226, 227, 228, 229, 230, 234, 235, 237, 238, 240, 245, 253, 254, 257, 259, 260, 261, 262, 263, 264, 265, 266, 267, 268, 269, 270, 271, 274, 275, 278, 279, 280, 282, 283.

C

Community Profiles, 144, 341.
Concluding Remarks, 62, 127.
Corporate Events, 2, 11, 36, 206, 207, 214, 257.

E

Economic Conditions, 143, 341.
Engagement Marketing, 233, 235, 236.
Event Budget, 191, 215, 256, 311.
Event Equipment, 16, 157, 163, 214, 215, 226, 233, 244, 245, 292, 299.
Event Planning, 5, 6, 21, 37, 38, 45, 46, 157, 164, 179, 188, 189, 191, 198, 200, 201, 206, 210, 215, 216, 299, 309.
Event Safety, 316, 318.

F

Finding Participants, 16, 338.
Food, 5, 7, 10, 12, 14, 16, 22, 23, 24, 31, 39, 54, 75, 79, 88, 141, 147, 167, 171, 175, 177, 181, 184, 185, 186, 187, 188, 189, 198, 200, 227, 228, 265, 269, 272, 274, 277, 279, 283, 286, 287, 288, 289, 290, 291, 301, 308.

M

Marketing Budget, 141, 145, 150, 260, 301.

Marketing Strategy, 68, 143, 146, 149, 150, 157, 233, 236.
Methodology, 113, 167, 168, 169, 171, 248, 323.

P

Personal Events, 171, 290, 341, 343.
Planning, 1, 2, 4, 5, 6, 11, 12, 14, 16, 17, 20, 21, 22, 24, 37, 38, 39, 40, 47, 50, 51, 52, 53, 56, 59, 62, 63, 66, 71, 87, 133, 136, 137, 138, 139, 142, 143, 147, 148, 149, 161, 165, 167, 171, 175, 176, 177, 180, 181, 182, 187, 190, 191, 192, 193, 194, 195, 196, 202, 207, 209, 210, 213, 220, 221, 222, 223, 225, 226, 227, 228, 229, 232, 235, 236, 247, 248, 249, 277, 278, 279, 281, 284, 286, 289, 291, 293, 295, 297, 299, 300, 301, 303, 305, 308, 311, 317, 320, 321, 322, 324.
Policies, 46, 72, 82, 84, 92, 93, 94, 95, 111, 113, 287, 319.

R

Rationalize, 130, 340.
Relationship Marketing, 238, 239, 240, 241, 243, 244.

S

Social Media, 23, 172, 175, 234, 235, 268, 320, 321.

T

Technology, 17, 18, 22, 55, 121, 134, 193, 205, 218, 223, 224, 227, 228, 235, 246, 259, 263, 266, 273.
Tourism, 42, 43, 44, 45, 46, 47, 48, 49, 50, 51, 52, 53, 54, 55, 56, 57, 59, 60, 61, 62, 63, 64, 65, 66, 67, 68, 69, 70, 71, 72, 73, 74, 75, 76, 77, 78, 79, 80, 81, 82, 83, 84, 85, 86, 87, 88, 89, 90, 91, 92, 93, 95, 96, 97, 98, 99, 100, 101, 102, 103, 104, 105, 106, 107, 108, 109, 110, 111, 112, 113, 115, 116, 117, 118, 119, 120, 121, 122, 124, 125, 126, 127, 128, 129, 130, 131, 132, 133, 134, 135, 136, 137, 138, 139, 140, 141, 142, 143, 144, 146, 147, 149, 151, 152, 153, 155, 156, 157.
Tourism Development, 47, 49, 50, 51, 52, 57, 59, 60, 61, 62, 63, 70, 77, 82, 85, 86, 90, 98, 101, 102, 103, 107, 111, 113, 115, 116, 117, 118, 122, 124, 125, 126, 127, 129, 131, 142.
Tourism Marketing, 68, 76, 84, 99, 156.
Tourism Planning, 50, 51, 52, 53, 56, 57, 59, 62, 110, 115, 116, 117, 118, 121, 122, 124, 127.
Training Event, 22.

V

Vision, 3, 44, 47, 67, 76, 87, 91, 95, 99, 100, 114, 128, 132, 138, 139, 148, 150, 159, 161, 175, 177, 181, 182, 183, 191, 199, 218, 235, 236, 244, 249, 256, 259, 263, 264, 277, 280, 283, 298, 312, 313, 315, 319..

❑❑❑